W9-BJL-950

Citizen Democracy

People, Passions, and Power

*Social Movements, Interest Organizations,
and the Political Process*

John C. Green, Series Editor

After the Boom: The Politics of Generation X edited by Stephen C. Craig and Stephen Earl Bennett

American Labor Unions in the Elected Arena by Herbert B. Asher, Eric S. Heberlig, Randall B. Ripley, and Karen Snyder

Citizen Democracy: Political Activists in a Cynical Age by Stephen E. Frantzich

Cyberpolitics: Citizen Activism in the Age of the Internet by Kevin A. Hill and John E. Hughes

Democracy's Moment: Reforming the American Political System for the 21st Century edited by Ron Hayduk and Kevin Mattson

Gaia's Wager: Environmental Movements and the Challenge of Sustainability by Gary C. Bryner

Multiparty Politics in America edited by Paul S. Herrnson and John C. Green

Rage on the Right: The American Militia Movement from Ruby Ridge to Homeland Security by Lane Crothers

Rethinking Social Movements: Structure, Meaning, and Emotion edited by Jeff Goodwin and James M. Jasper

Social Movements and American Political Institutions edited by Anne N. Costain and Andrew S. McFarland

Teamsters and Turtles? U.S. Progressive Political Movements in the 21st Century edited by John C. Berg

The Social Movement Society: Contentious Politics for a New Century edited by David Meyer and Sidney Tarrow

The State of the Parties: The Changing Role of Contemporary American Parties, 3rd ed., edited by John C. Green and Daniel M. Shea

The State of the Parties, 4th ed., edited by John C. Green and Rick D. Farmer

Waves of Protest: Social Movements since the Sixties edited by Jo Freeman and Victoria Johnson

Forthcoming

Chimes of Freedom: Student Protest and the American University by Christine Kelly

Coalitions Across Borders: Transnational Protest and the Neo-Liberal Order edited by Joe Bandy and Jackie Smith

Ralph Nader, the Greens, and the Crisis of American Politics by John C. Berg

The Art and Craft of Lobbying: Political Engagement in American Politics by Ronald G. Shaiko

The Gay and Lesbian Rights Movement: Changing Policies! Changing Minds? by Steven H. Haeberle

The U.S. Women's Movement in Global Perspective edited by Lee Ann Banaszak

Transnational Protest and Global Activism edited by Donatella della Porta and Sidney Tarrow

Citizen Democracy

Political Activists in a Cynical Age
Second Edition

STEPHEN E. FRANTZICH

ROWMAN & LITTLEFIELD PUBLISHERS, INC.
Lanham • Boulder • New York • Toronto • Oxford

ROWMAN & LITTLEFIELD PUBLISHERS, INC.

Published in the United States of America
by Rowman & Littlefield Publishers, Inc.
A wholly owned subsidiary of The Rowman & Littlefield Publishing Group, Inc.
4501 Forbes Boulevard, Suite 200, Lanham, MD 20706
www.rowmanlittlefield.com

P.O. Box 317, Oxford OX2 9RU, UK

Copyright © 2005 by Rowman & Littlefield Publishers, Inc.

All rights reserved. No part of this publication may be reproduced,
stored in a retrieval system, or transmitted in any form or by any
means, electronic, mechanical, photocopying, recording, or otherwise,
without the prior permission of the publisher.

British Library Cataloguing in Publication Information Available

Library of Congress Cataloging-in-Publication Data

Frantzich, Stephen E.
　　Citizen democracy : political activists in a cynical age /
Stephen E. Frantzich.—2nd ed.
　　　　p.　cm.—(People, passions, and power)
　　Includes bibliographical references and index.
　　ISBN 0-7425-2952-5 (cloth : alk. paper)—ISBN 0-7425-2953-3
(pbk. : alk. paper)
　　1. Political participation—United States.　I. Title.　II. Series.
JK1764.F73　2005
323'.042'0973—dc22

　　　　　　　　　　　　　　　　　　　2003026324

Printed in the United States of America

♾ The paper used in this publication meets the minimum requirements of
American National Standard for Information Sciences—Permanence of Paper
for Printed Library Materials, ANSI/NISO Z39.48–1992.

Contents

Preface

The stories told in this book originated as classroom examples designed to temper the cynicism of my students at the U.S. Naval Academy. Over the years, I increasingly wondered that if my students who had committed themselves to a minimum of five years of government service were cynical, what were students in the "real world" like? Rather than repeating rosy dictums like "you *can* fight city hall" or giving overly optimistic examples of going from log cabin obscurity to White House power, I wanted to provide real examples of relatively typical individuals who overcame cynicism to affect public well-being. In the telling and retelling of these stories, my students helped me hone their content by asking penetrating questions and helping to tease out broader lessons. In selecting the stories and determining the portions to emphasize, a serious attempt was made to present an honest view of the opportunities and potential limits of civic activism in contemporary America.

We all owe the individuals profiled in the following chapters a debt of gratitude for stepping onto the political playing field and challenging the status quo. As an author, I owe many of them a personal debt for subjecting themselves to numerous interviews and sharing original materials. Personal quotes that are not annotated come from those interviews.

The stories have been refined and new ones added to the second edition from suggestions of many readers, especially the teachers going through "We the People" training at summer institutes sponsored by the Center for Civic Education (www.civiced.org). The universality of many of the stories was confirmed as I tried them out on my students at Charles University in the Czech Republic while on a senior Fulbright Grant. The major addition to the second edition is a number of "kidizen" democracy stories focusing on the efforts of activists under the age of twenty-one. While it is always agonizing to drop stories, it was necessary to do some trimming in order to make room for more timely examples.

A number of teachers have augmented reading and discussing the vignettes from the first edition with having students write their own stories of individuals in their communities who have made a difference, following the same template as the book. Others have asked students to present "what if " scenarios, speculating on what might have happened if the profiled individual in a vignette had not stepped forward at that particular time. I am particularly interested in hearing how teachers have used the book. Please contact me at *frantzic@usna.edu.*

Research funding for this project came from the Dirksen Center and the U.S. Naval Academy Research Recognition Grant Program. Jennifer Knerr and her coworkers at Rowman & Littlefield Publishers encouraged the project and helped mold the manuscript into a much better product. My wife, Jane, served as my initial editor and "reality test" for the value of various stories and their presentation.

Throughout our lives we learn and interpret our life experiences through listening to and telling stories. It is hoped that the stories that follow will enrich your life experiences.

Introduction

Countering the Culture of Cynicism: Keeping the Fans in the Stands

A democracy can accommodate many things in its people—passion, ambition, selfishness, even corruption. But it cannot long endure on a foundation of public cynicism and indifference.

—Michael Nelson[1]

The erosion of our confidence in the future is threatening to destroy the social and the political fabric of America. . . . Our people are losing faith. Not only in government, but in their ability as citizens.

—Jimmy Carter[2]

Our history is not a story of perfection. It's a story of imperfect people working toward great ideals. . . . American children are not born knowing what they should cherish—are not born knowing why they should cherish American values. A love of democratic principles must be taught.

—George W. Bush[3]

Individual excuses for not participating in politics and society abound. Some individuals spend more time and energy avoiding involvement than they would taking action. Their excuses, "I don't have the time," "You can't fight city hall," and "I wouldn't have any impact anyway," express their attitude more than they describe empirical reality. Political scientists call these feelings about participation "efficacy," the degree to which individuals feel that political activity is an efficient and effective use of one's time. A person's sense of efficacy answers the question, "With everything else I have to do, just how worthwhile is it for me to expend my precious resources of time and psychic energy to get involved in the political game?" The cynic concludes that it is simply not worthwhile to get involved. The costs are too high and the potential for success is too remote.

1

The patterns of public attitudes are clear. The last three decades have witnessed a steady decline in the general public's sense of efficacy and an increase in commensurate cynicism. Since 1960, there has been a nearly ten-point increase in the percentage of people who feel that "people like me don't have any say about what government does," with over one-half of respondents now expressing the cynical response. There has been a similar increase in the percentage of the population feeling that "public officials don't care much about what people like me think." Over two-thirds of the public do not expect public officials to be responsive to their thoughts. Younger voters seem to be the most affected by the increase in cynicism.[4] The partisanship and conflict surrounding President Clinton's impeachment and trial in 1998–1999, the controversy over the 2000 presidential election results, and debate over the legitimacy of the war with Iraq and its aftermath all gave the wheel of cynicism another downward spin, reducing the level of trust even more.

The tragic events of September 11, 2001, led to a dramatic and visible outpouring of patriotism reflected in the appearance of American flags in almost every imaginable location and increased support for American political instutions and processes. Some felt that the slide into cynicism had miraculously reversed itself. The optimism turned out to be misplaced with levels of cynicism increasing to pre 9/11 levels within a few months.

Increased cynicism emerges in the form of reduced political participation. Election turnout in the United States is lower than in most democracies, with a general decline over time. Voting is probably the least intrusive and time-consuming political activity. More difficult political tasks are even more likely to be negatively affected by growing cynicism. Participation in activities such as writing letters to public officials, attending meetings, and joining political groups has also declined over time, with only 10 percent of citizens having written a public official and about the same percentage claiming to have "attended a public meeting on town or school matters."[5] Taking leadership in public affairs is so rare that it does not appear in public opinion polls at all. The generational differences emerge starkly when one considers these more difficult tasks of citizenship, as table I.1 indicates.

Focusing on "traditional" modes of participation such as voting, writing letters, and attending meetings may seem quaint given the potential of new social conditions and technologies. The 2004 race for the Democratic Party presidential nomination generated significant discussion of new approaches such as computer fund-raising, "blogging" (interactive web discussions, or "logs"), and "meet-ups" in which a candidate's supporters made initial contact on the Internet followed by face-to-face meetings. The ultimate failure of Howard Dean's campaign, which deftly used such techniques, dampened the view that they were clearly the wave of the future. The loss of one skir-

TABLE I.1
Civic Participation and Age

	"DotNet" Generation (Under 25)	*Over 26 years of age*
Follows what is happening in government	49%	78%
Ever contacted a public official	16%	36%
Worked in or contributed to a political campaign	9%	29%

Source: National Conference of State Legislatures national survey, August 2003. Available at www.ncsl.org.

mish does not doom the entire war over political power. Future activists will clearly learn from the past. While the political system is not ready for such new techniques to replace the old ones, there is clearly some room for creative applications to augment the more established modes of participation. Despite the availability of new techniques, there is little evidence that declines in political involvement have, or will be, stemmed in the foreseeable future.

FROM BOWLING TO PARTICIPATION

Wide dissemination of data and of opinions such as those outlined above has stimulated a great deal of thinking among academics, citizen activists, and the media. Harvard political scientist Robert Putnam captured the attention of both the academic and the popular worlds with his cleverly titled and thoughtfully argued article, "Bowling Alone: America's Declining Social Capital."[6] Putnam raised the specter of a disengaged society that would ultimately undermine the performance of government and other institutions, drawing on empirically based observations that reflect (1) declining public involvement in traditional social groupings such as bowling leagues and civic clubs and (2) declining trust in fellow citizens and political leaders. His comments generated a firestorm of reaction, pro and con. Political columnist David Broder asserted, "His conclusion seems to me irrefutable: Unless more Americans start working with each other on shared civic enterprises, and learning to trust each other, the formal government of this nation will probably lurch from one credibility crisis to the next."[7]

Putnam's seminal thoughts were tempered and refined in the blast furnace of public debate.[8] In reasserting his arguments, he attempted to more carefully discuss their origins. Although recognizing alternative venues of participation such as mailing list organizations, he continues to assert that "the weight of available evidence confirms that Americans are significantly less engaged with their communities than was true a generation ago."[9]

In analyzing the causes of this trend, Putnam sheds light on a conundrum that teachers and contemporary civic activists regularly confront. Although well-established correlates of civic trust and activism such as educational level and easy access to political information have increased, each new wave of entrants into the civic community seems to have less trust and less willingness to become political movers and shakers. The physical mobility of Americans and privatizing technologies such as the Internet and contemporary television have tended to disassociate individuals from the local communities in which much political activism begins.[10] A number of societal phenomena, including the cynical focus of the news media and a succession of contemporary political scandals, are blamed for this new reality. Putnam focuses more on *who* is cynical than on *how* they got that way and flatly points out the correlation between cynicism and generation. Trust and activism depend less on who you are in demographic terms (region, gender, socioeconomic status, etc.) and more on when you came of political age. Each generation of political activists faces the task of activating generations of citizens who distrust political activism and increasingly see such efforts as quaint and peculiar at best.

RISING ABOVE CYNICISM

Never doubt that a small group of thoughtful, committed citizens can change the world; indeed it is the only thing that ever has.

—Margaret Mead[11]

Anthropologist Margaret Mead's call to action seems alien to many contemporary Americans. Cynicism is debilitating and becomes a self-fulfilling prophecy. As David Broder sees it:

Cynicism is epidemic right now. . . . It saps people's confidence in politics and public officials, and it erodes both the standing and standards of journalism. If the assumption is that nothing is on the level, nothing is what is seems, then citizenship becomes a game for fools and there is no point to staying informed.[12]

If you believe you cannot control your destiny and affect the policy goals you support, you fail to act. By failing to act, you assure political impotency.

Although trust in politics and willingness to take action have declined, some individuals still step into the void and act either as individuals or in groups to affect political outcomes. The nature of a particular battle affects one's degree of commitment. Joining the political game to save the life of one's child or to protect one's personal economic well-being is more likely to overcome the natural hesitancy to get involved than goals such as improving the lot of the neighbor's children or improving the world. The benefits of political involvement fall into two broad categories. "Collective benefits" affect a broad range of individuals and hinder any attempt to limit who gains and who loses. If we as a society pass legislation to improve air quality or protect free speech, the benefits will accrue to a large segment of society, not solely to those who sought its enactment. "Selective" benefits affect the lives of a narrow segment of the population; in the most restrictive case, one individual.

In general, it is easier to motivate individuals to pursue selective benefits than collective benefits. Individuals are often drawn into political battles for selective benefits, only to find that in seeking to gain benefits for themselves collective benefits come along as part of the package. An individual's problem or irritation highlights a broader cause also requiring amelioration. Lois Gibbs (whose efforts are detailed later) interested her neighbors in toxic waste to protect their children and recover personal economic losses only to find herself part of a larger movement that affected national environmental policy. Howard Jarvis, whose story is also part of this book, convinced his friends that their tax problem was a symptom of a broader policy failure that required the establishment of a new general precedent. Bernice Sandler began challenging sex discrimination out of personal frustration and ended up being part of a much larger cause.

Not all activists are drawn into the process by personal benefit. Jean Anne Hlavacek did not have AIDS, and Carl Cohen was not directly affected by affirmative action laws. Their selective benefit lay in doing what they saw as the right thing in fighting for the collective benefits of others.

In rising above cynicism, the activists profiled in this book averted the immobilization that results from self-doubt and distrust in the political process. Also, they avoided the unrealistic expectation that any desired political outcome is possible through passionate commitment and hard work. Successful activists worked smart as well as hard, recognizing the nuances of the various decision-making arenas. They began with a healthy skepticism, recognizing that success is elusive, but were empowered by knowing enough to target the right decision makers. They framed the issues in human terms and pursued their goals with creativity and persistence.

Contemporary political policy decisions are still strongly dominated by individuals who work within the system as opposed to those who stand outside it, ignoring the political game or simply carping at the officials. Democracy implies responsiveness from decision makers and the principle that the "squeaky wheel gets the grease."[13] By paying attention to those who make the most noise, the American political game almost assures that "you can't win if you don't play." In abandoning the playing field, the cynics leave room for less desirable participants to dominate: "the only thing necessary for the triumph of evil is for good men to do nothing."[14] The cynics expend so much effort railing against the system that they have little energy to work it to their benefit. But in the American political system individuals can make a difference, policy decisions are not maliciously preordained by a malapportionment of resources, and good can prevail over evil. The activists included in this book emphasize strategy over resources, adding to the familiar stories of how a few dedicated individuals forced the system to change, overcoming resource disadvantages with clever strategy.

HEEDING A CIVIC CALL TO ACTION

Model citizen activist Lucius Quincticus Cincinnatus was said to have laid down his plow on his small farm in 458 b.c. to serve as Roman dictator. Unmoved by power, he returned to the fields as soon as he completed his civic duty. The stories that follow are largely about Cincinnatus-like activists who either found themselves in challenging positions or created opportunities to participate. Their activism may have taken years to produce a plan of action or may have involved a split-second review of available options. Most often the decision was based on a clear calculation that recognized a variety of realistic outcomes, not invariably victory.

The activists portrayed here focused on what could be done, as opposed to what could not be done. You have probably heard of some of them. Rosa Parks, whose actions injected new life into the civil rights movement, has become a mythic folk hero. Candy Lightner's journey from grief to political activism in founding MADD (Mothers Against Drunk Drivers) shows how channeled energy can reach into the lives of Americans. The latest twist in her story reveals just one of the many anomalies of American politics. Jack Kevorkian's stand against restrictions on suicide has challenged both the legal system and the moral principles of millions of Americans. Some citizen activists have become perpetually attached to legislation or legal cases, whereas others faded into oblivion, known only to a few key participants. For every Rosa Parks, Candy Lightner, and Jack Kevorkian there are scores of less well-known but nevertheless effective activists. Both well-known and unknown heroes of civic action are profiled in the pages that follow. In collecting these stories, I tracked down activists and had them relate in their own words what they did, why they did it, and how they evaluated the importance of their actions for themselves. Political action changed some of them into full-time activists; for others, it was little more than a minor blip on the radar screen of their existence.

As case studies, these stories have their limitations. They focus on particular individuals attacking specific problems and include a fair amount of detail. From such richness of detail, generalizations emerge only with difficulty.

Civic activism takes on a large number of forms. Some of the stories here emphasize individuals who capitalized on the attitudes of their fellow citizens to lead a very public charge. As in the 1980s movie *Network,* they spurred on the crowds who exploded, "We are mad as hell and are not going to take it anymore." Others worked quietly outside the spotlight, even in secret, with few knowing their contributions. Each supported the principle that "the value of government to the people it serves is in direct relationship to the interest citizens themselves display in the affairs of state."[15] They overcame any lingering cynicism, used their remaining skepticism to guide their strategies, and expended the effort required for success.

These stories emphasize successes, some partial and some full. For each success, there are probably dozens of failures. Failures are harder to chronicle, in part because the participants are less willing to tell their stories. As John F. Kennedy once observed, "Success has a thousand fathers and failure is an orphan." Politics is a continuous game with many rounds, and a failure at one point in time may well set the stage for success when the issue is revisited. The real failures in the political game are those who refuse to take action and doom themselves and the causes they promote to the sidelines.

If we believe that active involvement in the body politic is important, how can we as a society reinfuse this ideal into coming generations of potential activists, who will undoubtedly be smart, aware, and data-oriented? The challenge is daunting. Preaching the values of civic life will have less impact than presenting hard evidence. The vignettes that make up the bulk of this book are an attempt to breathe some life into the dictums that "civic activism is worth it" and "one person can make a difference." They originated as classroom examples from which meaningful lessons could be learned. Optimally, the stories will be repeated and analyzed, and their relevant lessons internalized. The stakes are high: the continued existence of a true democracy hangs in the balance. If the wall of civic activism is crumbling, it needs to be rebuilt from the bottom, one brick at a time.

The individuals profiled herein took action that resulted in raising a national policy issue to public debate, placing an issue on the public agenda, affecting the nature of enacted public policy, and/or changing the nature of the public policy process. They are a lot like you and me. Each had shortcomings, doubts, and reversals that could have doomed their efforts. Many of their stories remain unfinished, with the final policy outcomes yet to be written.

The world of politics deals with issues over which reasonable people can and do disagree, and not every reader will see all of these individuals as heroes. Some pushed for policies that you may abhor. But there are broader lessons to take away from reading their stories. They glorify the democratic value of subjecting public policy to public debate instead of leaving it to backroom collusion. The stories are intended to highlight personal characteristics like dedication and hard work, and to analyze the variety of political strategies available to would-be activists. Serendipity plays a part too.

Over forty years ago, John F. Kennedy challenged all Americans, "Ask not what your country can do for you—ask what you can do for your country."[16] The individuals profiled in this book took that challenge to heart. These are ordinary people who took extraordinary action. The good news is that if they could succeed, so might you. This effort is a call to skeptical activism. In the words of Theodore Roosevelt, who believed passionately, acted boldly, and proceeded strategically,

> It is not the critic who counts; not the man who points out how the strong man stumbles, or where the doer of good deeds could have done better. The credit belongs to the man who is actually in the arena . . . who at best knows in the end the triumph of high achievement, and who at worst, if he fails, at least while daring greatly, so that his place shall never be with those cold and timid souls who know neither victory nor defeat.[17]

PRACTICING ACTIVISM

A democracy must ask itself a series of questions. What if we held an election and no one showed up at the polls? What if problems emerged and no one took the initiative to put them on the public agenda? What if everyone simply said, "let somebody else do it," and nobody did? Abandoning the political arena does not mean that nothing will be done but rather that the agenda and preferences of others will dominate. Politics abhors a vacuum and is controlled by those who take the initiative to guide it.

Democracy is a participatory game of contact and blocking, not a spectator sport. It may be able to survive with some of the population simply cheering from the sidelines or even blissfully unaware that the game is being played. But the number of participants can decline to the degree that democracy exists in name only, since as the level of participation declines, so does its representativeness. The fewer the people who get involved, the less likely they are to reflect the concerns of the general population.

The almost two dozen individuals profiled in the following chapters have little in common except for the fact that they avoided the tendency to sit back and let others get involved. Few would pick them out of a crowd as likely activists. They hail from all walks of life. Many found the political realm both mystifying and repulsive. Their motivations and strategies varied significantly, but they are bound together by the fact that as individuals they all made a difference in the public policies that affect everyone.

ENTERING THE POLITICAL ARENA

American politics can be compared to a game. This game analogy is not intended to imply frivolous enjoyment; people literally live or die because of its outcome. Analogies allow us to take familiar concepts, apply them to new situations, and improve our understanding. Like all games, politics has players, rules, strategies, winners, and losers.

Playing Politics

Politics, like many games, includes fans in the stands who cheer their favorite partisan or ideological teams but seldom get involved personally. The focus of this book is on fans who became *players*. They are the heroes of the American political process, who make it legitimate for us to be called a democracy.

Their motivations for running onto the playing field vary. People like Howard Jarvis and Lois Gibbs took on the political system out of frustration with existing laws governing taxes or the environment. In the process they changed the face of American politics by leading the drive to cap property taxes and helping enact the most expensive environmental legislation in the history of the world. Two families, the Clerys and the Kankas, rose above the murders of their daughters; their victimhood led to their involvement in the political game. By adding a human face to the inadequacy of current policy, they helped pass legislation to alert students of shortcomings in campus security and to warn families of the presence of sex offenders in their communities. Some of our heroes focused their efforts on facilitating the political participation of others. Frances Fox Piven and Richard Cloward fought to make voting participation easier and thereby broaden the base of participation. Just barely out of college, Brian Trelstad capitalized on his experiences of using activism to revolutionize energy use among his classmates and worked to expand the political participation of college students on the national scene. Bernice Sandler channeled her frustration over losing jobs because she was a woman into a crusade providing opportunities for others.

Understanding the motivations, resources, and effectiveness of the players reveals a great deal about the way the game will be played and what the likely outcome will be. Players seeking personal benefit play the game in one way; players getting more joy out of playing than winning, in another. Players expecting to be on the field for a long time play in one way; those recognizing politics as a passing fancy, in another. Some players are professionals who spend entire careers in elective or appointive office. Much has been written about them and for our purposes they will be treated as part of the political context. Less is known about the amateur "walk-ons" who enter the game for shorter periods of time and mix it up with the professionals before returning to their private lives. These citizen politicians add a new element to politics. Many of them have lived through the problems they attempt to solve. It is one thing to abhor drunk driving in principle or to oppose discrimination as a concept; it is quite another to live through the death of a child at the hands of a drunk driver, like Candy Lightner did, or to experience racial intolerance on a daily level, like Rosa Parks. What differentiates the individuals profiled in this book is their unwillingness to wallow in their frustration or to be consumed by their grief. They jumped into the political arena, seeing it as a vehicle for alleviating personal suffering and as a tool for improving the lives of others.

Acting Strategically

Strategies are established plans for reaching an objective. Acceptable strategies are often defined by the rules associated with particular institutions and processes. What is allowed in a congressional campaign (i.e., direct contributions to candidates) would be illegal when dealing with Supreme Court justices. The feasibility of strategies is determined by the resources and capabilities of the players. The political game welcomes a variety of different strategies. Some of the strategies are traditional. Barbara Brimmer and Valerie Schoen wrote letters to their members of Congress and in so doing began a dramatic move toward gender equality in one of the last bastions of gender exclusivity. Dr. Kristen Zarfos used her pen to alert members of Congress about a dangerous medical insurance practice and saw her ideas become part of the president's agenda. Jean Anne Hlavacek and Diane Nannery enlisted the help of others to write letters and petitions to a little-known bureaucratic agency and in the process saw their causes promoted by millions of tiny postage-stamp "billboards."

Information is critical in the political process, with victory often depending on whose information is available and/or accepted. Professor Carl Cohen challenged the practice of affirmative action on his campus (and eventually in the nation) by disclosing hard data that revealed racial discrimination in his college's admissions process. Merrell Williams became a thief in order to expose the duplicity of the tobacco companies and eventually helped shift the balance of power in tobacco liability suits.

Political protest has been a tool of American politics since the Revolution. Rosa Parks stood up against racial discrimination by remaining seated on an Alabama bus. Martha McSally challenged the power of her military superiors by refusing to wear clothes she felt were a violation of her civil rights. Jack Kevorkian forced a national debate on issues of life and death by facilitating suicide among terminal patients and eventually performed the medical actions he supported.

Often the effective players are those who find new methods of reaching their goals. Shabbir Safdar and Jonah Seiger tapped the power of the Internet to help protect free speech. Most of the persons profiled in the following pages simply resurrected traditional strategies such as writing letters, using the power of the media, and forming groups. What sets them apart is their creativity and level of persistence in making the system work to their benefit.

Winning and Losing

Players, rules, and strategies all affect the final outcome of the policy game. Citizen-politicians affect who wins and who loses the political game, and the stakes of the game are high. Lois Gibbs forced the government to fund the toxic waste cleanup of her Love Canal neighborhood and in the process stimulated passage of Superfund legislation providing for massive cleanups around the nation. Gregory Watson's frustration with his political science grade led to the passage of a constitutional amendment affecting congressional salaries. Megan Kanka's parents helped pass a law bearing her name, which many believe will save other parents from losing a child needlessly. Bernice Sandler entered the political arena to improve women's access to the classroom and in the process had a dramatic unanticipated impact on men's and women's athletics.

The political game determines how we as a society gather and use our collective resources. The laws and regulations emerging from the political process reflect the values our society attempts to uphold. Howard Jarvis's campaign against property taxes significantly affected policies governing both taxation and spending. By supporting flag burning, Joey Johnson forced American policy makers to define the limits of their commitment to free expression.

Not all victories are complete. The young anti-smoking activists have seen government activity only touch the surface of teen smoking. Sex offenses, child abduction, and drunk driving have decreased, but they still present society with significant problems. Legislation supported by Dr. Kristin Zarfos to limit insurance companies still languishes in Congress, yet the companies themselves have changed their policies in the direction she sought.

Public policies reflect the winners and losers in our society and often determine who will win and lose the next round of play. At times the stakes of the political game involve life-and-death situations, such as going to war or enacting laws concerning assisted suicide, drunk driving, or health care benefits.

There is no need to accept the specific policy goals and accomplishments of these profiled activists or to applaud their efforts. They are not heroes because of the causes they promoted; they are heroes of democracy because they took a stand in the first place. They identified significant problems and proposed solutions in the appropriate place in a democracy: the public forum.

At least one activist or cause profiled in the following chapters is likely to offend at least one value of every reader. Read the chapters that follow before concluding that we would be better off if Jack Kevorkian had never raised the issue of assisted suicide, if Joey Johnson had dutifully saluted the American flag rather than burn it, if Martha McSally had quietly followed the rules, or if Howard Jarvis had simply accepted rising property taxes.

Democracy is the reoccurent suspicion that when properly informed, more than half of the people are right more than half of the time. It assumes that ideas are no threat to a truly democratic political system and that the public is competent enough to ferret out the bad ones. The founders of American democracy rested their support for the principle of free expression on the views of individuals such as Voltaire who purportedly asserted, "I disapprove of what you say, but I will defend to the death your right to say it."[18] The corollary principle of political activism in a democracy is, "I disapprove of the issue you are promoting, but I will defend to the death your right to promote it." The activists profiled in these pages lay down a challenge to the rest of us. If their initial results fail to please our preferences, there is always another round in the political game. The appropriate response to an undesirable policy is not shame on them for promoting and enacting it, but rather shame on us if we do nothing about it. Ideally their success stories will inspire a new round of activists, revealing effective strategies and redefining winners and losers.

1

Rewriting the Constitution: One Man's Journey to Lend Madison a Hand

OLD WORDS WITH A CONTEMPORARY RING

The assignment seemed too vague and too broad: "write a paper about the governmental process." Gregory Watson followed most of his classmates and pursued a contemporary topic in his political science course at the University of Texas. In 1982, debate raged over the propriety and legality of Congress's decision to extend the time limit for state ratification of the Equal Rights Amendment. The ERA looked like an easy, if mundane, topic. Along the way, however, he got sidetracked. In the university library, a book published by the Government Printing Office caught his eye. It listed constitutional amendments sent to the states by Congress that did not receive approval from the necessary three quarters of the states. In the dustbin of history remained proposed amendments allowing slavery, prohibiting U.S. citizens from accepting titles of nobility, and outlawing child labor.[1] Gregory remembers focusing on an amendment proposed by James Madison in 1789, which jumped out at him "as something both timely and important." A few months earlier, Congress has passed a special tax provision to a bill on black lung benefits treating members of Congress as a special class and effectively giving them a pay increase. Public and media cynicism toward Congress had begun to grow. The proposed amendment simply stated: "No law varying the compensation for the services of Senators and Representatives shall take effect, until an election of Representatives shall have intervened."

During the constitutional convention, Madison lost the battle over who should set the pay for members of Congress. He forcefully argued that to let Congress set its own pay "was an indecent thing and might, in time prove a dangerous one."[2] With the decision that Congress, not the individual states, would both set the amount and the way it would pay its mem-

Gregory Watson

bers, Madison took another tack. In the first Congress, he introduced an amendment as part of the package that would eventually become the Bill of Rights. He argued that "there is a seeming impropriety in leaving any set of men without control to put their hand in the public coffers, to take out money to put in their pockets; there is seeming indecorum in such power." In his day, congressional pay amounted to less than $1,000 per year, but clearly the seeds of public scorn for lawmakers who raise their own salaries had been sown. The proposed amendment, disallowing members from granting themselves midterm pay raises, passed easily in Congress. It was then sent to the states for ratification and languished for almost two hundred years. Six states approved it immediately, far short of the eleven then needed for ratification. As new states were admitted to the union, the number of rat-ifications required grew. In 1873 Ohio added its support after Congress raised its pay. Frustrated by a congressional pay raise a century later, Wyoming signed in 1978. By the time Watson made his discovery, thirty more states would be required in order to reach the necessary thirty-eight for a three-fourths approval.

The issue of Madison's amendment raised two questions: Was it still a good idea? Was the potential for ratification still alive after all these years? When Watson started his research, members of Congress made over $76,000 per year and regularly pushed for more. In the next decade their salary increased to over $129,000. The public became increasingly cynical about the process, and members of Congress feared retribution. Between the 1960s and the 1990s Congress relied on a succession of methods to increase its members' pay. Most fair-minded observers agreed that congressional pay levels had fallen far behind increases in the cost of living and failed to take into account the unique financial demands on members of Congress who often must establish two households, one in Washington and one back in the district. Initially, Congress gave up voting directly on pay increases and attempted to avoid public retribution by relying on an independent pay commission whose recommendations would be approved unless Congress or the president objected. When this failed to work, Congress imposed a revised system that further removed members' fingerprints by granting automatic cost-of-living adjustments in pay. Each revision of the process was an attempt to avoid blame for feathering one's own nest. Members in office regularly accepted pay increases enacted during their term. Only a few members rejected the increases—most with a flourish of self-congratulation and public relations. Eventually the House bit the bullet and proposed a significant increase to make up for past inaction. The Senate, however, held back out of fear of public reaction, and for a number of years House members' salary was higher than senators'. The Senate finally faced the issue, tying its pay raise to a prohibition on accepting honoraria for public speeches.[3] The sequence of congressional machinations over pay served to keep the issue in the public eye. Watson could see that Madison's amendment was still a good idea.

Untangling the legal question of whether the amendment remained a live issue led Watson to analyze Supreme Court decisions and found that precedents led in different directions. In the 1921 *Dillon v. Gloss* (256 U.S. 368) case, the Court considered the time limit of seven years placed on Congress in regard to the Eighteenth Amendment, which prohibited the sale of alcohol nationwide. The Court accepted the limit as legitimate, indicating that the Constitution did not suggest "that an amendment once proposed is to be open for ratification for all time."[4] Eighteen years later in *Coleman v. Miller* (307 U.S. 433) the Court took a different stance on the issue, arguing that a child labor amendment proposed in 1924 was still open for ratification. They asserted that since the Constitution did not provide nor require clear time limits, the timing of ratification was a political issue best left to congressional discretion.[5] Siding with the more recent decision, Watson argued that the Madison amendment remained a live issue. He turned in his paper, satisfied that he had fulfilled the requirements and had raised some important issues about the political process.

A GRADE SURPRISE

When the paper was returned, Watson was in for a shock. Not only was he not rewarded for his efforts and creativity but he was chastised. The teaching assistant made it clear that Watson's paper strayed far from the norm set by his classmates, who focused on contemporary issues. Watson appealed to the course instructor with no success. He remembers her "throwing it back at me and ruling there would be no change in the grade, arguing that the assertions were unrealistic."

Sharon Waite, the instructor of the course, dredges up somewhat different memories. The name Gregory Watson fails to register on her radar screen and the incident with his paper evokes no recollection. She does remember the challenge of teaching classes of over three hundred students and assigning papers despite the advice of her colleagues to stick with multiple-choice exams. She also remembers the difficult task of riding herd "on a United Nations group of teaching assistants and attempting to maintain reasonable fairness in their grading." Course meetings with teaching assistants over grades were rife with conflict and required significant negotiation skills.

Although embarrassed about Gregory Watson's grade, Sharon Waite was "delighted to hear about his subsequent efforts" and took some pride in having established a situation that "ignited such a spark in a student." Frustrated with the life of an untenured instructor forced to teach large sections allowing very little interaction with students, she shifted her career by earning another graduate degree in human resource development. She now serves as business manager for her family's grapefruit and onion farm in Mission, Texas, where she remains active in the politics of agriculture.

The experience of strenuous effort unrewarded soured Gregory Watson on his educational pursuit but sparked a journey that changed both the process and the document Watson was writing. He quit school and determined to make the assertions in his paper about the value and potential success of the congressional pay amendment come true.

WRITE IF YOU FIND WORK

With little more than some spare time and a typewriter, Gregory Watson went to work. He knew that the key to ratification lay in the state legislatures, but he had little idea of where to start. He even found it difficult to determine which states had passed the amendment in the last two hundred years.

Needing allies, he wrote to several members of Congress from states that had not ratified the amendment. He focused on members whose records supported legislation to limit congressional pay increases. He asked them a simple question, "Who in your state legislature might be willing to sponsor a bill to ratify the amendment?" One of the first respondents was Senator William Cohen of Maine, who passed Watson's letter on to a state senator, Melvin Shute. In 1983 Maine became the first of the new round of states to ratify the amendment. Watson next wrote to the majority and minority leaders in each state legislature. Colorado House majority leader Ron Strahle suggested he "give it to Don Mielke to carry out." Within a few months, Colorado joined the list of supporting states.

By 1984, Watson was batting 100 percent, but "the process was just going too slow." At one state a year, victory was a long way off. Watson decided to crank up his efforts by writing letters to all state legislators in states that had not ratified the amendment. Lacking a computer, Watson stayed up until all hours of the night cranking out letters. He describes the effort as "practically my life's work at this time, taking up all my spare time and making the question of a social life academic."[6]

Through his day job as a staff member in the Texas state legislature, Watson knew that form letters seldom make much impact on legislators. He thus attempted to create personalized letters mentioning the legislator and his district in the text. Slowly, the effort began to pay off. In numerous legislatures, it was possible to find "one or more ambitious members who wanted to use support of the amendment as a feather in their cap." He included a revised version of his paper as a rationale and offered to help interested legislators draft the necessary resolutions.

In most legislatures the opposition arose from inertia more than substantive or procedural complaints. In some cases a token opposition arose, arguing that the date for ratification had passed decades ago. Supporting resolutions were seldom voted down but died in committee. No organized opposition arose in any state. Watson concluded that whatever opposition emerged remained "very, very secretive, so secretive in fact that in some cases the sponsors themselves are unable to pinpoint exactly where it's coming from." He felt strongly that "it's probably someone from the congressional delegation in each of these states who has said, 'Don't you dare pass that.'"[7]

No one had been keeping "score" over the last two hundred years of ratification activities. His list with its detailed information on resolutions and dates became the official record. Despite his tenacious commitment to setting the record straight, monitoring low profile activity in fifty states eluded him. He learned about Wyoming's ratification by chance, six years later.

Watson's efforts stand out as low tech and inexpensive, but not costless. He estimates spending over $6,000 for stamps, stationery, and photocopying. Even though no one offered to help pay for the effort, Watson would have refused help anyway: "I wanted to do it on my own and I'll be damned if anyone else is going to get the credit."

A CONSTITUTIONAL STITCH IN TIME

As is often the case in politics, time was on Gregory Watson's side. Public esteem for Congress fell rapidly during the 1980s (see fig. 1.1), accelerated

Figure 1.1
Based on national polls asking, "Please tell me how much confidence you,
yourself, have in Congress—a great deal, quite a lot, some, or very little."
Source: Gallup Poll Monthly 313 (October 1991): 37, and the RPOLL file
of the LEXIS-NEXIS database.

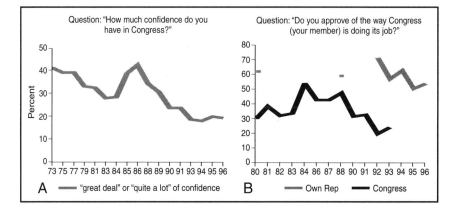

by a series of scandals. Members and former members found themselves
charged with bribery (the Keating Five and Koreagate cases), sexual mis-
conduct (Reps. Howe, Hayes, Studds, and Frank), and inappropriate official behavior (bouncing checks at the House credit union). Speaker of the
House Jim Wright (D-Tex.) and key party leader Tony Coehlo (D-Calif.)
faced forced resignations. On the institutional level, the public became increasingly frustrated with growing legislative branch appropriations and
legislative inaction characterized as "gridlock." Although Congress has
never enjoyed great popularity with the public, the existence of hard
polling data, extensive media attention, and members' own willingness to
accept the depth of public enmity made this period stand out as unique.[8]

Concern over both the amount and the process of congressional pay
raises was consistent with this disillusionment. Polling data indicated that
over 80 percent of respondents opposed a pay raise, and over 70 percent felt
that they would be less likely to vote for a representative who backed such
an increase.[9]

If Congress as an institution was perceived as not working well and
many of its most visible members were acting inappropriately, why not
hit them where it hurts—in their pocketbooks? During the height of his
battle Watson was quick to point out that "the American people are fed
up with the sneaky, tricky and deceptive ways that Congress increases
salaries. . . . No one trusts the members to make their own pay raise
reforms."[10]

PAY AND CREDIT

As the number of states ratifying the amendment grew, others began to show interest in Gregory Watson's efforts. As John Kennedy once said, "Victory has a thousand fathers and failure is an orphan." Watson willingly shared credit when warranted but exhibited single-minded tenacity about dishonest attempts to grasp the spotlight. He found that a good idea seemed to inspire "a lot of dishonesty and political plagiarism." About the time Watson reached the halfway point, consumer activist Ralph Nader put his prestige and the support of his organization, Congress Watch, behind the effort. Watson appreciated the support of this "Johnny-come-lately" but not its attempt to claim credit: "When I think of all the nights I've stayed up until three or four o'clock in the morning typing letters and licking stamps, it just absolutely outrages me that some other person would come in like some white knight in shining armor and snatch it away; it's very insulting."[11]

Watson reserves much of his frustration for Representative John Boehner (R-Ohio). Boehner spearheaded a drive to make the amendment the "class project" of the freshman House members elected in 1990. Political scientists have long recognized that credible credit claiming stands out as a major key to political success. It is not so much what you actually do in Congress but what you can claim credit for that determines your political fate.[12] Press reports of Boehner going on the House floor to congratulate his freshman colleagues for creating the climate necessary for the approval of the amendment ignited Watson's fury. Boehner "was running around the country telling people he was the one that got the last three states to pass it and that was not factual. John Boehner had nothing to do with it."[13]

State legislators in the final states to ratify give most of the credit to Watson. Michigan state senator John F. Kelly (D-Grosse Point) firmly asserts, "There is no question that [Watson] deserves credit for keeping the issue alive. His persistence paid off. The beauty of our system is that every individual counts, if they want to."[14] Senator Kelly's assistant, Joe Howe, provided additional insight on how Watson moved the process along. "It was because of Gregory Watson's efforts that it passed. At one point, the measure was stuck in a legislative subcommittee, and we wouldn't have realized it except that Mr. Watson called and reminded us that we needed only one more state for ratification."[15]

The disagreement over Boehner's role illustrates the difference between visibility and effort. As an elected official with access to the national media, Boehner "probably attracts more press attention than Gregory."[16] His role involved attaching himself to an issue Watson cultivated for years. There is no way to definitively determine whether Boehner's comments on the House floor or his supportive resolution even reached the ears of the state legislators involved. Clearly his support did not undermine Watson's activities. Boehner does not deny Watson's efforts but sees his own role as crucial to revitalizing the effort in the final stages. Based on his aggressive leadership among the emerging Republican majority, Boehner succeeded in his campaign for selection as House Republican Conference chairman in the 104th Congress, making him the fourth-ranking party leader only four years after entering the House. Watson still bristles at the mention of Boehner's name, referring to him as "that Boner guy."

AN IDEA WHOSE TIME HAD COME

Much of Greg Watson's frustration disappeared on May 7, 1992, as the Michigan state legislature became the crucial thirty-eighth state to ratify Madison's amendment, 203 years since its inception and almost ten years to the day after Watson began his one-man crusade for ratification. He remembers it as "the happiest day in [his] thirty-year life."[17]

After living with the process intimately for over a decade, Watson had not become enamored with the process, viewing the ratification system as "sloppy, extremely unprofessional, and terribly haphazard."[18] He wonders if any other ratifications remain unreported.

With the thirty-eight verified ratifications, the pay raise amendment was out of Gregory Watson's hands, but it was still not home free. Constitutional scholars differed widely as to whether the delayed ratifications were legitimate. Some congressional leaders made similar arguments. Given public opinion and legal arguments, Don W. Wilson, archivist of the United States, cut the debate short by certifying the requirements for ratification met. Wilson's decision quieted opponents both inside and outside of Congress. Within six months, the amendment emerged as the basis of court decisions questioning congressional cost-of-living adjustments.[19]

The experience changed Gregory Watson. His tenacity and orientation to detail make him the kind of person you would rather have as an ally than an opponent. He remains an angry young man. One of his legislative goals as a state legislative staff member includes changing Texas law to require state schools to expunge previous grades when a student retakes the course. His C in American government still grates on him. He also expends considerable effort to maintain his rightful parentage of the Twenty-Seventh amendment.

Gregory D. Watson takes pride in the fact that "one person can still make a difference in the United States of America, even today in the era of megabucks politics. If they are stubborn, if they know how to nag and pester, they too can make a difference. While the meek may inherent the earth, they do not pass legislation."[20]

LESSONS

- *Persistence and attention to detail pay off.* Watson established the first complete and detailed records of state legislative action.
- *Information is an important power resource.* By becoming the expert on the substance of the issue and the status of the ratification process, Watson became the person to be consulted. He often knew more about what particular legislatures had done than they knew themselves.
- *Timing is important.* Promoting a limit on pay increases during a slump in public approval of Congress facilitated its passage. When an issue entrepreneur joins forces with public pressure, the likelihood of success increases.
- *Apathy is a more important detriment than outright opposition.* Few state legislators disliked the idea, but there was little passion for change. Watson's key role was becoming a thorn in the side of apathetic state legislators who failed to realize the importance of their individual action.
- *Success has many claimants.* It is hard for a policy activist to retain credit for his or her efforts. Numerous individuals are motivated to take credit for successful endeavors.

2

Do Ask, Do Tell

The high school senior was intense as she framed her questions for the college admissions office representative. The questions flowed like a litany during her sixth college visit:
"Do you offer anthropology?"
"Do freshmen have to live on campus?"
"How many rapes happened on campus last year?"

The young couple took turns trying to keep their three-year-old quiet as the realtor outlined their options. Focusing on the last house they saw, they began a series of rapid-fire questions:
"Would the owner hold a mortgage for us?"
"How much would we have to put down?"
"Are there any sex offenders in the neighborhood?"

It would be impossible to assign a date to the scenes above, but the question about sex offenders probably would not have been asked, nor would the recipient be capable of giving an answer, until the 1990s. It is not because sex crimes are anything new but because until recently they were not monitored in many settings.

WHEN CRIME STRIKES HOME

The initial "crimes" seemed pretty trivial. Residents in the Lehigh University coed dorm had taped doors open to allow easy access. It was a common practice, regularly recorded in campus security logs. Students hired as security guards regularly broke regulations and failed to secure the doors during their rounds. Two wrongs provided the right of access to Joseph Henry, a student with a record of criminal assault. Shortly after being dropped off by her parents after spring break in 1986, freshman Jeanne

Clery was about to become another statistic. What began as a robbery after a drinking binge ended with Clery being raped, sodomized, mutilated with a broken bottle, and strangled to death. The five-cent plastic rape whistle that Lehigh had passed out during freshman orientation lay useless and ineffective in a drawer in her room.[1]

Megan was a typical seven-year-old, and the puppy was so cute. Her parents had warned her about talking to strangers, but this was a neighbor from across the street whom she had seen dozens of times. Could it be wrong to go into his house to see the new puppy? A few hours later Megan Kanka was found dead in a field not far from her Hamilton Township, New Jersey, home. She had been raped and murdered. The quiet thirty-three-year-old neighbor turned out to be a twice-convicted sex offender living in a house with two other convicted sex offenders. None of the neighbors knew of the danger in their midst. They all exclaimed, "If we had only known." Megan Kanka lay dead and her parents and friends asked themselves what they might have done to protect her.

ZONES OF PROTECTION

We all know that the world is a dangerous place. Bad things happen "out there." The feeling of comfort and safety most of us build around ourselves reflects the artificial boundaries of "our" campus or "our" neighborhood. Since medieval times, college and university campuses have been viewed as safe and legal entities responsible for their own residents. Campus security forces police the campus, often denying access to police officials from outside jurisdictions. Acting in loco parentis (in place of one's parents), college officials were long viewed as responsible for the safety of those on their intellectual "island." Most children feel a similar sense of safety in their neighborhood. Parents admonish their children, saying, "You can go outside and play, but don't leave the neighborhood." Increasingly these artificial boundaries fail to protect their residents from crime.

WHOM DO WE PROTECT?

All educational institutions seek to protect their students from harm out of both personal concern and practical necessity. Educators have an interest in the well-being of students but also recognize the public relations and economic implications of campus crime. Colleges and universities have become big businesses, bidding for applicants in a shrinking pool of college-age students. College administrators fear any news that might drive away potential students, thus preferring to handle crime discreetly. Discussions of campus crime have the potential for affecting enrollments.

*Maureen and Richard Kanka with
U.S. Representative Dick Zimmer (R-N.J.)*

Since 1974, colleges have had an important legal tool for limiting access
to student records. Based on the right of privacy, the Family Educational
Rights and Privacy Act—often called "the Buckley act" because of its sponsor—allows colleges to withhold academic and police records about individual students. The result was that campus police often kept the barest
of details in their campus crime logs.[2] Without details, it becomes impossible to effectively summarize the characteristics of victims, perpe-
trators, or crimes. Although state and local governments are required to
report crimes to the Federal Bureau of Investigation's Uniform Crime Report, no such requirement existed for colleges and universities, which often have their own police force and are viewed legally as autonomous governmental entities. As a result, some educational institutions reported and
others refused.

There was little doubt that colleges and universities supported punishing criminals, especially nonstudents, but they wanted it done without
implicating the institution. Student criminals often received more leeway
as educational institutions treated "minor" crimes (often including rape,
breaking and entering, and physical attacks), as potential "learning experiences," dealing with them via on-campus judicial hearings that would
not permanently damage the record of either the accused or the institu-

tion. The bottom line was that campus crime statistics were inconsistent and woefully underreported.[3] Existing procedures did a good job of protecting the reputations of colleges and universities but did little to warn potential campus crime victims of possible dangers.

On the surface, informing neighbors of a sex offender living in their area sounds completely reasonable. Assuming that sex offenders are likely to strike again, such warnings make sense, even in a society that allows convicted criminals to "pay their debt to society" and then go on without forever displaying a "scarlet letter" of punishment. We clearly want to protect children from predators. But lonely voices caution the need to balance the rights of potential victims against those of the rehabilitated offender. They point out that the recidivism rate for sex offenders is relatively low[4] and that they might "actually become more dangerous if driven from communities where family and friends help control their behavior."[5] The issue involves balancing the ex-prisoner's right to liberty and privacy and to begin anew against the community's right to protect itself and its children.

UP FROM VICTIMHOOD

Victimhood serves as a powerful motivator. Crime cuts a broad swath of victims, as friends and family of the victim find their lives turned upside down, thus becoming victims themselves. Some crime victims turn inward, feeling angered, perplexed, or even guilty about the disruption in their lives; others turn outward. Political involvement fills the days with activity and thus pushes out some of the pain. Howard and Connie Clery and Maureen and Richard Kanka found themselves unwitting victims of senseless crimes. As Howard Clery put it, "When your child dies, you're left with a completely empty feeling—beyond grief. We wondered, 'What is our life about?' In that sense [our] campaign helped."[6] Maureen Kanka echoed the same thought, saying, "If I had not started the movement, I would have died. When Megan died, I died with her. I needed a purpose to go on; in a way, this campaign has been a blessing. . . . I have come to feel that it was Megan's destiny to die, and mine to campaign in her name, so other children will be saved."[7] Victims' families want their relatives' deaths to mean something. Political activity can lead to living memorials for the deceased. Less selfishly, political activity may lead to an understanding of why the crime happened and how others may be protected from the same fate.

Society grants victims certain rights. Passion, emotionalism, and single-minded devotion are accepted from victims of crimes more readily than from those who only think about a category of crimes. The Clerys found that as "victims we were able to speak out in media of all sorts. . . . They would listen and write about campus crime."[8] The Kankas used the publicity from their status as victims to find like-minded allies among their neighbors and to put their legislative goals on the fast track.[9] Facts and figures help build the case that a problem exists, but victims give a human face to abstract ideas. The Kankas "used their visibility to work on behalf of children's safety issues. While academics and lawyers debated over the dueling constitutional rights of victims and sex-offenders, the emotional power of . . . victim's families prevailed."[10] In the competition for public attention and decision-maker interest, "the anecdote wins out over the . . . bean counters."[11] What moves legislators is often the latest headline, and victims are headline makers.

ORGANIZATION

The trial of Jeanne Clery's murderer revealed several lapses in security by Lehigh University employees. After the murderer was convicted, the Clerys sued the university and received a large (reportedly $2 million)[12] out-of-court settlement, which they used to help start Security on Campus, a nonprofit information clearinghouse and lobbying organization. Initially located in the Clery's house, the organization was later moved to allow more room for its three paid staff and five volunteers. The move also reflected some normalization in the Clery's life, which had been consumed by the murder for four years. Connie Clery pointed out that "it was just too hard, always seeing those grim headlines every time we turned around."[13]

Maureen and Richard Kanka were thrown into the battle over legislative reforms dealing with sex criminals in midstream. Maureen Kanka expressed

Connie and Howard Clery

the common theme of victim-motivated militants, saying, "Never in my wildest dreams, I thought, I would be an activist. . . . I was at home for twelve years raising my children."[14] Existing victims' rights groups were pushing for everything from the death penalty or chemical castrations to enhanced community notification laws. Laws on the books in more than half of the states required that local prosecutors be informed when offenders were released, but not the public.

Despite their grief, the Kankas eschewed revenge and defined the issue as one of informing parents about sex offenders residing in their neighborhoods.[15] The Kankas found themselves at the center of events as citizens of Hamilton Township channeled "what would otherwise be unmanageable rage, fear and grief [into] the more manageable demand for notification."[16] The reaction began almost immediately. On their way home from identifying their daughter's body, Megan's parents saw neighbors collecting signatures for a community notification law.[17] Pink ribbons sprouted on lapels, in young girls' hair, and around fenceposts, symbolizing both the memory of Megan and the demand for community notification. Over 200,000 New Jersey residents signed a petition demanding legislative action. Within a week of the murder, the Kankas would be speaking at a New Jersey rally supporting "Megan's law" as a tool to help parents better protect their children. The proposed law, modeled after legislation in other states, would require New Jersey authorities to notify communities when a child sex offender moved into their neighborhood. The Kankas would spend the next few months talking to the public and to legislators about their experience and serving as a visual reminder of a significant societal problem. As they sat in the public galleries of the state legislatures during the debate on the proposed law, each wearing a pink ribbon with Megan's name on it, they reminded legislators that the abstract goal of crime prevention had a human face.[18]

"THE FACTS, MA'AM, JUST THE FACTS"

Random acts of violence provide an elusive target for both law enforcement prevention and political action. Concerted action requires the establishment of patterns, trends, and projections.

One of the first steps taken by the Clerys involved collecting data on the legal rights of victims[19] and the pervasiveness of campus violence. Over the months, the piles of clippings grew. Organized data collection allowed them to present sound bite summaries of the problem with comments such as, "Eighty percent of the crimes committed on college campuses are committed by students."[20] Campus murders are rare, but 21,000 students fall victim to violent crimes each year. To give these mind-boggling figures some meaning, the Clerys began talking about the fifty-seven violent acts committed every day.[21]

The issue for the Kankas involved recidivism, the potential for sex offenders to commit repeat offenses after punishment and supposed rehabilitation. There is little justification for informing neighbors of harmless past offenders. The extreme difficulty of assessing an individual's danger to society varies by the nature of the crime and the effectiveness of rehabilitation. Research shows that between 7 percent and 35 percent of convicted rapists strike again.[22] The imprecision of the figure engenders considerable doubt. Proponents of Megan's law emphasized the higher figure, whereas opponents jumped on the lower.

STATING THE OBVIOUS

The U.S. Constitution creates a federal system with powers explicitly allocated to either national or state governments. All powers not specified are reserved by the Tenth Amendment to the states or the people. Proponents of federal legislation must pass three hurdles, convincing decision makers that the problem cannot be handled on the state level, finding a constitutional basis for federal action, and establishing a method of enforcing federal mandates on the states.

Crime prevention is largely a state responsibility, complicating any attempt to attack it nationally. Starting on the state level, the Clerys helped secure the passage of the Pennsylvania College and University Security Information Act of 1988 by gathering the relevant data and lobbying state legislators. Within three years, ten states had passed legislative mandates requiring postsecondary institutions to report crime statistics or lose state financial aid. Some states added more teeth to the legislation by including civil and criminal penalties for failure to comply.[23] Variations in state reporting laws made it difficult to compare risks across state lines. Arguing the need for consistency gave the proponents of federal legislation a basis for action.

In a federal system, individual states serve as models to be copied or "laboratories" for testing the effectiveness of new laws and assessing their unanticipated consequences. Experience with existing state variants of Megan's law raised some significant questions. In Washington State, local notification led to vigilante "justice" when the home of one sex offender was set on fire, and another offender was punched in the face.[24] Opponents of the law fear that it will create a class of pariahs that moves from community to community upon being identified.[25] Little hard data existed about the impact of notification laws on perpetrator deterrence or potential victim prevention. Some anecdotal examples emerged of sex offenders, with the threat of public notification hanging over their heads, facing up to the need for treatment.[26] In general, state experience with notification laws revealed few serious problems and allowed one proponent to claim, "I regard the safety of the children who are unsuspecting victims to be infinitely more important than the comfort of the repeat sexual-offender. . . . the Washington state law has been very good for our communities and has probably saved a number of children from grievous harm."[27]

MAKING A FEDERAL CASE OUT OF IT

State laws can be effective, but working on a state-by-state basis is slow and arduous. Variation from state to state also creates inequalities in the application of laws. Differences in crime reporting laws could put educational institutions from "tough statute" states at a competitive disadvantage relative to those in states not requiring reporting. Although potential students are more mobile, variations in reporting requirements may well disadvantage those looking at colleges in states without strict reporting laws. Sex offenders are mobile, which may become a necessity if they are driven from their communities by disclosure laws. States without strict disclosure laws could find themselves "dumping grounds" for offenders not wanting to face the glare of disclosure, thus increasing the dangers to their students.

Taking the Case to College

With over 20,000 violent campus crimes per year,[28] the need for a tough and uniform national standard became clear. The Clerys contacted Senator Arlen Specter (R-Pa.) and Representative William Goodling (D-Pa.) about their concerns. The two legislators responded by introducing the Crime Awareness and Campus Security Act of 1989. Involving the federal government in an essentially local issue such as campus crime requires some creativity in a federal system. Protection from such crime was not specified as a federal responsibility in the Constitution and it did not involve crossing state lines, where federal involvement was accepted on practical grounds. Normally the "reserved powers" clause of the Constitution kept such protection at the state level. The federal government's primary wedge for involvement stemmed from its ability to limit funding. The federal government often employs a "carrot-and-stick" approach to entice and/or threaten states or private entities to cooperate. The "carrot" might be the promise of increased funding in exchange for abiding by federal guidelines. The "stick" often involves the threat of reduced funding. Using the "stick" approach, the Crime Awareness and Campus Security Act of 1989 threatened colleges and universities with the loss of federal funds unless they made their crime statistics and campus security policies public. With over 8,000 colleges and universities involved in federal student aid programs, the potential threat was significant.

The Crime Awareness and Campus Security Act was explicitly promoted as a consumer bill of rights for students, providing them with adequate information regarding campus crime to make an informed decision before choosing to attend a college or university. The debate included arguments that "sunlight is the best disinfectant." The title of the bill was eventually changed to the Student Right to Know and Campus Security Act, reflecting the consumer aspect. The bill was expanded to include the requirement that schools also report their student athlete graduation rates, broadening the reasons for legislative support. Implicitly, a secondary goal involved encouraging colleges to tighten campus security in the hope of improving their criminal activity profile. In supporting the bill, Senator Kennedy (D-Mass.) pointed out that "making this information available will help students decide which institution to attend, will encourage students to take security precautions while on campus and will encourage higher education institutions to pay careful attention to security considerations."[29]

Some spokespersons for higher education worried about government intervention in their industry and the danger that crime and graduation statistics could hurt their reputations and/or be misinterpreted. With all the direct costs for improved security and record keeping borne by the schools, the debate raised the issue of unfunded mandates in which the federal government coerces both governmental units and private institutions to expend their own funds to carry out federal legislation. The appeal of a bill that cost the federal government nothing and held some promise for protecting students proved overwhelming. It passed unanimously in both House and Senate.[30]

But the battle over publicizing campus crime statistics was not over. Relying on the same privacy laws colleges previously invoked, the U.S. Department of Education blocked the implementation of the law by introducing a second "stick," the threat to block federal funds from any school opening its police logs.[31] Two years later, in 1992, Congress cleared the way for reporting by passing the Buckley Amendment Clarification Act, declaring that records kept by campus law enforcement offices are not confidential "education" records.

Bringing the Case Back Home

Forcing federal action often requires years of effort. Using states as "laboratories" can slow down the process as national opponents suggest waiting until the evidence from the states is in. Megan Kanka's case touched the hearts and minds of so many people that federal action virtually preempted state activity. Experience with existing state notification laws revealed few problems. Within a month of her murder both the House and Senate dealt with amendments to an existing crime bill to require convicted sex offenders to register with state authorities. The amendment permitted local authorities to alert communities when such criminals are released but did not require it. Especially in light of a case involving an eleven-year-old Minnesota boy abducted in 1989,[32] Megan's death served as a timely reminder of the danger, pushing the amendment to victory. It was a first step toward direct notification of neighbors. When a conference committee threatened to drop the amendment, President Bill Clinton weighed in. Just over a month after their daughter's funeral, Maureen and Richard Kanka sat through another ceremony. This time they were on the White House lawn for the president's signing of the 1994 Federal Crime Bill, which encouraged states to pass Megan's laws.

The original federal Megan's law lacked teeth. Permitting community notification turned out to be a far cry from requiring it. Some states, such as New Jersey, the site of Megan Kanka's murder, acted quickly, but others hung back. With the 1996 elections approaching, many elected officials scrambled to be on the popular side of the crime issue. Using the New Jersey law as a pattern, Congress passed more stringent legislation. Proponents argued that New Jersey's law served as "a model for other states to emulate. [It is] battle-tested by state and federal courts and looks like it balances interests of children and parents with the rights of offenders."[33] The law made it mandatory for local law enforcement officials to notify schools, day care centers, and parents about the presence of dangerous offenders in their area. The federal "stick" encouraging enforcement involved the threat of losing up to 10 percent of federal law enforcement funds. Although it was another unfunded federal mandate, requiring states and localities to spend money for administration with no extra federal funding, the momentum for passage was strong, leading to a unanimous vote in Congress. Again President Bill Clinton took time from his reelection campaign to sign the new legislation, with Maureen Kanka prominently leading other victim's parents as onlookers. Within a year, virtually every state had passed a community notification law. Again capitalizing on the laboratory function of states in a federal system, states are experimenting with different methods and degrees of notification. About half the states are using active notification initiatives, with the other half simply providing public access to registration records.[34] California established the most aggressive notification procedure, placing information about 64,000 registered sex offenders on a CD-ROM and prominently providing access to it at county fairs and other community events.[35]

Other states have used postcard notification, community flyers, and the Internet to provide access to the information. The widely diverse approaches reveal variations in crime rates, ideological commitments to federal intervention, and local traditions. This variation has also raised a wide range of legal issues that will keep the courts busy for years. In Louisiana, for example, newspapers are required to publish the photographs of released child sex offenders, whereas in New Jersey, leaking sex offender information to the press is prosecutable.[36]

Measuring the effect of Megan's law is probably premature. On the negative side, it forced states and localities to reshuffle scarce resources to comply with the law and potentially shortchange other crime-fighting initiatives.[37] At least one bogus attempt to embarrass an innocent victim[38] and one suicide of an "outed" sex offender have occurred.[39] Most nonoffenders and law enforcement professionals, however, believe we are better off with the law than without it.

KEEPING THE PRESSURE ON

The potential effectiveness of a legislative remedy can often be measured by the energy expended in circumventing the law. Benjamin Clery, Jeanne Clery's brother, charges that "the vicious cycle of student-on-student crime is quietly perpetuated by image conscious administrators who adjudicate felonies and misdemeanors in closed campus disciplinary hearings," which are now considered confidential under privacy law. Security on Campus (www.securityoncampus.org) successfully pushed for revision of the Campus Security Act to tighten requirements. In 1990, an amendment required that schools afford rape victims specified basic rights. The 1998 amendments expanded the reporting requirements and formally named the law the Clery Act in memory of Jeanne Clery. In 2000, amendments linked the Clery Act to Megan's law, requiring colleges to provide information about where sex offender information could be obtained. The battle over implementation continues. A study conducted by the Education Development Center at the University of Cincinnati discovered that less than 40 percent of colleges and universities accurately follow the act's requirements, leading to a new round of pressure to strengthen compliance.[40]

The effectiveness of notification laws depends largely on state and local implementation as influenced by judicial rulings. The Kankas formed the Megan Nicole Kanka Foundation for the state-by-state fight, quickly securing new laws in New Jersey, New York, Connecticut, and Maryland. A number of other states implemented Megan's laws on their own initiative.

Less than three months after the passage of New Jersey's Megan's law, a convicted rapist secured a federal court order blocking neighborhood notification on the grounds that it would cause "irreparable harm [to his] quality of life." This turn of events brought the Kankas back into the battle, filing a legal brief to protect the law.[41] Legal challengers in this and other cases questioned whether those convicted of a crime prior to the passage of

Megan's law could still be forced to register, or whether that would breach the constitutional guarantee against ex post facto laws, imposing punishment beyond that on the books when the offense occurred. Convicted offenders released after the passage of the law argued that public notification imposed a second punishment, violating the constitutional guarantee against double jeopardy. In 1998 and 2003, the Supreme Court validated the applications of Megan's law, initially by refusing to reconsider a set of supportive lower court rulings and later by taking two cases on appeal and directly rejecting constitutional challenges. The Court invalidated arguments that the law inflicted retroactive punishment (violating the ex post facto clause in the Constitution) and rejected the argument that ease of access to information on the Internet changed the basic nature of public records.[42]

To alleviate the pain of having to look across the street to see the rape and murder scene, the local Rotary Club bought and razed the house, making room for "Megan's Place," a small park with a fountain and a place to play hopscotch—one of Megan's favorite games.[43] Megan's murderer was convicted and sentenced to death.

Neither story is over. Lives were clearly changed. Connie Clery admits that her daughter's death has "torn her apart, [but] in one sense it's been good, because we're helping so many others."[44] The Clerys remain active in Security on Campus, attempting to educate parents and students about the potential dangers of campus life. The Kankas continue an active speaking schedule committed to making neighborhoods safer. Maureen Kanka describes their efforts of the last four years by saying that "it started as a little rolling stone and ended up as a boulder by the time it was at the bottom of the hill."[45] Both the Clerys and the Kankas remain vigilant, recognizing that laws and their interpretation are almost as fragile as the lives of the children they lost.

FROM ROCKING CHAIRS TO SUVS

It is one thing to identify potential repeat sexual offenders and another to stop them *before* they do any harm. Megan's law and the Clery Act look a lot like "locking the barn door after the horse is gone," at least to the victims of the first abuse.

In the not so distant past neighbors sat on front porches and looked out windows to keep track of all the children in the neighborhood. Kids played in the streets or on the sidewalks and could keep track of each other. Crimes were harder to pull off without someone observing them. Lifestyles change. Both children and adults spend more time away from home, running to soccer games and ballet practice. Soccer moms cruise the beltway strategizing their next pick-up and drop-off. Many people spend more time in their cars commuting each week than they spend eating, shopping, attending religious services, or participating in community activities. Anonymity is easier to maintain and crimes go unobserved.

It is no surprise that pedophiles would take advantage of unobserved children and hide their crime by slipping away in the flow of traffic. Even when a crime is observed, the complexity of modern society creates confusion and hesitancy. If the potential crime stopper wanted to get involved they would have to ask "Who do I call? The city police, the county police, the state police?" The multiple and overlapping boundaries mean that a criminal acting in one nested set of jurisdictions can quickly scamper across boundaries with impunity.

BE ALERT: THE WORLD NEEDS MORE LERTS

An attempt to tighten the net on fleeing pedophiles began in 1996 with the disappearance and murder of nine-year-old Amber Hagerman in Dallas, Texas. She was dragged screaming from her bicycle and kidnapped. The discovery of her nude body in a creek shocked the community, leading a local radio station to begin broadcasting news bulletins about missing children in the same manner as severe weather alerts.[46] Using a clever acronym

Donna Norris, Amber's mother, with President George W. Bush

based on Amber's name (AMBER- America's Missing: Broadcast Emergency Response), the program quickly spread to over forty states and has been credited with saving dozens of children.[47]

Local success stimulated pressure for national action. President George W. Bush convened the first White House Conference on Missing, Exploited and Runaway Children in 2002, directed the attorney general to create an AMBER coordinator in the Justice Department, and strongly endorsed national AMBER legislation.[48] The Senate acted quickly, passing the legislation twice by unanimous votes. The House was more hesitant, with Republican leaders holding out for stricter federal penalties for sexual abusers, kidnappers, and "virtual" pornographers on the Internet.[49] The March 2003 safe return of kidnapped Elizabeth Smart in Salt Lake City after nine months gave her father a national platform to successfully argue for immediate House action.[50] The national legislation is designed to speed the news of missing children to the public over radio, television, and electronic highway signs. The eyes and ears of the peripatetic population can be harnessed to spot criminals like the civilian posses of the Old West. As President Bush put it, "These criminals can know that any driver they pass could be the one that spots them and brings them to justice."[51]

Donna Norris, Amber's mother, found the bill-signing ceremony a "bittersweet" moment, pointing out that "I'm proud and happy and very excited, but our little girl was murdered for this bill."[52]

LESSONS

- *Federalism provides state laboratories for testing the consequences of legislation.* Passing a national law without prior testing courts disaster. The ability to try out new legislation in a variety of forms on the state level limits the breadth of potential unanticipated consequences.

- *Constitutional limits on federal activity can be overcome.* Despite severe constitutional limits on federal government power and responsibilities, creative members of Congress can find ways to enforce federal mandates. Using the "carrot" of increased benefits and the "stick" of reduced funding, states hesitate to not go along with federal government desires.

- *Politics is a continuous game.* Few fixes are final. Laws passed with great fanfare often require almost immediate revision.

- *External events can stimulate action.* Elizabeth Smart was not returned because of an AMBER alert, but her safe return focused media attention on kidnapping and gave her parents a platform to urge action.

- *Abstract ideas can be made more forceful by giving them a human face.* The images of Megan and Amber add potency to the issue of pedophiles and demand more action than sterile bill numbers or names.
- *Victimhood provides motivation but no guarantee of action.* Not all victims have the energy, skill, or obvious legislative solution for meaningful political action. The risks of some senseless crimes are simply not subject to governmental action. Successful victim-activists need to define problems in such a way that a legislative remedy seems both legitimate and likely to succeed.

Civil Rights

3

Taking the Bus and Driving
Public Policy for Us

It was an unlikely place for the birth of the modern civil rights movement—Montgomery, Alabama, still proud of its footnote in history as the city in which Jefferson Davis took the oath of office as president of the Confederacy. Most of its white residents reveled in their southern heritage. Intellectually they knew the Civil War was over, but emotionally they had not yet accepted losing the "war of northern aggression." Segregated housing, elevators, drinking fountains, restrooms, and transportation were a way of life. Negro (the accepted term in the 1950s)[1] bus passengers were accustomed to paying at the front door and then exiting the bus only to reenter at the back door, often standing while empty seats remained in the "whites only" section. Bus drivers were known to drive away as a Negro passenger was dashing for the back door. White citizens largely accepted their status as a right while "years of this degradation had largely anaesthetized the black population, which passively accepted its second-class citizenship."[2]

A CHANGE IN PATTERN

Rosa Parks, a forty-two-year-old department store seamstress, was no newcomer to the civil rights movement. She had served as secretary of the local NAACP (National Association for the Advancement of Colored People), had helped start the local NAACP youth chapter, and was well acquainted with many local Negro leaders. She was fully aware that E. D. Nixon, a local leader, had been trying to persuade the local Negro community to boycott the bus company, arguing that "the only way to make the power structure do away with segregation on the buses was to take some money out of their pockets."[3]

Parks was not the first person to protest bus segregation. At least three local cases of minority women refusing to give up their seats were well known in Montgomery. After the most recent situation, in which fifteen-year-old Claudette Colvin was arrested for disorderly conduct and taken away in handcuffs, Negro leaders protested to the city commission and received a "first-come, first-seated" commitment, although segregated seating areas were retained. The plan was torpedoed by the bus company's attorney, who declared that state law required segregated seating.[4] Once it became known that Colvin was pregnant and unmarried, she could not serve as a good vehicle for rallying support because her pregnancy would become the focus of attention.

No one on the bus that day, December 1, 1955, would have seen Rosa Parks as a "pushy Negro" itching for confrontation. She seated herself in the "colored section" toward the back of the crowded bus. Finding a seat in the "colored section" was no guarantee of retaining that seat. By law and tradition,[5] bus drivers could ask Negro passengers to give up their seats if the white section was full. Bus drivers were granted the powers of a police officer while in "actual charge of the bus," requiring them to "separate the white people from the Negroes."[6] Seeing a white man without a seat that afternoon, the bus driver asked the four Negroes in the front seats of the "colored section" to move and make room, calling over his shoulder, "niggers move back."[7] Parks stood (or perhaps more accurately sat) her ground, explaining, "the driver saw fit to have the four of us—the man who shared the seat with me and the two women across the aisle—stand up so this white man could have a seat. From where I was sitting there were no seats left in the back. The people were standing up just as close as they could together. There wasn't even any possibility of my having a choice to take a seat in the back."[8] The scene grew tense. The driver repeated his order and everyone craned to see who the troublemaker was. The driver "swore under his breath, pulled over to the curb, put on the brakes and came to stand above her," saying, "I said to move back. You hear?"[9] Parks continued to stare out the window, giving no recognition.

Rosa Parks was arrested and taken to the police station, where her request for a drink of water was refused. E. D. Nixon, the local NAACP leader, liberal white attorney Clifford Durr, and his activist wife, Virginia, obtained Parks's release on a $50 bond.[10] Over the objections of Parks's husband, Nixon and the Durrs encouraged Parks to use her situation as a test case to challenge the bus segregation laws.[11]

SORE FEET OR BRUISED EGO?

Rosa Parks greets the frequently told story that she refused to move because of her "tired feet" with a combination of bemusement and frustration, arguing that "my real reason was that I didn't think that I should have

Rosa Parks

to stand up on order of this bus driver and be deprived of my seat. I figured that as long as we did take that kind of treatment, they [the white segregationists] were becoming even more overbearing and cruel in their way of treating us."[12] She says, "My feet were not tired, but I was tired—tired of unfair treatment. Tired of being pushed around. Tired of seeing the bad treatment and disrespect of children, women, and men just because of the color of their skin. Tired of Jim Crow.[13] Tired of being oppressed. I was just plain tired."[14]

In response to charges that Parks's arrest was a setup orchestrated by the NAACP, one participant stated:

> No one can understand the action of Mrs. Parks unless he realizes that eventually the cup of endurance runs over and the human personality cries out, "I can take it no longer." Mrs. Parks's refusal to move back was her intrepid affirmation that she had had enough. It was an individual expression of a timeless longing for human dignity and freedom. She was not "planted" down there by the NAACP, or any other organization, she was planted there by her personal sense of dignity and self-respect.[15]

Often called the "mother of the civil rights movement," Rosa Parks had a defiant streak not always associated with the term *mother*. Parks grew up in a household "with an attitude." Her grandfather was hostile toward whites because of the cruelty he had endured. Parks says, "While I do not think I inherited his hostility, my mother and I both learned [from him] not to let anyone mistreat us. It was passed down almost in our genes."[16]

FORGET THE BUS AND LEAVE THE DRIVING TO US

Parks's case might have remained one of those thousands of indignities suffered by Montgomery Negroes after she paid her $50 bond and waited for her court date, but E. D. Nixon had other plans. He saw Parks's arrest as an ideal vehicle for galvanizing the local Negro community and carrying out a bus boycott that would force the end of bus segregation once and for all. The task was daunting. The chill of the Montgomery winter was setting in, and the city's 50,000 Negroes had little reputation for protest politics, the city having been called as "caste-ridden as any country in the world except India."[17]

The first call for a boycott came from the Montgomery Women's Political Council, a group of three hundred middle-class Negro women. Professor Jo Ann Gibson Robinson had "made it," with a prestigious teaching position at Alabama State University, but she still smarted from the discrimination and intimidation she had experienced on buses. Hearing of Rosa Parks's experience galvanized her to the point that she was willing to risk what she had. Robinson and a colleague stayed up all night running the university's mimeograph machine. The next morning, she and her students distributed 52,000 leaflets announcing a one-day boycott for Monday, December 5, 1955, Rosa Parks's day in court.[18] Tired of cautious male leaders, the women had decided to strike out on their own.[19]

On the surface, a bus boycott seemed rather tame, but it was a major step for a community that had largely accepted its lot with little more than private frustration. The backbone of an effective boycott would not be enlightened middle-class Negroes who owned cars, but the day laborers and service workers who depended on buses to get to work. Many could not afford losing even one day's wages. Recognizing the church as the mainstay of the Negro community, Professor Robinson made sure to drop off a set of circulars at a previously scheduled meeting of Montgomery's Negro ministers.[20] The ministers called a meeting at the Dexter Avenue Baptist Church for that evening and enlisted the help of the Reverend Ralph Abernathy and the church's new pastor, Mike King. King was an unknown factor, having recently arrived from a fashionable Negro church in another southern town. His Ph.D. from Boston University was impressive, but he had no record as an activist. Busy with his new duties at work and a new baby at home, King welcomed the meeting to his church but almost decided not to attend. His change of mind had significant repercussions for both the civil rights movement and King personally.[21]

The forty participants at the hastily-called evening meeting agreed to support the proposed one-day boycott. Since many Negroes lacked televisions, radios, or even telephones, getting the word out proved a significant challenge. Announcements from church pulpits and leaflets handed out at local stores proved more effective. Negroes with cars were encouraged to provide rides to their neighbors. The Negro cab companies, which also operated under segregation rules, were encouraged to transport passengers for the ten-cent bus fare. Boycott leaders were up early Monday morning hoping against hope to meet their goal of a 60 percent drop in ridership. The scene amazed even the most optimistic. "Sidewalks were crowed with Negro pedestrians. College and high school students were thumbing rides. Cars driven by Negroes were overloaded with ride-sharers. There were a few old-fashioned buggies on the street, and one man was seen riding a mule."[22]

But the joy of the early morning gave way to harsh reality. At 9:30 a.m., Judge Fred Gray found Rosa Parks guilty and fined her $10 plus court costs without ever considering the conflict between state and local laws or the constitutionality of her case. The importance of the verdict was heightened by the fact that it was one of the first clear-cut cases in which the segregation law was used as the basis for conviction. In previous instances, either the case had been dismissed or the defendant charged with disorderly conduct. It is probable that prosecutors had no idea what this change in strategy would unleash.[23]

The verdict spawned another meeting, this time at the Holt Street Baptist Church. By the time of the meeting, it was standing room only in the church and loudspeakers had to be installed on the roof for those in the street. At Abernathy's suggestion, Reverend King—who would make history as Martin Luther King after shedding the "Mike King" moniker—was named president of the newly formed Montgomery Improvement Association (M.I.A.).[24] In a revival-style atmosphere with music like "Onward Christian Soldiers," King rose to the occasion with a powerful sermon combining a call to action with Christian love. Speaking without notes, King asserted that

> we are here this evening to say to those who have mistreated us so long that we are tired—tired of being segregated and humiliated; tired of being kicked about by the brutal force of oppression. . . . If you will protest courageously, and yet with dignity and Christian love, when history books are written in future generations, the historians will have to say, "there lived a great people—black people—who injected new meaning and dignity into the veins of civilization." This is our challenge and our overwhelming responsibility.[25]

The final decision was a forgone conclusion—the boycott would continue. Carpools were formed on the spot. The Negro cab companies continued their ten-cents a ride policy.[26] For many, the new transportation system was more convenient than the buses.

The city of Montgomery chose to play hardball and began enforcing a city code that set the minimum cab fare at forty-five cents per passenger. This compelled the organizing committee to recruit over 150 volunteer drivers and establish routes. Rosa Parks, who had lost her job as a seamstress over the incident, became one of the clerks directing volunteer drivers to locations where pickups were needed.[27] Some white housewives lightened the demand by driving their Negro maids and cooks in order to "protect them from harassment." Martin Luther King established his credentials as a symbol of nonviolence after a bomb exploded on his front porch. Later King and other M.I.A. leaders were arrested for violating a state antiboycott injunction. Their case would join Rosa Parks's through the appeals process.[28]

THE END OF THE LINE

Montgomery, once a social and political backwater, became the focus of extensive media coverage, with local leaders on both sides realizing that the repercussions of their actions would extend well beyond the city limits. Rosa Parks began traveling around the country telling about the boycott and raising funds to cover the costs of providing transportation.[29] She was more powerful as a symbol than as a speaker.[30] Nationwide attention focused on Montgomery, and the $25 a week seamstress's protest was commemorated with a song, "When Momma Parks Sat Down, the Whole World Stood Up."[31]

After forty years it is hard to imagine the depth of frustration felt by Montgomery Negroes and the profound fear in the hearts of many white citizens. One prominent and respected white attorney argued earnestly that Rosa Parks was an NAACP "plant" and that goon squads were keeping the responsible "niggra" residents off the buses through intimidation. Expressing a widespread fear of losing a way of life that had been good to most whites, he asserted, "Hell, we don't care whether they have two seats or ten seats—this bus boycott is piddling stuff. Everyone knows what the NAACP is after—complete integration, even to intermarriage."[32] White officeholders reflected the fears of their supportive voters. As the boycott extended to almost a year and the legal cases dragged on, the city prepared a frontal attack, requesting an injunction "to stop the operation of the carpools or transportation systems growing out of the bus boycott."

At the darkest hour, the U.S. Supreme Court stepped in. On November 13, 1956, the justices upheld the decision of a federal district court that segregation on public transportation in Alabama was illegal. The final indignities of the boycott battle were still not over. The city of Montgomery appealed the original decision and also succeeded in getting its injunctions against carpools granted, condemning many Negroes to walk many extra miles until the final judicial mandate took effect.[33] On December 20, 1956, the Supreme Court ruled Montgomery's segregated seating laws unconstitutional. A little over a year after it began, the bus boycott was over. Rosa Parks celebrated by riding a newly integrated bus with James Blake, the bus driver who originally had her arrested.[34]

The celebration was tempered by the realization that Rosa Parks's act of defiance was a beginning rather than an ending. Martin Luther King characterized the bus incident as a "precipitating factor rather than a cause."[35] It unified and mobilized a previously complacent minority population, giving them strength, courage, and their first taste of victory. Many more battles remained to be fought. Success in Montgomery stimulated renewed commitment to civil rights activism around the country. The dark days of church and home bombings lay ahead. Other courageous acts of defiance would be necessary, of which it might well have been said that "this is where it all started." But for most on both sides of the segregation issue, the starting point of the modern civil rights movement was the "colored persons" bus seat that Rosa Parks refused to relinquish. Parks became a symbol for future generations of civil rights leaders: "I knew someone had to take the first step and I made up my mind just not to move."[36]

A TRANSFER FOR A NEW JOURNEY

On the heels of its bus boycott success, the Montgomery Improvement Association transformed itself into the Southern Christian Leadership Conference, launching Martin Luther King into a position of national leadership.[37] Rosa Parks had given the wheel of social reform another spin and intended to step back and watch the movement progress. She never felt totally comfortable with her notoriety. "Never having desired fame, she carried it as a simple person wears an ostentatious garment—uncomfortably, wishing with all her heart that she could trade it in for an honest cloth coat."[38]

Rosa Parks's courage guaranteed her a place of honor in the history of civil rights activists, but despite her wishes, she was not finished. Celebrity turned Parks into a full-time activist. Her husband lost his job as a barber when white customers deserted him, and they moved to Detroit to avoid the threats and conflict that plagued them. She spent twenty-three years on the staff of Representative John Conyers (D-Mich.). Retiring at seventy-five, Parks cofounded the Rosa and Raymond Parks Institute for Self-Development organized for "encouraging, motivating and training young people to reach their highest potential."[39]

Parks rose above racist explanations for every phenomenon and focused on identifying broader causes. Although she was beaten and robbed in a random act of violence when she was in her eighties, she eschewed bitterness and despair, asserting that "I pray for this young man and [deplore] the conditions in society that have made him this way. . . . I regret that some people, regardless of race, are in such a mental state that they would want to harm an older person."[40]

Rosa Parks's ride as a civil rights activist continued into her nineties with attempts to protect the symbolism of her efforts and promote equality. In 2003 she took to the courts and won a judgment against the hip-hop music group OutKast for naming one of their tunes "Rosa Parks," falsely suggesting its content.[41] That was also the year the Henry Ford Museum discovered the original bus in an Alabama field and spent almost $500,000 to buy it in an auction and restore it to its original condition for public display. In the most delicious bit of irony, the state of Missouri named a stretch of highway the "Rosa Parks Highway" after the Ku Klux Klan went to court to secure the right to erect an adopt-the-highway on that section of road. The Klan's limited interest in highway beautification as opposed to publicity was revealed when they never actually cleaned up the assigned section and were dropped from the program.[42]

Parks experienced a dramatic change in American society and deserves credit for its timing. The legal underpinnings of segregation completely evaporated, with society eventually attempting to redress years of indignity and harm through affirmative action programs.

As children subject to insults, we learn to repeat the palliative "sticks and stones may break my bones, but words will never hurt me." We didn't believe it then and don't now. Words continue to make a difference. The term *Negro* now sounds quaint at best, with the more derogatory variants of the "n word" totally unacceptable. The more neutral term *colored people* served as a bridge between less acceptable earlier terminology and contemporary nomenclature. Some readers may find the word *Negro* disconcerting after becoming accustomed to terms like *African American* or *black.* In this chapter I used the term *Negro,* which was accepted in the 1950s by blacks and whites alike, both to give a legitimate flavor for the era and to show how things have changed. Rosa Parks clearly played a role in bringing about changes that have occurred both in our behavior and in our language.[43]

Hollywood has a penchant for explaining social change in terms of dramatic events. Yet we mark the modern civil rights movement from a relatively simple individual act and a massive miscalculation by public officials. "Who would have thought . . . that a $14 fine against a Negro seamstress named Mrs. Rosa Parks for refusing to move to the 'Jim Crow' section of a municipal bus in Montgomery, Alabama, would galvanize a show of passive resistance . . . a symbol in another struggle for independence."[44]

LESSONS

- *The power of tradition.* We today look back at the unfairness and indignities of segregation and wonder how any white person could support it and why so few Negroes actively protested it. Through years of experience, individuals on both sides came to accept tradition and found ways to justify the existence of segregation and their own personal failure to confront it.

- *The power of a galvanizing incident.* Rosa Parks exemplified the importance of "being the right person at the right time." Her spontaneous action served as a rallying point for portraying bus segregation for what it was, an indefensible power play designed to "keep Negroes in their place." The fact that a respected Negro woman who had paid her fare was being asked to stand to allow a white man to take her seat symbolized the outrageous indignities of segregation in a country publicly dedicated to the principle that all persons are created equal.

- *The vehicle for protest strengthens or undermines a cause.* Rosa Parks engendered respect by her demeanor and her reputation as an unassuming, hardworking, churchgoing citizen respected by others. She had no skeletons in her closet that could undermine the cause by focusing the issue on her as a person.

- *Don't underestimate the pettiness of the opposition.* In an attempt to cling to the past and defeat the boycott, city officials took a no-holds-barred approach in harassing both boycott leaders and participants, passing discriminatory regulations and enforcing petty laws.

4

Being a Good Sport, or, Won't You Be on My Team?

The next time you hear the crowd in a college basketball arena shouting "Jump, Judy," or "Go for it, Sue," you can thank Bernice Sandler. In fact the next time you see female athletes play in any collegiate game, Bernice Sandler deserves some credit. No, she was not a star athlete who showed the way by example. At her height she would have been trampled by most of the female athletes of the day. She was not even an avid sports fan trying to make athletics better for women. Her story began with a much more personal plight whose unanticipated consequences revolutionized sports and, eventually, educational opportunities for both women and men.

Bernice Sandler's resume prior to taking on the issue of sexual discrimination in education does not read like the background of the high-powered activist she became.

She describes her experience at that time as "part-time visiting lecturer at the University of Maryland; Instructor at Mt. Vernon College; research assistant at the University of Maryland; nursery school teacher; guitar instructor; census taker; and secretary."[1]

It was her part-time teaching that got the ball rolling. With her doctorate in counseling psychology in hand, she looked forward to a career in higher education. When her department had seven openings her hopes built only to be dashed when she was not even considered for any of them. The tip-off came from a colleague who asserted that it was not her qualifications but, "Let's face it, you come on too strong for a woman."[2] The words stung like a body bloc. She initially accepted the evaluation with private tears. The next assaults driving her from the working world court came during two interviews for a position. One interviewer stated flatly that he would not hire a woman since they stayed home when their children were sick and

46

Bernice Sandler

told her that she was "not really a professional [but] just a housewife who went back to school."[3]

FINDING A WAY TO GET ON THE COURT

With her interest in gender discrimination piqued, Sandler began to read everything she could. Her search began with the landmark Civil Rights Act of 1964 which signaled increased attention on the rights of individuals. Inspired by the intentions of the Civil Rights Act, President Lyndon Johnson issued Executive Order 11246 making it illegal for companies bidding on government contracts to discriminate in employment. Sandler snatched the figurative "jump ball" while reading a report by the U.S. Commission on Civil Rights. Buried in a footnote lay the information that the original order had been amended by Executive Order No. 11375 in 1967 to prohibit such discrimination based on sex. She remembers, "Even though I was alone, I shrieked with my discovery."[4]

Cleverness counts and the oft called "Mother of Title IX" certainly saw an opening no one else had perceived. The textbooks emphasize a legislative process in which laws are passed by Congress and carried out by presidents. This misses a whole class of government dictates with the force of law. Presidents approve federal executive orders in a number of realms, often with innocuous and widely supported purposes. Federal Executive orders 11246 and 11375 were viewed as a method of giving minorities and women equal access to federal construction jobs and access to jobs providing materials to the government. Sandler's reading included a keen insight. Even though no existing laws prohibited sex discrimination in education, this order could be interpreted to include this intent since most educational institutions depend on federal grants and were therefore "doing business" with the federal government.[5]

WHO IS RUNNING THE GAME ANYWAY?

Executive orders are seldom self-implementing. They require bureaucratic action, often spurred on by citizen demands. Most federal bureaucrats have plenty to do and are not out shopping for new duties. Sandler went straight to the director of the Office of Federal Contract Compliance to make sure she was reading the order correctly. He said he "had been waiting for someone to use the Executive Order in regard to sex discrimination."[6]

Bolstering her credibility with the backing of the Women's Equality Action League (WEAL), Sandler filed a class action charge against all universities and colleges in the United States, asking the Department of Labor for an immediate compliance review and charging "an institution-wide pattern of discrimination against women in the academic community."[7]

"THE FACTS MA'AM, JUST THE FACTS"

Sandler recognized that hard facts trump weak impressions and personal experiences. It is just too easy to dismiss random impressions as not representative. She began doing her homework, documenting campus sex discrimination in the most precise and empirical ways possible. She used existing statistics about the availability of Ph.D.s in various fields and compared them with the number of female faculty members reported by female faculty members around the country in their institutions and departments. The patterns were hard to refute; many departments had no women faculty members even though as many as 25 percent or more of the doctorates in those fields had been granted to women. While it might be possible to argue that earlier hires had been constrained by lack of available female candidates, that would not wash for the present. On the advice of the director of the Office of Federal Compliance, Sandler created an eighty-page appendix of data, which he said "was important; even if no one read it [since] they would assume that the many pages confirmed the charges."[8]

Sandler sought out women with stories such as her own to bolster her case. Recognizing the hesitancy of the bureaucracy to act, she encouraged these women to write their representatives in Congress. Her efforts generated hundreds of letters and under congressional pressure the Department of Labor charged all field personnel to include sex discrimination in all contract compliance investigations.[9] While she felt strongly the executive order was clear, her cause would gain legitimacy if sex discrimination were part of a formal law, since executive orders can be rescinded or amended at any time.

ROUND ONE: FINDING THE TARGET FOR ONE'S BEST SHOT

As in most sports, Sandler targeted her shot strategically, focusing on Edith Green (D-OR). Green was not only a woman and senior member of the majority party in Congress, she was also chair of the relevant subcommittee of the Education and Labor Committee, and a long-time supporter of liberal issues. The seven days of hearings on what became Title IX produced a two-volume committee report of nearly 1,300 pages that was widely distributed, "helping to make sex discrimination in education a legitimate issue."[10] Signaling the limited awareness of potential implications, no postsecondary institutions bothered to testify at the hearings.[11]

There is a time to speak and a time to remain silent. When Representative Green introduced Title IX to the 1972 Education Act, she "requested women's groups *not* to lobby on behalf . . . because she believed that if members of Congress were not aware of what was included in Title IX, they would simply vote for it without paying too much attention to its content or its ultimate implications."[12] The women agreed not to lobby and members of Congress were distracted by other "hot button" issues in the legislation such as school busing.

Sandler and the organizations involved were presented with a choice to lobby or not lobby. They chose the latter.

The content of Title IX of the Education Amendments of 1972 was not created out of whole cloth, but rather emulated the Civil Rights Act of 1964 which had provided equal protection for racial minorities. Title IX reads: "No person in the United States shall, on the basis of sex be excluded from participation in, be denied the benefits of, or be subjected to discrimination under any educational program or activity receiving federal financial assistance." In many ways, the full implications of this portion of the bill were not anticipated. Title IX generated little controversy and no organized constituency opposed its passage. It was not until the full implications of the law were understood by the male sports establishment that conflict arose.[13]

AWAKENING FROM THE FIRST ROUND

Political battles, like many games, have a series of rounds. In the case of Title IX, the first round involved passing the legislation, but success at that stage harbored no guarantee that the law would do what was intended. The second round involved the crucial determination as to which aspects of a school's educational program it would apply. The third round involved the battle over how the law would be applied. "Equal opportunity" is a slippery term needing definition and enforcement. Definitions of an even playing field differed depending from which side of the slope one was looking. The third round let loose the creative juices of experienced competitors as they sought to test the rules using end runs and sneak plays.

ROUND TWO: EXPANDING THE PLAYING FIELD

Bernice Sandler was one of the first to admit that "We didn't really think of it (Title IX) as a sports thing, and the sports people were not watching and didn't know it covered them."[14]

Ralph Waldo Emerson boldly declared that "foolish consistency is the hobgoblin of little minds, adored by little statesmen and philosophers and divines."[15] Emerson was obviously never under the pressure of modern political forces. Politicians who change their position over time are charged with doing a "flip-flop," with the implication that either their former or latter position was somehow fraudulent. Holding two seemingly inconsistent positions at the same time implies that the politician has either not thought through his or her beliefs, or that self-serving duplicity rules. Describing someone as "talking out of both sides of their mouth" is not a compliment to their dexterity. Much political argumentation proceeds by analogy and comparison, with proponents asking the questions, "if the law applies in this situation, why shouldn't it apply here?" In the case of sex discrimination in education it had long been argued that a well-rounded education involved improving students in mind *and* body, with athletic programs fulfilling much of the body development goals. Given that opening, it became easy to take the argument about gender equality in education one step further and apply it to sports programs. For Sandler and her early supporters, it was an unanticipated consequence, but anticipated or not, consequences are consequences.

ROUND THREE: SCORING WHEN IT COUNTS

As with most legislation the impact was not immediate. Congress passes laws in general form and turns them over to bureaucratic agencies to spell out the details. Although passed in 1972, the Department of Health, Education and Welfare did not promulgate the specific regulations for implementing Title IX until 1975. The process of writing the regulations was complicated by the passage of the 1974 Education Amendments providing for a "legislative veto" giving Congress forty-five days to disapprove specific regulations. In a classic case of the "devil is in the details," the process of writing the Title IX regulation became the battleground. The male-sports-oriented National Collegiate Athletic Association awoke from its political slumber to oppose strict equality as a threat to their sports programs. Some feminist groups spoke out but wisely recognized the need to speak with one voice. Taking a new role in the fray, Bernice Sandler became a prime mover in the National Coalition for Women and Girls in Education. Coalition lobbying is often difficult to pull off since constituent groups fear losing their identities and ability to take credit. Supporters began asking constituent groups, "Why do we need to support you any more?" The National Coalition was careful to limit its area of concern, leaving many issues for constituent groups to claim as their own. They also worked hard at sharing power among participants.[16]

Seeking an enforceable set of rules, the Department of Education brought in representatives from the National Collegiate Athletic Association, American Football Coaches Association, and women's organizations. The women's groups led with a proposal to simply split all athlete support 50–50. Donna Lopiano, representing the women, remembers that the "football guys just about fell off their chairs, [but] came back with a proposal that I think was an effort to gain a perpetual advantage."[17] They proposed a proportionality standard, arguing that the percentage of athletes should mirror the gender split among undergraduates. Lopiano asserts that agreeing to such a split was a wise and forward-looking strategy by pointing out that "in the 1970's most schools were about 65% male, and I think the coaches thought it would stay that way, so they were protecting their football rosters. . . . We figured that participation was so miniscule that going from 5 percent to 35 percent was enormous."[18] Dislocations from making the initial adjustments to proportionality and a growing female percentage in the undergraduate pool led to dramatic changes in opportunities.

CRYING FOUL

On paper the penalties for discrimination under Title IX were serious. "If any educational institution was found to discriminate in any of its programs—including admissions, athletics, financial aid, counseling, facilities, and employment practices—federal funds would be cut off."[19] Feminists felt that the Office for Civil Rights (OCR) was lackadaisical about enforcement, while others pointed out the numerous decision points policy decisions had to go through. OCR regulations had to be considered and acted on by 16,000 school districts and 2,500 colleges to be fully effective.[20] "Ultimately all implementation of this law resides with school districts and college and university officers. The actual effect of the law has been therefore determined to a significant degree by the willingness of local officials to act in accord with the spirit as well as the letter of the law."[21]

Proponents of strict enforcement were also frustrated by the low priority subsequent secretaries of HEW gave to the law and the fact that the OCR staff were largely males who had come from the black civil rights movement of the 1960s and "seemed to be in questionable sympathy with the goals of women activists."[22]

WORDS MAKE A DIFFERENCE

The regulation used terms like "reasonable provisions" for female participation in intercollegiate athletics, and "substantially equal per capita expenditures" for items such as scholarships, travel, and equipment. This still left room for interpretation of words like *reasonable* and *substantially*. Representatives of male sports urged flexibility and continually tried to exempt revenue-producing sports. The final regulation clearly included all sports and required "proportionally equal" scholarships for men's and women's athletic programs and "equivalent benefits."[23]

FAKE RIGHT, CHARGE FORWARD

Legislation and its implementation are seldom straight-line phenomena. Challenges and counter challenges serve to refine the application of laws. A challenge by Grove City College questioned whether an entire educational institution could have its federal funds withdrawn for discrimination, or whether the prohibition against discrimination applied only to the specific educational program in question. The Court's 6–3 1984 decision in *Grove City v. Bell* limited punishment to specific programs, dramatically weakening the potential threat of Title IX as well as a variety of other discrimination laws. Enforcement of Title IX by the Department of Education Office of Civil Rights was slowed down awaiting further guidance from Congress. A broad coalition of civil rights groups began pushing for a legislative remedy.[24]

The opening for legislative action lay in the fact that the Court had ruled on legislative intent in *Grove City v. Bell* and had not questioned the constitutional basis of the legislation. It took four years of maneuvering and the ability to override a veto by President Reagan for the *Civil Rights Restoration Act of 1988* to reverse the Court interpretation and clearly spell out that legislative intent was to ban federal funds to an entire institution if any of its programs or units was guilty of illegal discrimination.[25]

WINNERS AND LOSERS

Most schools (about 75 percent) sought to meet the mandate by simply adding women's sports without dropping men's teams. Often the sizes of men's team rosters were reduced and high volume, low cost women's sports were added. Some creative accounting was allowed with a female runner competing in cross-country, indoor, and outdoor track counting for three female athletes in the proportionality ratio.

In many cases, lack of resources, will, and creativity turned the battle into a zero sum game, with gains by women coming at the direct cost to men's sports. Some teams with long histories of excellence, such as winning Olympic medals and national championships, were dropped.[26]

TITLE IX BY THE SCORE CARD

Sports teams keep score. If Title IX had a score card it would look something like this:

	Pre–Title IX	2002	Change
Number of women in intercollegiate sports	30,000	157,000	+523%
Number of men in intercollegiate sports	248,000	206,573	–17%
Number of women's teams in the NCAA	4,776	8,400	+175%

Men's teams cut 175 wrestling programs, 80 tennis teams, 70 gymnastic teams, 45 track teams; while 39 colleges have added high-income football teams in the last 10 years.[27]

On the softer side of the score card, it is impossible to accurately measure the impact Title IX has had on both the individual lives of athletes and on sports as a whole. Reallocating scholarship money to women undoubtedly has given some women the chance for a college education they would not have had. Self-confidence and other life skills commonly associated with athletic participation are now available on a more equitable basis. In the broader scheme of American sports, "Many now sug-

gest that the U.S. victory in the Women's World Cup [soccer], the existence of the Women's National Basketball Association, and America's
1998 Olympic gold medal in women's ice hockey were made possible by
Title IX."[28]

THE GAME GOES ON

The political process is a continuous game with numerous rounds. The arrival of the George W. Bush administration and its more conservative outlook heartened supporters of threatened, lower-profile, limited-means
sports teams who hoped that conservative opposition to government involvement would lead to changed levels and nature of enforcement for
Title IX. Public support and the "growing realization that the law is, in
large measure, working" led to a blue ribbon commission appointed by
President Bush to recommend upholding the current standards of compliance.[29]

MONDAY MORNING QUARTERBACKING AND
ANTICIPATING THE NEXT ROUND

The interconnections between changed laws, changed behavior, and
changed attitudes are difficult to sort out. Each can be a driving force.
Now, thirty years after Title IX's passage, two participants who have lived
through the fray come to complementary conclusions. Susan Hofacre, athletic director at Robert Morris University, points out that "twenty years
ago, when I taught about these kinds of things [women's opportunities in
sports] males in the class didn't have a clue that women should have equal
opportunity. Now it never occurs to them that girls can't play sports at a
high level."[30]

Still active in a broad range of issues associated with woman's rights,
Bernice Sandler has overcome her initial assumption that the battle would
be short and sweet. More than twenty years after her quest began she admitted that she had "thought I would work for two years [on Title IX] and
then go on to something else."[31] Now a decade later she maintains her optimism, pointing out that "I anticipated that most people would see that
[academic equality] was right, that most people would follow the law. And
in fact, that's what happened."[32]

Sandler sees Title IX's broader importance as having helped change the
public mindset about equality. In her words,

> What Title IX has done, it gave it [sex discrimination] a name, it gave us a lens
> by which we would look at things and say, "Is this fair? Are they treating
> women fairly?" Once you look at it that way, it is hard to ever go back.[33]

LESSONS

- *It is important to know the rules and how to use the rules to one's benefit.* The "devil" or perhaps "angel" is in the details. Read the footnotes.
- *Arguing for consistency is a powerful strategy.* It is hard to argue against "What is good for the goose is good for the gander." There is an appealing neatness to equality in the application of laws.
- *Unanticipated consequences are often more important than anticipated ones.* The impact of Title IX on athletics at all levels of education was largely outside the dreams of the supporters and the fears of the opponents.
- *There is a time to act and a time to keep quiet in order to minimize opposition.* Keeping quiet may be difficult for activists, but it can be the key to success.
- *Much can be done if one is not concerned with who gets the credit.*
- *Don't assume that those charged with enforcing the law will do so without prodding.*

5

Let's Just Run That One Up the Flagpole

Rude? Yes. Disrespectful and childish? Sure. Intended to offend? Without question. Unconstitutional? That is another question.

Critical issues of civil liberties seldom arise out of one-sided situations. The true test of a society's commitment to liberties is sparked by controversial behaviors. Schoolchildren are taught respect for the American flag through both words and examples. Classes begin with pledging allegiance *to the flag*. Proper handling, folding, and disposal of the flag are taught by organizations such as the Girl Scouts and Boy Scouts. We learn to stand when the flag passes and "read" its public presentation for symbols of societal mourning (flying at half staff) or danger (flying upside down). Children learn that the flag is not just a piece of cloth but rather a powerful symbol imbued with supernatural power and requiring extraordinary respect. Perhaps no lesson taught by the schools is more pervasive and consistent than honoring the flag.

Capitalizing on the pervasive societal norm of respect for the flag, a small group of demonstrators cleverly decided to "hit us where it hurts," and in the process forced society to decide whether our loyalties lie with the flag itself or with the values it represents.

A FLAG OF CONVENIENCE

Gregory Lee (Joey) Johnson came to Dallas from Atlanta to test the patience of the police and protest Reagan administration policies, but not necessarily to test Texas law against flag desecration. In fact, he and the other protesters began their quest without the symbol for which their protest would be remembered.

As a military brat following his stepfather around the world, little Joey Johnson became a kind of mascot to enlisted personnel as he tried to peddle the *Stars and Stripes* newspaper around the barracks. What might have

Gregory Lee (Joey) Johnson

been a training school for patriotism turned into something else as Johnson, who happens to be white, "rapped" about the war with disenchanted black draftees.[1] With the Vietnam War in full force, his formative years were dominated by "a whole generation of radical GIs who went against the masters of war."[2] During high school, he became convinced of America's racism and decided he was "for revolution, not for reform."[3] After dropping out of high school and doing a stint in the merchant marine, Johnson returned to Tampa, Florida, in 1976, became more radical, and began his active involvement in the Revolutionary Communist Youth Brigade (RCYB). The depth and breadth of his hatred for the United States knew few bounds. He described the country as "an imperialist system which dominates and exploits large sections of the world" and charged that U.S. "crimes committed against the peoples of the world exceeded even what the Nazis were capable of." He welcomed "every defeat that the U.S. suffers in the world" and sought to use such defeats to "hasten the day when we can actually bring down the empire."[4]

Using the 1984 Republican National Convention as an excuse, the twenty-eight-year-old Johnson and his left-wing compatriots staged the "corporate war chest tour" through downtown Dallas. They carried out "die ins" at various locations to dramatize the impact of nuclear bombs, and they spray-painted buildings, overturned planters, and shouted obscenities.[5] In an act of improvisation, one of the demonstrators snatched an American flag from the Mercantile Bank building and handed it to Johnson, who shoved it into his shirt.[6] With no prior planning, this action set into motion a court test that would clarify Americans' rights of free expression. The protestors held up the flag and chanted, "America, the red, white, and blue, we spit on you," before dousing it with lighter fluid and igniting it.[7] It was never possible to prove who actually stole or burned the flag.

When the dust settled, ninety-six demonstrators were arrested, with Johnson and three others charged with flag burning under a Texas law outlawing "desecration of a venerated object." Of the four charged, only Johnson chose to show up for the trial and fight the charges, thus becoming the vehicle for an important test of civil liberties in the United States.[8] His actions surprised few of his supporters, who described him as a "real rabble rouser . . . [who] never backs away, goes to court, [and] when he gets time [in jail], he doesn't run."[9] Few outside of his inner circle of disaffected communists found Johnson's cause very appealing. His lawyer, provided by the Texas Civil Liberties Union, described him and his friends as "punk anarchists who despise the government and big business."[10] The lawyer quickly added that "a strong democracy should be able to tolerate this kind of dissent [peaceful and quiet], as long as it is not violent."[11]

APPEALING TO THE COURT STANDARD

Johnson's actions presented a significant test to both the court system and the government. "He chose to criticize power by attacking the state's most cherished symbol of power, its flag. The genius of flag-burning is that the emotions it provokes challenges the government to stay unemotionally reasonable."[12]

The evidence that Johnson personally burned the flag was largely circumstantial. Johnson himself denied doing the burning but admitted his approving of it. Under Texas law, he could be prosecuted for aiding and encouraging illegal activities committed by his coconspirators.[13] Against the advice of his lawyers, Johnson insisted on wearing a T-shirt at the trial emblazoned with the words "Revolutionary Communist Youth Brigade" and depicting a man carrying a rifle.[14] He refused to play the role of a nice middle-class kid wrongly charged by the police. He saw the publicity surrounding the trial as a vehicle for espousing his radical rhetoric.

The jury in the Dallas County Criminal Court found him guilty and handed down a sentence of one year in jail and a $2,000 fine. If Johnson's goal was publicity and national change, the initial reaction seemed disappointing; outside of Dallas, the story was largely ignored by the national media.

Johnson's supporters went beyond the constitutional guarantees of free expression to point out that prosecuting Johnson for disrespecting the flag was based more on what he attempted to communicate than his actions. A 1942 congressional resolution on the proper utilization of the flag prohibits using it on any commercial product or on any disposable item. No one protests when political candidates (usually of a conservative persuasion) bedeck their campaign advertisements with the flag, when used car dealers hang gigantic flags around their lots, or when the flag is used on a clearly throwaway item such as a stamp.[15] When Joey Johnson used the flag to castigate the U.S. government, patriots assigned his breach to a different category than improper "use" of the flag.

The Texas Court of Appeals in Dallas rejected the arguments that flag burning represented "expression" guaranteed by the U.S. Constitution and unanimously upheld Johnson's conviction.[16] The next avenue of appeal involved the Texas Court of Criminal Appeals. In a state as conservative as Texas, few observers anticipated the stunning reversal that the appeals court would hand down. By a 5 to 4 vote, the Texas Court of Criminal Appeals declared that the Texas venerated objects law had been used to violate Johnson's right to engage in peaceful symbolic political protest. The court accepted the Texas Civil Liberties Union argument that

> the right to differ is the centerpiece of our First Amendment freedoms.... Government cannot carve out a symbol of unity and prescribe a set of approved messages to be associated with that symbol.... [The state cannot] essentially license the flag's use for only the promotion of the governmental status quo.[17]

It now fell to the state of Texas, as the losing party, to pursue the final round of appeal before the U.S. Supreme Court.

Johnson used his newfound publicity to tour the country espousing his views on flag burning as well as his broader political agenda. Always good for a sound bite, Johnson ridiculed President Bush's volunteer recognition program by calling flag burning one of the "thousand points of light" and calling the Supreme Court threats to reinstate his conviction, "desperate steps [by a] sick and dying empire desperately clutching to its symbols."[18]

The issue gained momentum from a juried art display at the School of the Art Institute of Chicago (SAIC) in which Scott "Dred Scott" Taylor's entry invited visitors to step on an American flag to sign the guest book. Scott admitted being inspired by the Johnson case. The controversy resulted in new legislation by the Chicago City Council and the Illinois state legislature, which outlawed positioning flags on the floor. The U.S. Senate concurred with such prohibition by a vote of 97 to 0. The Illinois state legislature put some teeth in its legislation by reducing state funding for SAIC from $65,000 to $1.[19]

In 1989, the Supreme Court ruled by 5 to 4 in *Texas v. Johnson* (491 U.S. 397) that flag desecration was a means of public protest and an act of free expression protected by the First Amendment. In a rare act, symbolic of the importance of the decision, Justice William Brennan read the entire twenty-two-page decision to the packed court instead of the more typical practice of providing only a summary.[20] The decision in effect nullified various laws in forty-eight states prohibiting flag desecration. The voting coalition surprised many observers, with three of the Court's most liberal members (William Brennan, Thurgood Marshall, and Harry Blackmun) being joined by two of the most staunch conservatives (Antonin Scalia and Anthony Kennedy). The majority decision, written by Justice William J. Brennan, noted that "if there is a bedrock principle underlying the First Amendment, it is that the Government may not prohibit the expression of an idea simply because society finds the idea itself offensive or disagreeable"[21] and that "we do not consecrate the flag by punishing its desecration, for in doing so we dilute the freedom that this cherished emblem represents."[22] In his dissent, Justice William H. Rehnquist called the flag "the visible symbol embodying our nation" and stated that the "public burning of the American flag by Johnson was no essential part of any exposition of ideas."[23]

Although Supreme Court decisions officially settle only specific cases, they become precedents for future cases. Law enforcement officials shy away from enforcing laws when the likelihood of court reversal is high. Flag burners now seemed to have free rein, but there was no great rush to burn the flag. Only prohibited fruit seems irresistibly luscious and tempting. With flag burning now apparently legal, there seemed little point in doing it.

TRYING AN ALTERNATIVE FLAGPOLE

Decisions by an unelected group of nine justices do not necessarily settle political conflicts in America. In our system of checks and balances, interested citizens and elected officials may question the wisdom of Supreme Court justices through new legislation or amendments to the Constitution. Johnson's actions, if nothing else, ignited a national debate on the limits of the First Amendment and legislation appropriate to it.

With over 70 percent of Americans favoring unique protections for the flag via a constitutional amendment and over 65 percent disagreeing with the Supreme Court,[24] Congress responded quickly by passing the Flag Protection Act of 1989—by a vote of 91 to 9 in the Senate and 317 to 43 in the House. Twenty-five House Democrats and eighteen House Republicans made up the opposition block. The legislation required up to one year in jail and a $1,000 fine for anyone who "knowingly mutilates, defaces, physically defiles, burns, maintains on the floor or ground, or tramples upon any flag of the United States."[25] President Bush withheld his signature, allowing the legislation to become law without it, as a way to signal his belief that nothing less than a constitutional amendment would provide long-lasting protection for the flag.[26]

The inconsistency between the Supreme Court ruling and congressional action set the stage for another head-to-head conflict over the constitutionality of legislation against flag desecration. With Joey Johnson now off the hook for his role in the Dallas protest, the torch was passed to fellow RCYB member Shawn Eichman, who burned a flag on the Capitol steps to protest the Flag Protection Act. Present at the Capitol, Johnson expressed outrage that he was *not* arrested, calling it a "miscarriage of justice" and "profound cowardice" on the part of the government.[27] William Kunstler, Johnson's lawyer, called it a case of "selective nonprosecution," arguing that charging Johnson would have been "too much of an organizing tool" for opponents of the new law.[28] The issue would now turn on the decision in *United States v. Eichman* (496 U.S. 310) (1990) to determine the constitutionality of national legislation such as the Flag Protection Act. Few expected a different outcome. The Court struck down the Flag Protection Act of 1989 by the same 5 to 4 margin.

REDESIGNING THE CONSTITUTIONAL POLE

The Supreme Court evaluates legislation in terms of the Constitution. Flag protection advocates next attempted to amend the Constitution, undermining the legitimacy of the Court to use the document to justify flag desecration.

Positions on amending the Constitution to protect the flag largely divided along liberal and conservative lines. On issues confronting society with a choice between freedom and the maintenance of order, liberals generally favor *freedom* and conservatives *order*. House Speaker Tom Foley (D-Wash.) took the rare action of speaking directly from the floor, arguing that "the flag is a symbol of our national life and values. It is a symbol of liberty and freedom." Turning to conservatives on whose support he could seldom count, Foley explained, "If there is one underlying principle of conservatism, as I understand it, it is to preserve the basic institutions of liberty and not to change them idly or casually in the face of . . . transitory forces, influences or emotions."[29] Liberal House members such as Representative Ted Weiss (D-N.Y.) argued, "We have nothing to fear from the flag-burner. We have a great deal to fear from those who have lost faith in the Constitution."[30] Putting the flag burning issue in the context of contemporary international events, Representative John Conyers Jr. (D-Mich.) put our liberties in a broader framework, arguing that

Demonstrators who cut the communist symbols from the center of East German and Romanian flags prior to the fall of the Iron Curtain committed crimes against their countries' laws, yet freedom-loving Americans justifiably applauded their brave actions. If we wish to maintain our moral stature in matters of human rights, it is essential that we remain fully open to political dissent, regardless of the unpopular form it takes—even disparagement of the U.S. flag.[31]

Conservative president George Bush favored congressional action to outlaw desecration of this unique symbol, the flag for which thousands of Americans had died. President Bush asserted that "the flag [is] more than mere fabric, rather a mosaic of values and of liberty. What that flag encapsules is too sacred to be abused."[32]

Despite widespread public approval and supportive resolutions from forty-nine state legislatures (all but Vermont), achieving a two-thirds majority in both houses of Congress to send an amendment to the states for ratification proved elusive. After numerous attempts, the House adopted a flag protection amendment by a vote of 312 to 120 in 1995, but the Senate failed to reach the required supermajority by three votes (63–36). In subsequent years, the House voted overwhelmingly four more times to support the amendment (300 to 125 in the latest vote) but failed to get Senate approval.[33]

LONG MAY SHE WAVE

Joey Johnson is an angry, now middle-aged man spewing his anti-American venom widely. Despite the failure and discrediting of communism during the 1990s, he remains the national spokesperson for the Revolutionary Communist Youth Brigade. In 2002, Johnson redirected some of his efforts to oppose U.S. involvement in Iraq.[34] In reaction to the proposed flag protection amendment, he said, "I want to encourage everyone protesting the cutting off of affirmative action, the closings of clinics and hospitals, the cutting of educational benefits, the racism and brutality of the police, the discrimination against immigrants. Go ahead, burn the American flag in protest." Johnson sees the attempted amendment as "another attempt to enforce mandatory patriotism and define the boundaries of correct political dissent [and as] . . . an act of a sick and dying empire clutching to its symbols which rest on genocide and slavery."[35] The breadth of his charges and the virulence of his attacks on the United States make Johnson a hard person for most Americans to like, but the American political tradition takes pride in protecting views we dislike and individuals we disdain. As Voltaire put it, "I disapprove of what you say, but I will defend to the death your right to say it."[36] Speaking for the majority of the Court in another free speech case, Justice Oliver Wendell Holmes explained that free speech is "not free thought for those who we agree with, but freedom of thought that we hate."[37]

LESSONS

- *Constitutional guarantees of civil liberties protect those we adore as well as those we abhor.* The granting of liberty always includes the potential danger that the liberty granted will be used in ways we disapprove. As Representative John Conyers Jr. (D-Mich.) put it, "The genius of the Constitution lies in its indifference to a particular individual's cause."[38] An unfettered First Amendment stands ready to protect everyone's right to speak and protest.
- *The public is not necessarily the best repository for civil liberties guarantees.* The public generally supports civil liberties in the abstract but is considerably more willing to place limitations on individual actions.
- *The courts evaluate action, not rhetoric.* Talking about burning a flag or threatening to do so would not have brought about court action. Gregory Johnson made history for taking responsibility for his actions and in the process forcing a true test of the limits of free expression.

6

All Dressed Down and Nowhere to Go: A Pilot's Checklist

THE TAKE OFF: LAUNCHING MISSION IMPOSSIBLE

The *burqa,* a floor-length garment with veiled headdress, became the symbol of the authoritarian regime in Afghanistan, and abolishing the requirement to wear it became part of the U.S.-backed movement to liberate Afghan women. As First Lady Laura Bush put it, "The fight against terrorism is also a fight for the rights and dignity of women."[1] At the same time the United States was pushing for women's rights in Afghanistan, female U.S. troops in Saudi Arabia were not allowed to travel unless accompanied by a man, were required to wear a garment somewhat less restrictive than the *burqa* (the black head-to-foot *abaya*), and were forced sit in the back seat of vehicles when off their military base. Martha McSally, an Air Force pilot, saw the policy as clearly "off base."

Pentagon officials argued that the rule "respects Islamic law and protects troops from harassment from religion cops."[2] As one Defense Department official explained, "the policy is a security measure . . . [and] 'whether we like it or not,' Saudi officials are empowered to physically punish women who appear in public in violation of Muslim dress codes."[3] Arguing against this logic, libertarian columnist Vin Suprynowicz asserted, "Let us suppose U.S. troops were stationed in a nation which still practiced chattel slavery . . . would black American officers be ordered to dress up in tattered clothing and frayed straw hats, made to walk behind their white subordinates when off base . . . and respond 'Yassa, mass' whenever addressed by a white person . . . ?"[4] From a more legalistic perspective, the Universal Declaration of Human Rights declares that civil rights should not be subject to the specifics of local custom.[5]

THE PILOT

Taking on the Pentagon over this policy may be a first, but Martha McSally is a person of firsts. She graduated first in her class from high school where she also served as captain of the track team. She excelled at the Air Force Academy and successfully fought to get a waiver by proving her leg strength, allowing her to fly even though she was an inch too short. As a means of improving her strength, she became a triathlete, winning the military division of the Hawaii Ironman World Triathlon Championship in 1993. She was among the first seven American women to train as fighter pilots, the first woman to fly a combat mission, and was promoted to lieutenant colonel four years ahead of her peers.[6] Martha McSally entered her political mission as a walking recruitment poster for the military's attempt to effectively utilize women.

THE TEST FLIGHT: SPEAK SOFTLY BEFORE WIELDING THE BIG STICK

A good pilot knows that when a problem arises one makes the minor corrections first before going into emergency mode. Going public and launching a court case are often not the most effective strategies for affecting public policy, especially at the vehicle testing stage. Initially McSally quietly revved her engines by following the rules and using internal bureaucratic channels to ask for a policy change. According to Air Force secretary Whit Peters, she raised "legitimate questions in a very tactful way."[7] The Air Force treated her complaint as frivolous and probably distracting to their more important mission. Working behind the scenes McSally spent seven years trying to change the policy before going public and filing her lawsuit.

THE ULTIMATE MISSION: WHAT'S GOOD FOR THE GOOSE SHOULD BE GOOD FOR THE GANDER

McSally's complaint was less about the required clothing than about the different treatment of men and women. In her view requiring women to wear the *abaya* but not requiring men to wear traditional local clothing "abandons our American values that we all raised our right hand to die for."[8] To add insult to injury, male military personnel were specifically forbidden to wear traditional Saudi garb. In her first trip off base, McSally sat in the back seat and wore an *abaya* while male officers of lower rank sat in the front wearing blue jeans. The double standard for males and females was impossible to miss, but it went farther than that. The State Department did not require their in-country female employees to wear the *abaya* nor was it required of military spouses. Even the requirement for female mili-

Martha McSally with her attorney John Williams

tary personnel had not been applied during Operation Desert Storm, when the U.S. military drove the Iraqis out of neighboring Kuwait using Saudi Arabia as a staging area.[9] Pointing out inconsistencies is a powerful political tool forcing one's opponents to justify the often unjustifiable.

FILLING OUT THE FLIGHT CREW: POLITICS MAKES STRANGE CO-PILOTS

McSally received support in her attempt to change the Pentagon's "flight plan" from an unlikely crew of supporters. Liberal feminists from the National Coalition of Women's Organizations and the National Organization of Women saw it as a gender discrimination issue. Conservatives and libertarians saw it as an issue of big government trampling individual rights. The Christian Right viewed it as a case of forcing another's religious symbols on McSally and her compatriots. Key support came from the Rutherford Institute, a conservative protector of civil rights and liberties.

KNOWING ONE'S EQUIPMENT: USING THRUSTERS TO SHOOT FOR THE STARS

Good pilots are trained to know the tools available. It was one thing for McSally to argue for policy change as a matter of personal convenience, but such a goal smacks of selfishness. A more effective strategy lay in linking one's personal goals to broader transcendent values. As a practicing Christian, McSally chafed at wearing clothing implying adherence to Islam. Her case was framed as an assault against her First Amendment rights to freedom of speech and religion.[10] By framing the issue as a challenge to the Constitution, it had the potential to arouse public debate as well as to facilitate utilization of the legal system.

ASSESSING THE POTENTIAL FOR A CRASH LANDING

All flight missions involve danger. McSally's lawyer, Thomas Neuberger, frankly admitted that "she understands this is going to destroy her career, but she's doing this so that other women won't have to take the hit."[11] Fear that her career might be grounded was not idle paranoia. As her attempts to change the policy increased, a superior officer sent her an e-mail suggesting it would be "extremely regrettable if you were to place yourself at risk professionally by choosing to violate a specific command directive."[12] In other words, "Shut up and follow orders." McSally refused to listen, asserting that she should not be required to follow what she viewed as an illegal order. If the order was found to be illegal, military law and tradition would give her the right to dissent.

LANDING WITH A WHIMPER, NOT A BANG

Some policy decisions end with dramatic announcements by the courts or after cliff-hanger decisions in legislative bodies. After the issue attracted media attention and McSally was interviewed on CBS's "60 Minutes" the stakes increased and the Pentagon responded. The change in uniform policy for troops in Saudi Arabia ended with a brief classified directive simply stating that the "wear[ing] of the abaya in the Kingdom of Saudi Arabia is not mandatory but strongly encouraged."[13] Recognizing that the public policy process operates more like a "puddle jumper" than a direct flight, McSally refused to withdraw her suit, arguing the military was still pressuring women to comply by the implicit threat in the words "strongly encouraged."[14] In September 2002, a U.S. District Court denied the military's motion to dismiss the suit and the case remains to be settled.[15]

Turning to Congress, McSally sought a legislative remedy. In 2002, the House and Senate unanimously passed legislation prohibiting the Pentagon from requiring or urging servicewomen to wear *abayas*.[16] The final legislation signed by President Bush not only forbade requiring the wearing of the *abaya* but also required the military to inform servicewomen about the prohibition. It also made it illegal to use federal funds to procure *abayas*.[17] Lt. Colonel McSally remains on active duty with no clear impediment to her career for speaking out.

LESSONS

- *Politics makes strange bedfellows.* Support for a policy change often involves a "coalition of mixed expectations" in which supporters have widely differing ideas as to the changes the policies will facilitate.
- *Moving from personal concerns to framing issues as battles over principles increases potential media and public attention while opening expanded strategies.*
- *Choose your advocates wisely.* Martha McSally was a "poster child" for what a smart and dedicated female officer should be. Her reputation could not be sullied as a way of diverting attention from the substance of her complaint.
- *Pointing out obvious inconsistencies in the content and/or implementation of public policy opens the door to questioning the entire policy.* Showing that women fighting for human rights were denied those rights was a hard argument for McSally's opponents to counter.
- *Politics is a multi-front endeavor. Failure in one arena does not doom one to overall failure—nor does success in one arena guarantee overall success.* McSally carried out and continues to pursue her cause in multiple political arenas.

7

Citizen.Action.Org

The Founding Fathers would have loved the Internet. Their engine of revolution was the hand-powered printing press stamping out provocative newspapers and broadsides. Today, thousands of citizens are becoming high-tech pamphleteers in a planetary public square, using computers and modems to recruit and organize without leaving their keyboards. Many think the Internet will eventually become the dominant political medium.[1]

THE MEDIUM

The media constitute tools for communicating messages—if someone is listening. Individuals were once limited to relatively inefficient one-to-one communication media in a face-to-face mode, with rare opportunities for one-to-many communications to those within earshot. The telephone inexpensively increased the efficiency of one-to-one communications. Advances in one-to-many media progressed from microphones to radio and eventually to television. At each stage, the equipment cost all but dealt individuals out. Television and radio networks controlled the airwaves, showing responsiveness to ratings and advertisers. As the age of mass media matured earlier in this century, discussion often focused on who controlled the technology. With the arrival of the low-cost personal computer and the Internet, technology promised to even the playing field for one-to-many communications. The Internet is a unique medium because of its speed, low cost, easy capacity for forwarding messages, freedom from gatekeepers, and unlimited capacity.

Computer activist Shabbir Safdar captures the low-tech–low-cost facet of the Internet for individual users by comparing it to an earlier low tech one-to-many tool, calling the Internet a "megaphone" with which individuals can announce their views.[2] The "megaphone" can work in two directions.

Jonah Seiger (left) and Shabbir Safdar (right)

Viewing the sender as working from the small end, it expands one-to-many communications through postings on personal e-mail distribution lists, established list-serves,[3] or bulletin boards. Like a megaphone, the Internet may amplify false or useless messages or spread true and necessary information. Uncritically blasting inappropriate targets with undesired electronic messages has even created its own new verb, "spamming." Using the megaphone from the large end to the small one implies facilitation of many-to-one communications, as the Internet is used for on-line polling or data collection. Counting the "hits" (visitors to a Web site) serves as a low-cost method of measuring public interest.

THE MESSAGE

The First Amendment to the U.S. Constitution states, "Congress shall make no law . . . abridging the freedom of speech, or of the press." Although the Founders could not have anticipated the era of cybermedia, subsequent policy makers have expanded the principles those eighteenth-century thinkers espoused through analogy. The problem with the Internet lies in finding the right analogy. Viewing the Internet as an electronic medium, and thereby a scarce societal resource, opens the door to government regulation similar to that applied to radio and television. On the other hand, viewing the Internet as a publishing technology, like a newspaper, considerably reduces permissible constraints on the constitutional guarantees of free speech.

As one of the few countries enshrining free speech guarantees in its constitution, the United States is forced to struggle with applying it to new technologies. The right of free speech invites challenges to determine the outer limits of acceptability. Espousing free speech is of little virtue if it applies only to content that is personally acceptable (see chapter 4). The ability for a wide range of citizens to become low-cost publishers on the Internet threatens the publication of a wide range of undesirable material from pornography and hate speech to religious diatribes and unfounded conspiracy theories. Free speech advocates argue that the Internet contributor is like a newspaper publisher or a person on a street corner handing out leaflets, where public demand determines viability and the nature of the audience. Since potential recipients can choose what they tune in to, the range of government control should be limited to facilitating parental control. If those supporting increased content control of the Internet view it as a broadcast medium with a large inadvertent audience that needs protection, they raise the specter of children gaining access to undesirable material and government subsidization of unacceptable content.

The implications of U.S. policy toward free speech on the Internet go well beyond U.S. borders for both philosophical and practical reasons. Philosophically, U.S. policy serves as a model for other countries seeking to modernize. Practically, traditional borders and physical barriers fail to fully constrain communications on the Net. "In cyberspace, the First Amendment is just a local ordinance."[4] Some political jurisdictions such as Singapore use legal threats and employ extraordinary blocking techniques to provide censorship.

For many, Internet policy has become the litmus test of support for democratic principles as countries around the world attempt to accommodate to its advantages and dangers. Since the Internet is "far harder for oppressive governments to control than any other medium,"[5] governments desiring to limit its use must expend considerable effort. Broadcasting on the Internet requires very little equipment, thereby broadening the base of potential users. As Shabbir Safdar points our, "It only takes a couple of modems and phone lines to bring about a bit of democracy. . . . The Net can spread democracy as fast or faster and wider than any other medium."[6]

The honor roll of incidents in which the Internet circumvented government control and/or breakdowns in traditional media continues to grow. Boris Yeltsin's speech from a tank in front of Moscow's "White House" challenging old guard Communists reached the world via the Internet. Both e-mailed accounts of the massacre in China's Tiananmen Square in 1989 and Web chronicles of protests in Belgrade in 1996 circumvented government controls.[7]

ACTIVATING THE NETIZENS

Jonah Seiger began his political activism with traditional door-to-door canvassing of voters in suburban Detroit in 1991, trying to drum up support for campaign finance and auto insurance legislation. He discovered little interest and got tired of having the family dog set upon him.[8] He recognized there had to be a better way to activate citizens. Seiger drew on his degree in psychology and religious studies from the University of Michigan to help understand what motivates people and the importance of organization. In 1994, Seiger helped found and served as the communications director of the Center for Democracy and Technology (CDT).

Shabbir Safdar came of age with the rise of the Internet. Building on his B.S. in computer science from Purdue University, he worked on Wall Street as a computer security expert. In 1994, he cofounded Voters Telecommunications Watch (VTW) (www.vtw.org) as a purely volunteer effort. His first political venture was modest, a warning posted on two dozen bulletin boards: "Dear Net Citizens: Legislation has been introduced before the Senate which would severely restrict your freedom of speech."[9] Recognizing the limited access to the Net on the Hill, he urged computer users to use traditional "snail mail" to express public opinion to their elected officials. With forwarding "spreading the alerts across the Internet like ripples on a pond, 65,000 to 100,000 people read each posting within three to four days of posting."[10] In Seiger's words, the "multiplier effect of the Internet magnifies the impact of its messages as users pass along messages to individuals and through cross-posting on lists to which they belong. . . . If we had 100 Xerox machines and a fleet of trucks we could not get the word out faster than on the Internet." Safdar's early efforts were called "the most successful example of . . . going door to door in cyberspace."[11] As the demands of Net activism increased, he cut back his programming job to part-time and eventually moved to full-time activism. Proving the utility of the Net to change communications patterns, Seiger and Safdar worked together for a year on issues concerning free speech on the Internet before ever meeting in person.[12]

Becoming more proactive, Jonah Seiger helped spearhead an electronic petition drive by the CDT, eventually securing over 100,000 signatures in opposition to the Communications Decency Act (CDA). This figure almost doubled the over 55,000 electronic signatures he generated in opposition to the antiencryption "clipper chip" a year earlier.[13] The immensity of the response allowed crossover publicity in another medium. During the debate, Senator Leahy (D-Vt.) arrived on the floor bearing the 1,500-page petition with over 112,000 signatures and the "C-SPAN cameras captured for millions of Americans the image of Leahy carrying the document into the Senate"[14] as a clear representation of the public's voice.

A NET DEFEAT

Hollywood scriptwriters would end the story with legislative victory for the two brave and creative new activists who adapted a new tool for democracy. Unfortunately for Seiger and Safdar, Congress read a different script. In 1995, Congress overwhelmingly passed[15] the CDA, calling for fines and imprisonment for anyone sending "indecent" or "patently offensive" material on the Internet. The debate highlighted differing conceptions of the Internet. Congress seemed unwilling to listen to the cyberactivists' message, preferring to rely on public opinion polls that overwhelmingly supported restrictions on Internet content.[16]

Sending what many saw as a mixed message, President Clinton used an electronic pen on a digital tablet to sign the CDA. This launched his decision into cyberspace, utilizing the same Internet vehicle the bill sought to limit.[17] With approval by Congress and President Clinton's signature, the battle turned to the courts. After losing the first round, Seiger and Safdar geared up to more effectively utilize the new medium they sought to protect.

BLACK NET STALKING

The passage of the CDA ushered in the era of "digital demonstrations." Turning to the very medium the CDA sought to control, our two "cyber-savvy [activists] . . . raised on-line activism to an art form."[18] The sit-ins, protest marches, and black armbands of the 1960s took on a new twist under the guidance of Jonah Seiger and Shabbir Safdar. Their first eye-catching stunt involved convincing thousands of Web masters to turn their pages black for forty-eight hours to protest the passage of the CDA and to mourn the loss of free speech on the Internet. The response was overwhelming. Major service providers such as Yahoo! joined hundreds of free speech advocacy groups and individuals to protest "the chilling effect" the CDA would have on would-be Net publishers.[19] Safdar raised the fear for both individual "publishers" and commercial information providers that "information that would normally be legal in print, at a newsstand or in a bookstore . . . is now going to be criminal on line."[20] He admits that the protest was impromptu and grew out of frustration, saying, "We knew the bill was going to get signed and we didn't know what to do about it. . . . We put out an alert and it caught on like wildfire. People are falling all over themselves to turn their Web pages black. I'm having to write software to answer my e-mail."[21] Eventually over 2,000 sites wore the black crepe of protest.[22] One member of Congress, Jerrold Nadler (D-N.Y.) joined the protest, turning his page black and calling the CDA "the cyberspace equivalent of book burning."[23]

The importance of the black pages protest was not so much in killing off the CDA but in framing the next stage of the battle for the mass media. Up to that point, the visual television used to tell the CDA story was usually some sanitized porn picture. The issue was thus framed as pornography versus no pornography. With the black screen, television had an alternative visual that emphasized censorship as opposed to access. The strategy worked, since ABC News, USA Today, and CNN all used the black screen in their stories.

Seiger and Safdar recognized the ability of the Net to "move an issue" and organize people into action. The reaction goes beyond activity on the Net, since "online activism means off-line action."[24] In other words, individuals who use the Net are not going to stop there. They will use other methods to make their voices heard by policy makers.

A court challenge was inevitable. As the CDA case went to the courts, Safdar's and Seiger's organizations supported the Citizens Internet Empowerment Coalition (CIEC) made up of sixty-four commercial entities and nonprofit groups. The coalition filed parallel briefs to the American Civil Liberties Union. The ACLU emphasized the vagueness of the definition of pornography in the CDA while the CIEC emphasized the uniqueness of the medium and the inability to control it in traditional ways. The Supreme Court's decision eventually relied more on the CIEC rationale than that of the ACLU.

The primary supporter of the CDA was the Christian Coalition, which argued the importance of the legislation to shield children from Internet "smut" in the same way radio and television are regulated.[25] Awaiting the initial court decision, Safdar posted a countdown screen. As soon as Safdar got the call on the ruling, he powered up his computer and replaced the countdown graphic with the victory message of "Free Speech!" True to their commitment to the Internet as an effective vehicle for getting the word out, 4,000 Web sites with links to a page run by Voters Telecommunications Watch blared out the good news simultaneously. Well before television viewers or radio listeners, Web "rats" heard the outcome. Safdar excitedly exclaimed, "All over the Web, people suddenly knew. It was like fireworks going off."[26] The news raced through the Net with thousands of messages popping up on e-mail with the same subject line, "We Won!" True to the promise of the Internet's speed, within a half hour, at least four major Web sites made the full text of the court decision available.[27] True to Marshall McLuhan's assertion that "instant information creates involvement in depth," electronic interactions between interested individuals coursed through the Internet and eventually led to face-to-face victory parties in New York, Pittsburgh, and San Francisco. However, there was just no way the Internet could electronically provide the "live music, free beer and naughty words," promised by the San Francisco organizers.[28]

The final say on the CDA would come from the U.S. Supreme Court. Pointing out the growth of the Internet and increased interest in the issue, the Seiger-Safdar countdown for the Supreme Court decision involved over 12,000 Web sites, from "the humblest home pages to high-visibility corporate sites like Microsoft."[29] The pages showed a red question mark logo with the words "Will online free speech survive?"

Upholding lower court rulings, the Supreme Court unanimously rejected the CDA as "vague and unenforceable." Seiger was ecstatic, arguing that the strong wording of the Court "does not appear to leave much room for a 'son of CDA.' "[30] Summarizing the arguments they had been using for months, Seiger argued that "the CDA threatened the viability of the Internet. It would have made the Internet the most heavily regulated entity on earth. This decision says that the responsibility for screening material rests with parents, not the government."[31]

The Court agreed to release the decision simultaneously on hard copy and on disk. To get the message of the ruling out instantaneously, Seiger stood outside the Court, laptop and cellular modem in hand. Within eight minutes the full text of the decision was downloaded and linked to the 12,000 Web sites that were part of the countdown.[32] More than 40,000 Internet users logged onto the decision the first day.[33] In the not-so-recent past, the public was limited to summaries of a decision by the mainstream news media, and/or having to wait for weeks for printed copies to arrive. Seiger sees his historical feat as "symbolizing everything the case was all about—a technology that could publish important public information from the steps of the Supreme Court to the entire world with equipment as simple as a laptop."

WHOSE OPINION FLOWS ON THE WEB?

Individuals using the Internet, a.k.a. "Netizens," are an important target for politicians and organized interest groups. Surveys show they are better informed, are more likely to vote, and have more faith in the democratic process than their nonwired counterparts.[34] The estimated 36 million regular American Internet users make up "a real legitimate constituency that candidates have to reach out to. Those candidates that don't take advantage of what the Net has to offer . . . will really be at a disadvantage in the information age."[35]

Effective transmission of public opinion involves an interested sender and a responsive receiver. Recognizing that legislators are most interested in messages from their constituents, Seiger helped create the Internet Empowerment Coalition Web page to encourage individuals to communicate with their members of Congress (www.ciec.org). Capitalizing on the technology, the page electronically matches users with their member.[36] Safdar's Voter's Telecommunications Watch site helps voters find their lawmaker through an "adopt your legislator" feature.[37] Within a few months, over 12,000 individuals signed up. "Spamming" Congress with multiple untargeted messages has little chance of effect. This program helps users identify their representative, find out about his or her voting record, read about the issue, and discover what is happening on Capitol Hill on encryption and privacy issues. The system also sends out targeted alerts to constituents whose members sit on committees about to take action. Both Safdar and Seiger discourage individuals from using the Internet to contact members of Congress for practical and political reasons. Practically, few member offices have developed good routines for handing e-mail. Politically, they recognize that "the goal of the activist is to register on a member's radar screen. That requires making a lot of noise. E-mail is too quiet and too unobtrusive. Letters, visits and making the phones ring off the hook are more likely to get the member's attention."

Although we normally think of the Web as a way for individual citizens to interact among themselves and with government, interaction between organized groups attempting to represent public opinion is also facilitated. As Jonah Seiger puts it, "There's a lot of untapped potential. There are so many groups organizing on various issues, to be able to share knowledge and tactics, what works and what doesn't work, that's powerful."[38]

PUTTING YOUR MONITOR WHERE YOUR MOUTH IS

Net activists such as Seiger and Safdar not only worry about government control and emphasize private sector utility of the Net but also promote positive political uses of the Net by government and the private sector. Recognizing the utility of the Net as an interactive tool, they have encouraged congressional use of the Net, providing equipment and serving as technical experts for Net-based initiatives such as broadcasting hearings, accepting hearing testimony, and developing chat rooms.[39]

Seiger and Safdar seek to make the Net community "the most mobilized, active and educated constituency around," while touting the effort as "enhancing citizen participation through the Internet, [and] open[ing] up a dialog between those who are inside the Beltway and those outside it."[40]

Strategically, Safdar and Seiger use the Internet to send out relatively simple messages. As policy decisions approach a deadline, their atypical e-mail alerts say, "Here's the issue, here's what you can do, and here's where you can find more information."[41] They treat their recipients as intelligent consumers of information who are willing and able to interpret and act on it.

Seiger asserts that the Internet "allows a level of participation in the legislative process that's simply unattainable in any other medium." By late 1997, the two cyberpioneers went commercial with a new high-tech firm, Mindshare Internet Campaigns (www.mindshare.net), designed to help trade associations, nonprofits, and political candidates use the Internet to educate and lobby. Even as a commercial venture, their goal remains "motivating citizens to participate in the democratic process."[42]

THE NET BALANCE

Safdar and Seiger see the Internet as "a healthy tool for informing citizens in the 21st Century." They recognize that the potential political impact of the Internet is not without dangers. "The speed and accessibility of the Internet allows anyone to speak and organize. The dangers of misinformation require diligence by smart users." The speed of the Internet puts pressure on politicians to act quickly in some cases where delay would be beneficial. The new technology reduces George Washington's "cooling saucer" role of elected assemblies to dampen the passion of hotheaded citizens. Although they recognize the danger of commercial domination of the Internet as large companies attempt to become gatekeepers for commercial gain, they believe that a relatively even playing field can be maintained; unlike previous media with clear capacity (column inches, airtime, etc.) limitations, the Internet is unlimited in terms of content capability.

Seiger and Safdar walk a fine line between critics and cheerleaders for the political potential of the Internet. They point out that "you need some skepticism in D.C. to get through the day, but we did not want to appeal to the lowest common denominator of cynicism. We found a message that resonated by saying, sure things are going to hell, but perhaps we can do something about it."

As Seiger summarizes their position, "The Internet is really about people communicating with each other. . . . It's perfectly suited to moving issues and developing support and reaching out to constituents. . . . It gives constituents an opportunity to really participate in a democratic process at a level . . . never before possible. . . . What it's about is . . . empowering citizens with the information they need in order to make informed and active choices."[43]

LESSONS

- *New media raise challenging issues of both technology and philosophy.* Traditional categories of "publishing" and "broadcasting" on which much of our public policy is based do not fit well with much of the new technology forcing a reconceptualization of issues.
- *New media gain attention and activate new segments of the public but do not guarantee victory.* Initial users of the Internet for political policy purposes lost dramatically in Congress on the Communications Decency Act. It was the courts, the institutions most shielded from the media, that eventually meted out a victory for Net activists.
- *The media are "neutral" tools.* Although a particular set of users may enlist various media to promote or oppose specific policy positions, a medium per se has no political agenda. The same medium can be used

on opposing sides of an issue. The political impact of a medium lies not in its technological characteristics but in the skill with which its human masters employ it. "Netizens"-citizens who use the net on a regular basis—are not simply a random subset of citizens. Their views represent "a" public opinion, not "the" public opinion.

Interest Groups

8

From Grief to Anger to Action: Making One MADD

A poised and confident middle-aged woman faced a bank of TV cameras as the spokesperson for the American Beverage Institute—an organization of restaurant, hotel, and liquor industry executives opposed to new measures limiting drinking and driving. She had become accustomed to the cameras and the shouted questions after years of sessions such as this one. Now she vigorously pressed the point that new initiatives to reduce the standard for declaring an individual legally drunk went too far and limited the rights of American citizens.[1] Groups such as MADD (Mothers Against Drunk Drivers) were pushing for what she called "de facto prohibition" and had shifted to an anti-alcohol agenda. She asserted that vindictiveness against moderate social drinkers had little to do with solving the drunk-driving problem.

The scene might have been ignored by both the media and the public as just another interest group representative doing her job in the political war of words, but there is more to the story. A decade earlier, this same woman, Candy Lightner, confronted her own words on a more personal level and then took action that would affect millions of people when words would no longer suffice.

LOST WORDS, LAST WORDS

Few of us can plan our last words to a friend or relative. Candy Lightner could have lived forever with the added grief of allowing her thirteen-year-old daughter to depart amid an angry exchange of words. Candy became annoyed when at the last minute Cari asked to spend the night at a friend's house early in May 1980. All the way over in the car she railed about the need to plan ahead. As Cari got out of the car, Candy heard her shrewish words reverberate and said, "Cari, you know that I love you, don't you?" Cari looked at her mother and said in typical teenage frustration, "Oh, Mother, don't be so mushy."[2] Less than twenty-fours hours later, Cari was killed by a drunk driver as she walked down a quiet street to a school carnival.

Candy, her ex-husband, her friends, and family got through the funeral. Once the shock of her daughter's death began to subside, Candy Lightner turned her attention to finding the driver. When word came back a few days later that the driver had been found, Candy and her friends let down enough to go out for dinner. On the way to the restaurant, they passed by the spot where Cari had been killed. Police officers were measuring something, and Candy jumped out to talk with them. They extended their sympathy and explained that the driver was drunk and had four prior arrests—one just two days before killing Cari. Candy responded, "He killed my daughter. So now he'll go to prison, won't he?" The officer responded, "Lady, you'll be lucky if he sees any jail time at all, much less prison. That's the way the system works."[3] If there was a moment when MADD (Mothers Against Drunk Drivers) began, it was then. The name came from Candy's friend, but the passion came from Candy herself.

Mentally Candy Lightner was well prepared to act with passion against out-of-control drivers. This was not Candy's first experience as a victim. When her twin daughters were eighteen months old, a drunk driver rear-ended her car. Serena received lacerations but Cari escaped unharmed. Six years later, Candy's four-year-old son was run over by a car whose driver was doped up on tranquilizers. He still suffers from brain damage caused by the head injury.[4] Candy was less well prepared in terms of skills, knowledge, and resources. Prior to her daughter's death she had been nonpolitical and "neither registered to vote nor able to distinguish Democrat from Republican."[5]

COOKING UP A HOME REMEDY

The organization started small. Sitting at her kitchen table, Candy Lightner scanned obituaries and news articles for the ominous words "killed by a drunk driver." She wrote letters to the families expressing her condolences and inviting them to capitalize on the benefits of democracy by joining together to stop this national tragedy. Thousands of individuals emerged from their private grief as victims and became participants in the political process. Over the months a significant mailing list emerged. Mothers Against Drunk Drivers moved with moral force and organizational skill to secure tougher drunk driving laws and increase the drinking age.

Candy Lightner

ACTION AND REACTION

Lightner's first real success came in California. It was not easy. She talked to anyone who would listen and parked herself outside of Governor Jerry Brown's offices for days on end. Finally publicity about her efforts forced the governor to listen to her and appoint a task force with her as a member. In 1981 California passed a tough new law imposing minimum fines and mandatory imprisonment of up to four years for repeat drunk driving offenders.[6]

Despite the grim reality of her crusade, Lightner is not without humor. She tells of marching into the office of a state legislator who had been convicted of drunk driving. Prior to relating her interest in pushing for stiffer fines, Lightner offhandedly suggested that she was pushing for the death penalty for drunk drivers. "By the time I told what we [actually] asked for, he was so relieved he would have voted for anything."[7]

In July 1984, MADD's drinking age initiative paid off at the national level. Candy Lightner was invited to join President Ronald Reagan as he signed a new law reducing federal highway grants to any state failing to raise the drinking age to twenty-one. The act exemplifies a key way in which the constitutional power of the federal government has been expanded. The reserve clause of the Constitution grants the passage of legislation such as drinking laws to the states, but the federal government can encourage (some would say "bribe") states into compliance by dangling federal grants in front of them. Associating drinking ages with federal grants was a classic example of the "carrot and stick" approach to nationalizing laws.

By 1985, MADD had 320 local chapters with 600,000 volunteers and donors. Its $10 million budget reflected a remarkable transition from its kitchen table origins to a national organization to be reckoned with. Even before the national legislation, its efforts had resulted in the passage of hundreds of state and local drunk driving laws.

DRIVING THE ISSUE HOME

Social activism can be a catharsis, a way to satisfy the human desire to "do something," when little can be done to rectify the real problem. Like most victims, Candy Lightner would desire most of all to turn the clock back to the time before the accident and expend all her efforts to protect her own child. She recognizes that "through MADD I found a way to deal with my anger, a way to address a serious social problem that had taken my daughter from me, and a way to fill my time for many years to come."[8] Lightner is realistic about the role MADD played in her life, saying that "most people think that MADD was my tribute to Cari. It wasn't. MADD was my reaction to her death."[9] She also points out that through MADD she has "made many friends, come to know some of the most interesting and influential people of our time, and become a savvy businesswoman. . . . I am grateful for all of that. But it does nothing to assuage the pain of losing my child. I would throw it all back in an instant if only my daughter could be with me still."[10]

There were also costs to her efforts. By turning her full attention to MADD, Candy Lightner kept herself busy but caused her other two children to become resentful. The activity also left little time for the grieving process to play itself out. "Rather than accepting her death, I kept her alive. I would take Cari's picture to TV stations and public events. Every time that picture was on a brochure, in a newspaper, or on television, I was able to postpone certain aspects of my grieving."[11]

DRIVING AND DRINKING, WITH A TWIST

Candy Lightner and MADD parted company in 1985. Some felt she was greedy to ask for a $10,000 bonus on top of her $76,000 annual salary. Some blamed her for criticism by the Better Business Bureaus and the National Charities Information Bureau that MADD was spending too much of its income on fundraising and too little on programs.[12] Lightner puts it more vaguely, saying, "There was a conflict between the board and me."[13]

Lightner now works as a lobbyist for Berman and Company, one of whose clients is the American Beverage Institute. Although some call Lightner a turncoat, she argues that she never supported prohibition or reducing the legal blood alcohol content to extreme levels. Commenting on the current efforts of MADD, Lightners says, "I worry that the movement I helped create has lost direction."[14] She sees herself as the voice of reason to "support legislation that will stop drunk driving and oppose that which doesn't work."[15] She argues (some say rationalizes) that by simply lowering the legal blood alcohol content, legislators may be "disinclined to pass more effective legislation that would crack down on the more dangerous hardcore offenders." She describes a Virginia state legislator who reacted to a proposal to reduce the limit by commenting, "If we pass this law, will you leave us alone for a while?"[16]

AFTERTASTE

Isolating the impact of Candy Lightner is difficult. Since MADD was founded in 1980, drunk driving deaths have dropped significantly. In that year 25,000 people were killed by drunk drivers; by 1992 the number had dropped to 17,700. Lower speed limits and safer cars certainly played a role in this decline, but so did the 30 percent decline in drunk driving, the increased stringency of drunk driving penalties, raising the drinking age to twenty-one years of age in all states, and changed attitudes toward drunk driving—all efforts spearheaded by MADD. Raising the drinking age alone is estimated to have saved eight hundred lives a year.[17] Not everyone gives MADD, nor the legislation it spawned, the credit. Research on drunk driving arrests indicates that much of the increase in arrests came before MADD was on the scene.[18] But such analysis misses the point that drunk driving itself and the deaths it caused did decline after the efforts of MADD took hold.

Candy Lightner and her fellow MADD activists did more than change laws—they increased public awareness and changed attitudes. Phrases such as *designated driver* have now become commonplace. Asking for "one more for the road" sounds rather silly today. Saying "Sorry, I can't have any more, I'm driving" has become a badge of responsibility, not a source of derision.

Even the liquor industry has climbed on the bandwagon of "responsible drinking." Those who see her as having gone to bed with the liquor industry and having gone soft on drunk driving forget how far we have come as a society when it comes to drinking and driving. At least some of that change can be directly credited to Candy Lightner.

Lightner is proud of her crusade. "I believe that for every problem there is a solution. We are changing the way people think about drinking and driving. But more than that, we have caused people to change their behavior, and that is saving lives. I believe in the rights of victims. And I do feel that if you believe in something badly enough, you can make a difference."[19]

LESSONS

- *Misery seeks company but needs a little help.* Candy Lightner did not create the issue of drunk driving nor discover the pain of its victims. Her contribution lay in channeling that pain into action. The relatives of drunk driving victims existed as a vast untapped resource of potential activists waiting for some direction to assure their loved one did not die in vain.
- *Choose the right target.* Focusing on drunk drivers assured a target with little potential for garnering sympathy. Driving while intoxicated is done by choice and reflects irresponsibility. MADD did not go directly after the producers of alcohol nor the retailers. They were not attempting to threaten the economic well-being of the industry; rather, they took on the irresponsible users of these products. Focusing on increasing the drinking age involved taking on eighteen- to twenty-one-year olds, whose political involvement and sophistication are quite low. Few individuals in this transitional age, who are passing from underage status to adulthood, exhibit a passion to change laws for those left behind.
- *Activists are human.* They are motivated by a combination of ideals, emotion, power, and financial benefits. The purists who criticize Candy Lightner for "selling out" and "changing sides" need to give her credit for what she did, not demean her for what she did not do.

9

Wouldn't You Just Love to Live Here?

The young, dark-haired housewife scanned the audience and found Wayne, her brother-in-law and now her public relations and scientific adviser. He had one finger in the air. The signal might have meant "you're number one" or "one minute left," but it did not. It was his signal that she had said "you know" again. Her conversations were sprinkled with "you knows," especially when she was in front of a crowd. She recognized her limitations, and the "you knows" were subtle requests for verification that she was on the right track. By the end of her speech, Wayne had all his fingers in the air. She certainly did not "know" and she hoped her audience did. A year earlier, she could not have imagined herself in front of a crowd, but here she was emerging as the president of her homeowners association.

THE BIRTH OF AN ACTIVIST

Lois Gibbs often describes herself as the "housewife who went to Washington."[1] As a twenty-seven-year-old high school graduate with two children, she lived with her husband, Harry, a chemical worker at Goodyear Rubber, in a modest single-family "starter" house in a nondescript neighborhood. Few would have expected the name of this shy homemaker and her neighborhood to dominate the headlines for years to come. When homes began to be built in the 1950s, Gibbs's neighborhood was given a romantic name, Love Canal. Harry and Lois had come to the neighborhood in what they thought was a fluke of good luck. Five years earlier, in 1978, a man had seen the for sale sign on their modest house a few miles away and offered to trade houses with them without even looking inside.[2] They found out that if it's too good to be true, it probably is.

The history of the land was checkered and reflected the limited concern of previous generations for environmental dangers. In 1892, William T. Love began digging a seven-mile canal to harness the Niagara River. Due

Lois Gibbs

to bad economic times, and new technology, the partially dug canal was sold at public auction in 1920 to serve as a municipal chemical disposal site. The primary user of this open trench of mixed chemicals (at least 21,800 tons) was Hooker Chemical. Over two hundred different compounds have been found at the site, including at least twelve different cancer-causing compounds such as benzene and Dioxin. In 1953, Hooker covered the ditch (full of loose chemicals and rusting barrels) with clay, abandoned it, and sold the land to the Board of Education for $1. The deed absolved Hooker of any responsibility for physical damage, providing them with the bragging rights that they had fully warned the officials in charge. Soon a housing development grew up on adjacent land, and an elementary school was built directly on top of the chemical waste site. The young, primarily blue-collar families moving into their new $18,000-$23,000 homes sought a little bit of the American dream of suburban living. No one anticipated the nightmare that would meet them there.[3] Roads and sewer lines crisscrossing the area disrupted the clay cap put over the chemicals by Hooker and allowed the chemicals to migrate over a wide area.[4] Since the land on which the homes were built was not part of the Love Canal transaction between the school board and Hooker Chemical, their deeds carried no warning of what was buried beneath the surrounding land. Niagara Falls residents had become accustomed to odors, skin irritations, and burns caused by emissions from the numerous chemical firms in the area. They accepted the situation as a minor irritant necessary for economic well-being.[5]

Gibbs's personal wake-up call came in June 1978 after she read a newspaper article about a school having been built over a dangerous chemical site. Although the article identified the location, in a typical "this can't happen to us" reaction, Gibbs first assumed it was another 99th Street School in the duplicate numbering system of Niagara Falls streets. She felt sorry for "those poor people over there," but she was not motivated to act.[6] A little investigation on her part revealed that the "them" was really "us," and her son Michael was a student at that school. The pieces soon began falling into place. Michael had begun having seizures after starting school, his white blood cell count had dropped dramatically, and urinary problems had developed. Her initial reaction was purely personal. She wanted to get her son out of that school and away from the chemicals. Organizing a broad political movement was well outside her personal agenda.

Gibbs's first round with government bureaucracy paled in comparison to her future battles. She naively called the school superintendent and asked to have her child moved to another school. The superintendent refused, saying it would not even be considered without the statements of two doctors. Armed with the doctors' statements, she was again rebuffed. At first the superintendent denied receiving the statements and then challenged the assertion that the area was contaminated. In a typically bureaucratic response, the superintendent concluded that by accepting Gibbs's individual request, he would justify the assertion that the area was contaminated, and if he accepted that assertion, the school would have to be closed.[7]

SEEING IF THE NEIGHBORS WOULD HELP

With fear and trepidation, shy and insecure Gibbs set out the next day going door-to-door with a petition demanding that children be given the right to change schools. Her first stop was a house near the school. She knocked on the door, and to her great relief, no one answered. She ran home, thinking, "Well, I tried." It took her a full day to build up her courage again.[8] It turned out to be easier than she had anticipated. Most people were receptive, but the more she heard, the more frightened she became. Neighbors who barely spoke on the street were sharing intimate details of their children's health problems such as birth defects and crib deaths. As her time on the streets increased, her time doing housework and being with her family diminished. Her days were filled by front porch discussions with concerned neighbors and the initial wave of frustrating encounters with government officials who refused to admit anyone was at risk.

While the petition drive continued, a lawsuit against the school board, the city of Niagara Falls, and Hooker Chemical was filed by Lois and her friends. As her efforts became more serious, opposition arose from some local citizens. Those who had worked for Hooker Chemical feared for their pensions; others, such as the mayor of Niagara Falls, feared that the publicity would lower property values and hurt tourism.[9] Hooker Chemical literally and figuratively had the mayor over a barrel, since they announced their tentative plan to build a ten-million-dollar office building downtown, an action greatly desired by urban renewal proponents.[10]

WHEN IN DOUBT, CALL A MEETING

Public pressure forced the reluctant government into action. A public meeting was in order, but in this case, the fewer local people attending the better. The meeting was called for Albany, 300 miles away. Gibbs who described herself as "a housewife whose biggest decision up to then had been what color wallpaper to use in my kitchen,"[11] was off to Albany to fight big business and government inaction. The state health commissioner shocked the crowd by announcing the evacuation of pregnant women and children under two. The hush after the announcement was deafening. Gibbs, the quiet housewife who hadn't even attended PTA meetings in the past yelled out, "You're murdering us."[12] Recapturing her composure, she maintained the initiative by asking, "If the dump will hurt pregnant women and children under two, what in God's sake, is it going to do to the rest of us?"[13] When the meeting ended, the incoming health commissioner announced a public meeting the next day in Niagara Falls almost sarcastically asking if there would be any people there. That night Gibbs spoke to her first street meeting to over four hundred people, with her brother-in-law counting the number of times she said "you know."

Gibbs immediately emerged as the unofficial leader and that night officially became the president of the Love Canal Homeowners Association, formalizing her leadership role. Like many other civic leaders she was blessed (some would say cursed) with a deep sense of responsibility. She describes herself by saying, "I always try to do the best I can when I have responsibility for anything, whether it be a child, a dog, or a piece of furniture."[14] As the biblical dictum reminds us, those who are faithful in little things can be counted on to be faithful in big things.[15]

It almost seemed too easy. The next day, President Carter declared that a "state of emergency" existed at Love Canal, making it the first man-made emergency in U.S. history. Four million dollars from the federal government was pledged for the cleanup. Gibbs started on the figurative ride from shy housewife to national spokesperson and on the literal ride to the White House, network television studios, and Capitol Hill. It all seemed too easy, and it was. As the initial euphoria died down, the real work began.

ORGANIZING FOR THE LONG HAUL

It soon became clear that this was not going to be a short-term problem with a simple solution. The homeowners had an inexperienced leader and few resources. There was little to do but to grow together. The organization eventually was given the use of abandoned buildings for offices, but support for the bulk of the effort stemmed from their own finances and labor. As Gibbs explained it,

> we financed our fight against the federal government and the state of New York with donations from individuals and with the proceeds from T-shirt and cookie-bake sales. You don't need money, but it helps; what you need most are determination, imagination, the conviction that you're right, and the knowledge that you are fighting not only for your family, but also for the good of everyone.[16]

Gibbs ended up in a strategically useful but unenviable position caught between two battling forces within the community on the extremes of the issue and a complex of competing interests among the residents. On the one hand were residents who feared that their property values would decline and/or depended on Hooker Chemical for their retirement and wanted to go slow or not go at all. This group also included other activists who felt Lois was horning in on their territory.

On the opposite end of the "go slow contingent" were activists calling themselves the Action Group who wanted immediate action and were willing to use confrontational strategies. Their confrontational approach went beyond the issues at hand and became personal. One activist leader exploded, "I don't know too many guys who'll follow a twenty-six-year-old high school dropout broad."[17] Gibbs held onto her leadership position with the barest of majorities, regularly having to fight off those who disliked her decisions, were jealous of her visibility, and/or who simply directed their personal frustrations her way. She realized that these deeply committed individuals were useful resources if they could be channeled. Adding further complexity were groups that either felt unrepresented or had legitimate fears about being accepted. The Concerned Renters Group feared being absorbed by the Homeowners Association and faced opposition from association members who saw them as having less of a stake in the outcome. The two groups worked together only when their interests coincided. Residents of the LaSalle low-income housing project also felt uncomfortable acting under the umbrella of the Homeowners Association. The split was exacerbated by the fact that LaSalle housed largely low-income minorities, whereas the homeowners were primarily a white and aspiring middle-class contingent who were only one economic step away from being low-income renters. These blue-collar homeowners tended to revel in their own progress, feeling little in common with those who had not progressed economically.[18]

EARNING THE LOVE AND ATTENTION OF THE MEDIA

Despite the organizational problems engendered by such a diverse and contentious community, Gibbs emerged as the legitimate spokesperson for those affected by Love Canal. Government officials and the media needed a single spokesperson, and residents needed one trusted source of information.[19] The mantle of leadership carried with it both rights and responsibilities. Important messages can be lost in a cacophony of competing voices, even if their messages are relatively consistent. Gibbs recognized her important role and the critical nature of presenting a united front to the media and public officials. She reminded members of the Homeowners Association and competing community groups that "we're a family. We can have our fights but we stick together against our enemies. Remember, we have to work together to get out of this mess."[20]

Lacking financial resources, Gibbs and her supporters relied on creativity to get media attention. Reversing W. C. Fields's famous warning to never share the stage with a child or a dog, the activists used a small child to confront the mayor of Niagara Falls at a speech. The toddler pointed a forefinger at the mayor and exclaimed, "Mayor Locklin, what are you going to do for me?"[21] It was a natural to get coverage. For a while the group picketed construction work at the canal. The arrest of a pregnant picketer got good publicity but not much else. After a few weeks, enthusiasm for this strategy waned. The group later took a child's coffin to Governor Carey to keep the story in the news.[22] The power of the mass media lay in "arousing public opinion and keeping the spotlight on decision makers [who] wanted to look good to the voting public."[23] Gibbs frankly admits that "we couldn't have gotten what we did without the media."[24]

The media campaign escalated with an appearance on the *Phil Donahue Show*. What a switch! Only a few months before, these housewives had been spending their time sipping coffee and watching *Donahue*. Now one of them was on the program. Gibbs found the appearance disappointing, but it did signal a nationalization of the issue.[25] She was more experienced by the time she testified before Congressman Al Gore's (D-Tenn.) hearings on toxic waste. She began to recognize that the stakes were high and that the ability to control the agenda affected how the story was told. The night before the hearing she was asked by committee staff members what kinds of tough questions the committee members could ask the state witnesses. "It was almost as if they were arranging the hearing to come out the way they wanted it to. . . . What if I had been on the other side of the fence?"[26]

Once one media outlet defines a situation as news, the others follow along. Gibbs and the Love Canal Homeowners Association became a national emblem of the victims of irresponsible stewardship of the environment. The story expanded into the public education realm as an ABC documentary called *The Killing Ground* raised public awareness among citizens more attuned to entertainment than hard news.[27]

THE PEOPLE VERSUS THE GOVERNMENT

The interaction between the Love Canal Homeowners Association and the government resembled a giant tug-of-war with an imaginary line demarcating the conclusion that government action must be taken. Between each gigantic tug, successive groups of affected individuals were dragged over the line and had their concerns alleviated. First, pregnant women and children under two were removed from "ring one," homes closest to the canal. Then the debate raged over removal of all residents in ring one. With the relocation of ring one residents, attention shifted to ring two, which included Gibbs's house. With the relocation of ring two residents, attention finally shifted to those in surrounding houses. All along there were a series of "time-outs" as government agencies asked for numerous studies of health conditions.

Civic activists feared the problem would be studied (literally) to death, whereas government officials sought definitive information to both buy time and justify their expenditures of public funds. The fear of establishing a precedent and assigning blame tempered the willingness of government officials to act. Love Canal was not the only (or even the worst) chemical disposal dump in the area. Chemical production is a necessity for maintaining America's lifestyle. Putting too much social or financial pressure on chemical companies could undermine their financial viability, force people out of jobs, and/or stop the production of necessary chemicals. Tightening local laws would only encourage companies to move to other areas. Each time dangers were identified, physical fixes such as drainage pipes and containment procedures were suggested as acceptable ways to keep people in their homes. Avoidance of cost and the precedent of government expending funds to relocate individuals facing environmental dangers and/or forcing chemical companies to accept retroactive responsibility for actions that were once legal was the bottom line.

As increasing numbers of individuals were relocated, there was considerable concern that they would forget those left behind and doom them to remain in a dangerous setting while their property values plummeted. As it turned out, few of the inner-ring residents who were first to leave remained active in the organization. Despite an idealistic desire to improve the lot of all, once people's personal demands were met it was hard to maintain a commitment. Indirectly, however, the experience of the relocated residents moved the cause forward, since at each stage of relocation, studies of the re-located families indicated that their health had improved.[28]

Gibbs's skills as a mediator and responsible leader received a real-world test in May 1980 after a pilot study indicated a high incidence of nerve damage among Love Canal residents. Residents began gathering at the Homeowners Association office looking for answers to numerous questions. Hyped with concern and frustration, the events of the afternoon were sparked by a newspaper headline proclaiming, "White House Blocked Canal Pullout." The quiet protest turned ugly as some residents began blocking traffic and one woman burned the letters E, P, and A into the lawn of an abandoned house, taunting the Environmental Protection Agency (EPA). That afternoon, Gibbs invited two Washington-based EPA officials to the Homeowners Association office. She initially hoped the residents would focus their anger on them instead of on the police, property, or innocent passersby. The tactic worked too well and talk of hostage taking rumbled through the crowd of over three hundred. Gibbs vividly remembers, "I really believed that half the crowd would have killed them if possible. I was as angry as anyone but I wanted to protect them."[29] Gibbs rushed them inside the office and away from the increasingly hostile crowd, explaining that they were being detained inside for their own protection. Her assurances sounded prophetic a few minutes later when a member of the crowd punched out one of the windows in anger.[30] Not wanting to turn an appearance before the crowd into a riot but also hoping to make the most of the situation, Gibbs alternately took on the good guy-bad guy roles police officers often use during interrogations. On the one hand, she fed the EPA officials homemade oatmeal cookies and ushered in members of the press to individually meet with them. On the other hand, she called the White House, explaining, "We are holding two EPA officials hostage." After threat of FBI intervention and assurances from the EPA that their concerns were being treated seriously and an answer would come soon, the officials were released. Gibbs commented that through this incident, "We've gotten more attention [from the White House] in half a day than we've gotten in two years."[31] Within a few days an expedited EPA decision arrived: "President Carter [upon the request of Governor Carey] . . . declared an emergency to permit the Federal Government and the State of New York to undertake the temporary relocation of approximately 700 families in the Love Canal area of Niagara Falls, New York, who have been exposed to toxic wastes by the Hooker Chemical Company."[32]

Politics and science are commonly viewed as competing realms with competing methods of proof and decision making. In its textbook form, politics involves deciding between values over which reasonable people can disagree. The winning side is the one that can convince more people—or more often the right people—that what you value should take precedence over what others value. Values such as maintaining housing values, maintaining area tourism, protecting residents from potential health problems, and being responsible about the use of government funds all came into play in the Love Canal situation.

Science, on the other hand, is supposed to base decisions on an objective analysis of observable facts. The winning side is defined in terms of which facts overwhelm those of opposing perspectives. What the distinction between politics and science ignores is that politics often determines what is studied, that values affect which facts are collected and how they are interpreted, that the facts seldom speak for themselves, and that human beings choose to accept certain sets of facts and base their careers and reputations on them. The epidemiological studies that attempted to determine the health effects of Love Canal spoke in terms of probabilities, not certainties. The question the scientists attempted to answer often involved determining whether more individuals in the area had a higher incidence of health problems than the general population after all other explanations had been explored.

It is all too easy for scientists to become hired guns in lab coats. Inevitably the scientists began to take sides. The government scientists were subtly reminded that concluding in favor of the Love Canal residents would involve admitting past errors and would require the expenditure of significant amounts of public funds, which would have to come out of other government programs. The burden of proof was expected to be very high. Love Canal residents and their scientific supporters were dealing with the lives and well-being of individuals and approached data analysis from the perspective of "better safe than sorry." Gibbs summarized the intermingling of politics and science in a way that represents one of the few areas in which those on both sides would fully agree: "Science is not separate from politics, no matter how much the scientists pretend it is."[33]

Despite assertions that the decision on federal involvement would be based on critical medical studies and health conditions, the decision to subsidize the relocation of all residents was made before the scientific studies had been completed. Public pressure and media attention had done what research and analysis could not do. Politics had trumped an orderly analytical policy process as President Carter and his staff recognized that further delay would further jeopardize his reelection chances. A few weeks before the election, President Carter (who had limited his early commitment to Gibbs, saying, "I'll pray for you,")[34] made a whirlwind tour of the Niagara Falls area to capitalize on the signing of the appropriations bill that would allow the government to purchase the 1,300 homes. Seated prominently on the stage, Gibbs was singled out by the president for praise. The proposed scientific health studies, once claimed as being so critical, were canceled a few months later.[35]

COSTS AND BENEFITS

The two years of activism and tension over Love Canal took its toll on marriages and families. Some of the women who became leaders grew in confidence and competence, whereas their husbands felt helpless and unable to protect their families. Many families lived with the guilt and reality that their children suffer permanent physical damage from the toxins they ingested. Leaving home and spending time in successive hotels and motels resulted in an insecurity that many of the children manifested in behavior problems. Gibbs's divorce was unfortunate but probably inevitable. She admits that the marriage was shaky even before the issue of Love Canal emerged. Her husband, Harry, supported her efforts but also wanted a meal on the table when he arrived home. The repeated argument became circular. "He'd say, 'Come home, your family is Number One,' and I'd say 'That's what I'm doing this for!' " It was a classic communications breakdown. She then more hesitatingly admits, "I outgrew him."[36] With their departure from Love Canal, the Gibbs children had no further health problems. Lois became something of a celebrity after a made-for-TV movie chronicled her efforts. People regularly recognize her in airports and ask, "Aren't you the 'dump' lady?"[37] Gibbs now lives and works near Washington, D.C., after establishing the National Citizen's Clearinghouse of Hazardous Waste, which works with over 8,000 grassroots groups.[38]

Love Canal might have represented an isolated, extreme case of corporate irresponsibility, bureaucratic red tape, and government inattentiveness. But it became a highly publicized shot in the larger battle to clean up toxic waste. It focused public attention on the question, "If this happened in bucolic upstate New York, I wonder what they have buried in my neighborhood." As Gibbs's two-year battle raged to save the already damaged residents of Love Canal, the Superfund legislation (Comprehensive Environmental Response, Compensation, and Liability Act of 1980) was wending its way through Congress. This landmark legislation initially created an unprecedented $1.6 billion fund to locate and clean up hazardous waste sites. Over the next fifteen years $24 billion more was appropriated.[39] The job is far from done—fewer than 300 of the 23,500 identified sites have been cleaned up.[40] Battles still rage over "retroactive liability" as the government attempts to take the Hooker Chemical companies of the world to task for their actions prior to the passage of the legislation. Gibbs's initial excitement about the Superfund has waned: "I'm the mother of the Superfund, but that's a child that went astray."[41]

For Gibbs, Love Canal is a reminder that all of us have spirit and skills that we may be unaware of. Love Canal taught that "ordinary people become very smart very quickly when their lives are threatened."[42] Gibbs summarized her story by saying, "I believe that ordinary citizens—using the tools of dignity, self-respect, common sense, and perseverance—can influence solutions to important problems in our society. To a great extent, we won our fight."[43] When civic activists confront government, they change government. Right seldom prevails easily. After a series of promises and disappointments, Gibbs came to the conclusion that "if anything is naive, it is the belief that government officials and politicians will do what they say they will do."[44] Success comes from keeping the pressure on, watching over the shoulders of policy makers and forcing them to live up to their commitments.

After the government declared Love Canal its first federal environmental disaster area, the area was cleaned up and a containment system was developed. Because the name Love Canal had come to mean toxic waste, the area was renamed Black Creek Village and the abandoned Love Canal homes went back on the market with buyers given significant financial incentives to buy once unmarketable homes.[45]

For the larger society, Love Canal is a powerful symbol that helped force a national consensus around government's responsibility to clean up the environment in a coordinated way, and it stands as a warning against ever again allowing such irresponsibility. "Part of the Love Canal story is a success story: government can be forced into accountability when citizens pool their strengths and use publicity and votes as bargaining chips in the game of power politics. But the story is, at the same time, sobering testimony to the eroded meaning of a phrase like public accountability in our modern, high technology society."[46]

Although the solution was not perfect and was long in coming, it is hard to read the Love Canal story as anything but a victory for citizen activism. "The Love Canal Homeowners Association was a true grassroots organization. It arose in a working-class community in a time of crisis, when citizens joined together because they felt their needs were not going to be met properly by their government. The organization became a strong countervailing force in opposition to corporate and government interests, which would have preferred to minimize the problem once they finally recognized that it existed. What began at Love Canal with one young woman knocking on doors grew into a force to be reckoned with by state and federal officials at the highest levels."[47]

After the federal government finally agreed to get involved, Gibbs was asked by a journalist whether her success in forcing action clearly demonstrated that "the little guy" had defeated the "big guys." Gibbs put the journalist in his place and the issue in perspective by saying, "No, that's wrong. We're not little people! We're the big people who vote them in. We have the power; they don't."[48]

LESSONS

- *Effective activists are made, not born.* Average individuals can rise to the occasion. Gibbs developed as a civic activist. She entered the battle with few of the typical experiences and skills we expect in leaders, but she dug down in her own personal resources to manage the battle.
- *Use the media to your advantage.* The media play a critical role in agenda setting by alerting people to problems and forcing officials to act when delay and inaction are the preferred course.
- *Voluntary citizen organizations are fragile coalitions.* Good ideas often fail in the face of human frailties and conflicts. Personalities, personal interest, and extraneous issues stand in the way of united action. Organizational leaders need to accommodate the egos and varying interests of those they lead.
- *Organizations keep the pressure on government and increase the potential for action.* Government officials prefer inaction to action, small steps to large steps, and credit claiming to problem solving. By watching over the shoulders of public officials, citizen-based interest groups with an immediate stake in the outcome decrease the likelihood of inaction.
- *Science and politics are inextricably intertwined.* Science emphasizes complete, objective analysis and precise determination of cause and effect. What is analyzed, how the analysis is approached, and the interpretation of the results often include judgments undergirded by little if any scientific basis. Personal biases, bureaucratic goals, and a desire for political support color the collection and use of scientific evidence. In the final analysis, scientific evidence is only one component in the policy process, with political considerations usually trumping scientific evidence when science and politics are in conflict.

10

Registering as a Protest, or, I'll Vote for That

What if we held an election and no one came? Or what if we held an election and the wrong people took part? Everyone approves of voting in the abstract, but few support expanding voter participation simply for the sake of expanding voter participation. Elections are vehicles for setting priorities; they go beyond being events in and of themselves. Who votes determines who wins, and who wins determines whose policy preferences prevail. If the policy outcomes satisfy you, there is little motivation to change the level of voting or the composition of the active voting bloc. Dissatisfaction with existing policy preferences forces a reassessment of the voter pool.

A CLASS ACT

Americans do not typically think in terms of social class. Almost one-third say they never think of themselves as a member of a class.[1] If forced to classify themselves, 87 percent call themselves "middle class" or "working class." Only 3 percent see themselves as "upper class" and 8 percent as "lower class."[2] The "land of opportunity" ethos creates a pervasive outlook that current economic status is not fixed. Why classify oneself if the status is transitory? Americans' optimism is reflected in the fact that over 70 percent of adults characterize themselves as "better off financially" than their parents and over 60 percent believe that their children will be better off than they are.[3]

Economic well-being and its correlates, such as secure employment and advanced education, are the prime predictors of voter participation. Socioeconomic status (SES), a combined measure of education, income, and job status, dwarfs all other variables in determining who will register and

97

Frances Fox Piven   *Richard A. Cloward*

vote. Voters tend to be drawn disproportionately from those who have reaped the benefits of contemporary society more than those whose hopes and wishes have been thwarted. Far from serving as a protest activity by the disadvantaged, voting participation is largely a reaffirmation ritual of those satisfied with the status quo.

In 1983 two academics, Richard A. Cloward from the Columbia University School of Social Work and Frances Fox Piven of the political science department at the City University of New York, wrote an article entitled "Toward a Class-based Realignment of American Politics: A Movement Strategy."[4] In it they laid out a scenario of social change based on class. Hoping to create a political climate more conducive to the economic interests of the poor, Piven and Cloward decried "the disenfranchisement of large sections of the working class" that precludes the emergence of a political party that could stimulate "greater class consciousness among American workers by articulating their class interests."[5] For Piven and Cloward, limited class consciousness is both a cause and an effect. Limited feelings of class association discourage lower-class political participation, whereas limited levels of participation in turn discourage the potential for increasing consciousness. Acting on their goals early in 1983, they organized Human SERVE (Human Service Employees Registration and Education Fund) to promote state executive branch action to increase voter registration.

THE POTENTIAL FOR CHANGE

With only about half the eligible voters casting ballots in presidential elections, America ranks among the least participatory of all democracies. The large group of nonvoters and the unique SES cast to those who do vote make massive political change mathematically possible. As political scientist E. E. Schattschneider asserted, "The whole balance of power in the political system could be overturned by a massive invasion of the political system, and nothing tangible protects the system against the flood."[6] The route to change lay not in simply expanding the electorate with a group of new voters who look and sound like those who have participated in the past but rather in mobilizing a large block of new voters whose political hopes, desires, and demands look and sound very different from the current participants. Parties and candidates are attracted to identifiable blocs of voters that they attempt to draw into their political orbit.

Piven and Cloward pointed out that America is the only advanced democracy without a viable socialist or labor party organized explicitly to promote the interests of the disadvantaged classes. Their goal lay in mobilizing large blocs of lower-income voters, forcing a party realignment along class lines.[7]

BLAMING THE VICTIM

For someone who believes that America is the land of social and political opportunity, it is a very small step to conclude that those who fail to achieve economic well-being or fail to take advantage of the right to participate are at fault. Blaming the victim challenges neither the economic well-being nor the social conscience of those who prefer the status quo. Concluding that economically unsuccessful nonparticipants lack the motivation, knowledge, and/or supportive attitudes to fully engage in the political process places the onus on their failure rather than on the structure of the political system. Also remaining unscathed by such an approach are the self-serving strategies perpetuated by those who currently participate in politics.

A more subtle variant of blaming the victim is the argument that nonparticipation is really a tacit expression of satisfaction with the outcomes of the political process. Piven and Cloward ask an interesting question: "If non-voting expresses happiness, why is it that such contentment is so consistently concentrated among the least well off?"[8]

BUILDING ON DISSATISFACTION

The 1980 election of conservative Ronald Reagan shook liberal political activists. Piven and Cloward took some perverse pleasure in the recession early in the Reagan presidency and the fact the 1982 midterm election resulted in an upsurge in voting by blacks, blue-collar workers, and the unemployed. Their hope was that "new voters from the bottom of the income scale could reverse the electoral tide that brought the right to power."[9] They looked toward 1984, hoping the Democratic party would see the potential and grasp the opportunity to redefine the electoral landscape. Piven and Cloward were not the only ones anticipating such a strategy. Conservative columnist James Kilpatrick laid out the challenge:

> Make no mistake. Democratic leaders will go after votes from blacks, Hispanics, welfare recipients and disenchanted women. . . . That is where the votes are. If the Republicans fail to mount a massive effort to register likely new Republican voters, the Republicans will take a drubbing in 1984.[10]

Republicans and conservatives took up the challenge, spending over $10 million in sophisticated targeted registration drives. The Democratic National Committee announced a multimillion-dollar voter registration drive that never materialized, leaving the liberal registration playing field to a set of unions, black church officials, women's organizations, and nonpartisan groups such as Piven and Cloward's Human SERVE. It became the first organization to recognize the ineffectiveness of door-to-door mobilization of poor voters and began to register people waiting for public services, "taking advantage of the way the welfare state concentrates nonvoters" who "congregate on its lines and in its waiting rooms."[11]

Human SERVE recruited volunteers to canvas the waiting rooms of public agencies and to encourage public and private social welfare agencies to allow their workers to register low-income clients. The pitch was far from subtle. Approaching individuals in line for food stamps and unemployment benefits, the volunteers handed out fliers "dramatizing past and pending cuts in food stamp programs" and warning "that food stamp benefits will be lost unless people register and vote."[12]

Capitalizing on the fragmented nature of American federalism, Piven and Cloward emphasized state rather than national action.[13] Working on a state-by-state basis, Human SERVE helped obtain six gubernatorial orders encouraging voter registration in state social welfare agencies. Human SERVE estimates that agency-based registration efforts helped place a million new voters on the rolls.[14]

Success bred publicity and controversy. In New Mexico, Governor Anaya was forced to rescind his registration plan after both parties perceived it as a ploy to register poor Hispanics. The Reagan administration threatened to cut off federal funding if any such funds were used to pay the salaries of state employers engaged in voter registration. In some states the threat had a "chilling effect," shutting down registration drives; other states shifted to a "passive" approach, setting up voter registration tables in waiting rooms but forbidding federally funded state employees from facilitating the registration process.[15]

The results of the 1984 voter registration initiative were a general success but a liberal failure. Ironically, the Republican party "galvanized itself to cancel out an electoral mobilization that the other party never attempted."[16] Overall, the national voter rolls increased by over 12 million voters from 1980 to 1984. A large number of those new registrants could have been expected to register on their own after reaching voting age or coming to realize the importance of voting. Piven and Cloward estimated that 7 million of the 12 million new registrants resulted from organized voter registration drives. The Republican party and conservative church organizations accounted for about half of the organized-drive registrants, whereas "nonpartisan" (but clearly liberal and Democratic party) efforts accounted for the other half. "Consequently, the 1982–84 drive expanded the electorate without reducing its upscale tilt; it was a class stalemate."[17]

Piven and Cloward look back at 1984 with frustration and resignation, realizing that they were naive in expecting the Democratic party to mount a significant registration drive. Democratic party leaders had become comfortable with a voting coalition that seemed to lock in their control of Congress and their domination of state and local politics. Recognizing that the Democratic party would be unlikely to give anything but lip service to mobilization of the lower classes, Piven and Cloward shifted their strategy from voluntary efforts by political organizations to institutional reforms.

SHIFTING THE BLAME

Policy shifts often result from a redefinition of the problem. As long as not voting was seen as a problem of limited awareness and motivation, the blame fell on the lower-class "victims" who failed to take advantage of the right to vote that had been graciously given to them. Piven and Cloward began a crusade to shift the blame away from nonvoters toward legal and institutional barriers keeping poor voters from the polls.

It was not enough to show that the United States imposes more barriers on voting than other developed democracies, nor that, unlike most democracies, American government units do not assume an affirmative obligation to register citizens.[18] These barriers seemingly affect all potential voters and thus cannot explain class variations in voter turnout. Piven and Cloward needed to show that the barriers affected low-income voters in a discriminatory way. Piven and Cloward argued that removal of the most obviously discriminatory measures, such as poll taxes and literacy tests, was not enough. They asserted that procedures requiring potential voters to periodically take time from work to appear before distant voting registrars imposed a heavier burden on the poor than on others. Travel costs and the requirement to forgo hourly wages imposed a subtle income test. Even more difficult to prove empirically was the assertion that registration laws were enforced by political appointees often hostile to minority groups and the poor.[19] In Piven and Cloward's minds the solution to reconstituting the electorate lay in changing registration procedures and personnel.

Combining their social passion and professional concerns as academics in a "publish or perish" world, Piven and Cloward became nationally recognized "activist scholars,"[20] using the strategy of publishing their concerns and proposed solutions in both academic and popular venues. Their book, *Why Americans Don't Vote*,[21] arrived with all the academic paraphernalia of theory, empirical data, and hypothesis testing before focusing on their reform agenda. Their book became the "bible" for registration reform proponents, with quotes, data, and descriptions appearing during congressional debates and reported in the *Congressional Record*.[22] Their more popular configuration of the arguments appeared in liberal publications such as *The Nation* and *Social Policy*.

MOVING TOWARD THE GOAL

At the outset, Piven and Cloward were forced to confront the fact that not all theorists of social change nor all their compatriots in the movement to empower America's low-income voters accepted the utility of focusing on the electoral process. Some analysts proposed that the symbolism and effort of elections channel disadvantaged citizens away from more effective strategies of social change such as protest and threats of civil disobedience.[23] Piven and Cloward recognized the often frivolous distractions of elections but also pointed out that the influx of new voters potentially threatens existing political coalitions. Political leaders are encouraged to make concessions favoring the emerging group of participants. Thus elections can provide social movements leverage with candidates and parties.[24]

The road to success was strewn with many obstacles. Numerous other voting participation groups existed. Organization leaders have a strong motivation to maintain and enhance their organizations and often saw complementary organizations as more of a threat than an ally. Piven and Cloward were not the only game in town.

In the battle over empowering more voters, Piven and Cloward also had to define the factual basis of their assertions against a powerful adversary. Curtis Gans, chairman of the Committee for the Study of the American Electorate, had become the media's favorite spokesperson on election statistics. His "sound bite" conclusion accepted by most of the media was that voter turnout was falling because registered voters were abstaining and not because of registration impediments. Shifting the blame back on the voters made changing registration laws of little importance. Seeing this as undermining their efforts, Piven and Cloward struck back, questioning both his logic and the veracity of his data.[25]

Piven and Cloward focused on registration as not only a legal requirement for casting a ballot but also as the linchpin for actual participation. Individuals who are convinced to register also vote. Although the United States ranks low among modern democracies with its close to 50 percent turnout of *eligible* voters, almost 90 percent of *registered* voters do vote, placing the United States among the top nations in terms of registered voter turnout.[26] They also asserted the interactive relationship between registration restrictions and partisan competition. The influx of new voters forces political parties to work harder to secure the votes of the new registrants by addressing their concerns. They echoed Walter Dean Burnham's conclusion that "when politics matters . . . people behave as though it matters."[27] When parties and voters begin going after the allegiance and support of voters, the voters respond.

One proposed route to greater registration among the poor and disadvantaged lay in reducing some of the impediments to voting. Reforms such as removing requirements for periodic reregistration and increasing the convenience of the registration procedure by expanding the number of official registration locations and increasing their hours of operation have the potential for expanding participation. Piven and Cloward advocated going well beyond such relatively passive approaches, preferring active outreach. With over 125,000 government agencies providing health and welfare services alone, they hoped to provide high-level encouragement that would stimulate social welfare workers to register their clients both as a service to society and as a way of protecting their programs and budgets. They recognized that bringing voter registration to the people worked better for low-income voters than previous attempts of trying to bring the people to the voter registration offices. They also recognized that not everyone appreciated their efforts to reconstitute the electorate and that success would require a broad-based national coalition and a national legislative mandate.

DRIVING TOWARD SUCCESS

Focusing solely on registration at social welfare agencies limited the potential political coalition. Only the most liberal political activist could get excited about such targeted activation. Piven and Cloward readily embraced the idea of "motor-voter" registration, which allows individuals to register at the same time they apply for or renew their driver's license, for two reasons. Such an approach would legitimize a more activist government role in the registration process, which could be broadened to include their more fervent desire to utilize welfare offices also. They also recognized that "while fewer poor and minorities own cars, many still register to drive or acquire photo identification."[28] Over 90 percent of voting-age citizens have driver's licenses or personal identification cards issued by motor vehicle bureaus.[29] The idea of voter registration by the motor vehicle administration was not new, having been pioneered by the state of Michigan in 1975.[30] From a political perspective, espousing motor-voter registration initiatives "nicely [took] the pro-welfare sting out of the project."[31]

The federal system of inconsistent laws allows using states as laboratories for experimentation. By 1991, fifteen states and the District of Columbia had active motor-voter programs and several states also provided registration at welfare and unemployment offices. As the debate developed on the national level, state action continued. By 1993 an additional thirteen states added motor-voter programs to the laws, although not all states actively promoted motor-voter options.[32] Another twenty-seven states allowed mail-in registration and a number of states provided for registration at the polls on election day.[33] These efforts clearly paid off as states with fewer registration barriers moved to the top of the list in terms of voter registration and voter turnout. Empirical studies prior to the conclusion of the debate on national legislation showed that motor-voter registration had "a positive and significant effect on turnout." Research comparing the impact of motor-voter legislation with other initiatives such as mail-in registration and welfare agency registration indicated that the effectiveness of other approaches paled in comparison to motor-voter laws.[34]

No consistent or significant partisan realignment emerged from existing studies of loosening registration laws, quieting the fears of many Republicans who saw loosened registration laws as a liberal plot to redesign the electorate. At least one detailed study of new registrants indicated that the largest number of new registrants in social welfare offices viewed themselves as independents rather than partisans,[35] removing some of the partisan sting (especially for Republicans) from such an approach. Party activists usually assume that they have more than an even chance to win over independents.

The battle lines developed over when and where federally mandated voter registration would be required. Republicans feared a flood of pro-Democratic voters onto the rolls. Republican public arguments sidestepped the partisan hesitation and focused on the potential for fraud, the cost, the fear that public assistance recipients would feel pressured into registering, and the inappropriate intrusion of federal power into state functions.[36] Democrats used the rhetoric of democratic (with a small *d*) empowerment and condemned bureaucratic disenfranchisement[37] while salivating over the potential for an influx of low-income Democratic party supporters. The threat of a Republican filibuster in the Senate was cut off by a compromise that dropped registration at unemployment offices from the bill while retaining registration initiatives at welfare and motor vehicle offices.

The National Voter Registration Act established three new procedures for improving voter registration on the national level: (1) requiring states to establish procedures permitting individuals to register to vote when applying for or renewing a driver's license or identification card; (2) requiring states to accept a mail-in voter registration form to be developed by the Federal Election Commission; and (3) designating public assistance offices and offices dealing with the disabled as voter registration agencies.[38]

A NEW SIGN ON THE ROAD

Just over ten years after the initial announcement of their plan in *Social Policy*, Piven and Cloward stood behind President Clinton as he signed the National Voter Registration Act. Their original goal, to target low-income voters at social service agencies, had emerged as a broad-based universal suffrage plan that retained the potential for having more impact among low-income voters than among those groups with currently high rates of participation. Recognizing that passing legislation is only one step in the process, Piven and Cloward committed their Human SERVE organization to monitor the implementation process.

One of the first challenges came in the courts. In January 1996, the Supreme Court rejected California governor Pete Wilson's challenge to the National Voter Registration Act by refusing to hear an argument advanced by several states that the law violates the Tenth Amendment reservation of powers to the states.[39]

The debate did not end with the passage of legislation. Human SERVE conducted a survey of election officials to collect aggregate data. They found that 11 million new voters registered between 1993 and early 1996. Not everyone credits motor-voter registration with the increase. Among the 5.6 million having registered at motor vehicle departments, a significant number would have registered in traditional ways and merely substituted the motor vehicle option because of its convenience. The 11 million also included the natural growth in the population and voters whose "registration" was nothing more than a change of address from the previous location where they were registered.[40]

Analysis based on individual polling data provided more details. Of the 19 million voters who report having registered between January 1, 1995, and November 1996, over a quarter (28 percent) used motor-voter procedures for registration, whereas only 3 percent registered at public assistance agencies. Motor-voter dwarfed other methods of registration such as voter registration offices (19.6 percent), mail-in procedures (18.8 percent), and registration booths (16.2 percent). The variation in registration location differed dramatically among various demographic groups. Blacks and Hispanics were twice as likely to have registered at a public assistance office as the general population of new registrants, and those with incomes under $15,000 were four times more likely to use the public assistance office venue.[41]

Although registration increased in 1996 and 1998, actual turnout levels showed record decreases to 49 percent in the presidential election and 36 percent in the 1998 off-year election. Perhaps significantly, the turnout of minorities and Democratic voters showed less decline in 1998 than that among Republicans, helping Democrats capture a number of key electoral contests.[42] The close 2000 presidential election brought more people to the polls, but the nature of the contest seems a more likely explanation than increased registration. Self-reported registration dropped from 66 percent in 1996 to 64 percent in 2000.[43] The motor-voter law initially could be associated with increasing the percentage of people *registering*, but it is another large step to get people to actually go to the polls.

The long-term partisan implications of the motor-voter procedures are not clearcut. Those most likely to take advantage of decreased registration barriers are the young and the physically mobile, the physical "movers" in society; neither group, according to surveys, has a significantly more Democratic party orientation than the electorate as a whole.[44] Physical mobility has a dampening effect on political involvement since uprooted individuals fail to establish roots in their community and are largely ignored by candidates and parties who recognize their low potential to vote.[45]

Although the more inclusive nature of the electorate with the addition of more low-income voters ostensibly should help the Democratic party, continuing low turnout rates for newly registered voters—especially those with Democratic proclivities—dampens the automatic partisan impact. For all the hype and focus on potential voting blocs, votes for candidates are still secured the "old-fashioned way," one voter at a time. "The real answer to the question of whom Motor Voter will help is that it depends on who does what it takes to earn it,"[46] that is, through appealing candidates and aggressive registration and get-out-the-vote initiatives.

LESSONS

- *The rhetoric of reform often differs from the reality.* Voter registration reform was publicly argued on the basis of "transcendent values" with which almost everyone agrees in the abstract. Behind the calls for democracy, avoiding fraud, and undoing bureaucratic impediments lay more potent partisan and ideological motivating factors.
- *Organization and activity breed counter organization and activity.* When challenged by a new political force, existing political interests organize and/or

redouble efforts to counter the challenge. The status quo of politics is really a balance of power between competing forces. The balance of power can change through luck, skill, or effort, but competing groups seldom simply roll over and play dead.

- *Not even the facts and data speak clearly.* Data require interpretation, with different interpretations implying widely varying predicted outcomes.
- *The line between the objective academic analyst and the activist political practitioner is not crystal clear.* Academics can use their analytical skills to promote policy outcomes. Academic analysts can willingly (or unwillingly) see their findings dragged into the political debate.

11

Changing the Ecology of Politics: Introducing a New Breed

Environmentalists have long championed the idea of thinking globally and acting locally. Brian Trelstad took the challenge seriously and focused on his own locale, the Harvard campus. Trelstad had always been an information junkie, always thinking in terms of the big picture. When someone mentioned the environmental dangers of Styrofoam cups, his first reaction was to establish a sense of scale by asking, "Is this a big problem or a little problem. How can we measure its consequences?" Transferring this concern to energy consumption in the residences, he asked similar questions about energy consumption at Harvard. He sought to develop a flow chart of the problem, using data to determine the soft spots amenable to change. Once he found out that the university kept track of usage on a building-by-building basis, he was on a roll.

Energy consumption in the dormitories ("houses" to Harvard students) had risen 17 percent in the previous five years. The Gulf War in the early 1990s heightened concern for a number of environmental/energy issues dealing with access to oil. Rising costs of heating oil created a practical problem for the Harvard physical plant officials, whose costs were running several million dollars over budget. In an almost desperate attempt to cut energy use down to size, the director of the physical plant gave Trelstad and his group $5,000 in seed money to promote conservation. The physical plant had good comparable energy data on the thirteen residential houses and the 1,600-person freshman residence. The houses were roughly of the same architecture and size, allowing "an apples-to-apples comparison." A fellow student created a computer program to organize the data. Building on the competitive spirit, Trelstad and his group publicized the past information of energy consumption and challenged the residents to do better in the future. After some brainstorming they came up with the idea of an

Brian Trelstad

Ecolympics. They "decided to use the inter-house competition . . . as a way to get conservation imbedded into the collective consciousness of the students [and] sought to build on the natural competitive, playful spirits among the Harvard houses."[1] It resulted in a high-profile way to encourage conservation by measuring progress against the previous year adjusted for the weather. Competition was based on comparisons: how much heat, water, and electricity were used, with extra points given for recycling. As a baseline, each house used the month-by-month energy figures for the previous year. The champion house for the first month reduced its heat and hot water consumption by 31 percent, receiving the first monthly prize. At year's end, the coveted Earth Cup was awarded.[2]

The Ecolympics program saved the campus over half a million dollars during its first six months. The $5,000 grant was used for posters and wool hats and socks for winning house coordinators. The physical plant manager's investment paid a handsome return. The route to energy savings involved a series of small, mundane steps that added up to major savings. For the first time students found out to whom they should be reporting broken windows. Students who had been compensating for dysfunctional radiators by opening their windows now had both the motivation and information to stop dissipating precious energy into the atmosphere. Finding clearly wasted energy such as the overheating of stairwells and hallways produced quick savings.

The program still exists on the Harvard campus, raising the consciousness of each new wave of students to the importance of conservation. Progress has slowed since the first year, when most of the "big apples on the low branches" were found, and it is harder to find obviously wasteful conditions. As Trelstad sees it, "We took a new look at existing information, presented it in a useful form, created a fun competition, gained a little media attention, and did something the university could not do on its own."

RECYCLING THE RECYCLERS

Looking beyond Harvard, Trelstad was introduced to the efforts of the National Wildlife Federation (NWF) as they geared up for Earth Day 1990. Becoming linked to a national organization gave him a sense of empowerment. He recognized that without such an association he "would have felt isolated and disconnected. It plugged me into a national network of like-minded individuals and the periodic meetings created energy and excitement." On the personal level, his association with students from around the country led to a legacy of enduring relationships. The cadre of activists would cross paths again and again as they developed their careers in various aspects of the environmental movement.

The success of the Ecolympics whetted Trelstad's appetite for civic activism and helped him make a name for himself within the environmental movement. After he graduated from Harvard in June 1991, the National Wildlife Federation recruited him to become a field organizer working with other schools to create their own Ecolympics. Trelstad helped establish over thirty similar campus competitions around the country. Success bred controversy. The U.S. Olympic Committee objected to the use of its trademark name, so the project was renamed the Campus Green Cup.

With his ten-month internship at the NWF winding down, Trelstad began looking for his new challenge. Chris Fox, a Yale student whom Trelstad had met in preparation for Earth Day 1989, expressed interest in getting involved in the impending 1992 presidential campaign. Fox felt that "if students could translate the energy of Earth Day into electoral power, they could have a big impact." It galled Trelstad that "students don't get taken seriously politically since they don't vote at significant levels. We wanted to do something about that."

IT'S THE ELECTION, STUPID

Local conservation efforts and raised environmental consciousness are important, but large-scale changes in society require changes in public policy. Changes in public policy require changed outlooks and/or a changed composition of policy-making bodies. With such logic, it is clear why Trelstad shifted his focus to the electoral arena.

The Trelstad-Fox duo received an offer of free space in old Earth Day offices in Palo Alto, California. NWF provided a $5,000 seed grant to get their effort off the ground. With only a few months left before the election, the learning curve for creating a new organization was necessarily a steep one. Trelstad and Fox had to learn about becoming a formal organization in order to open bank accounts and other infrastructure requirements. The movement received a shot in the arm with Al Gore's nomination as vice president on the Democratic ticket. His presence increased the ticket's appeal to young green voters. The nomination also activated a number of progressive and pro-environment groups who wanted to affect the outcome of the election but legally could not expend funds directly for political purposes. The Campus Green Vote (CGV) proposal developed by Trelstad and Fox, which had been sitting on a number of desks in Washington, soon began to yield a return. Being at the "right place at the right time," the organization took off. It was a good time to start such an initiative. CGV was part of a growing trend. The number of American college campus environmental groups grew from 400 in 1989 to over 2,000 in 1994.[3] The focus of CGV was relatively narrow, increasing the turnout of environmentally committed students and training them in strategies for influencing environmental policy through the electoral process.

NWF gave an additional $50,000, with more than $70,000 arriving from other organizations. Within a number of weeks of setting up, Campus Green Vote organized ten regional training sessions for students on the legal and practical aspects of voter registration. At its height during the 1992 campaign, CGV had five field organizers and a Washington staff of four.

DEVELOPING A VOTE OF CONFIDENCE

Trelstad promoted the importance of elections and electoral participation to a generation known for political apathy and cynicism. Expressing hope more than reality, Trelstad questioned the labeling of his generation of twenty-somethings as an example of nonquestioning self-absorption by claiming that "we're not generation X. We're Generation why?"[4] He argued that "everything can be traced back to the accountability of elected officials. There's been a culture of disinterest, but by making the environment a high profile issue, students have real potential to make a difference."[5] His message to young voters emerged clear and direct—"This year there's one single thing people can do to save the earth: vote!"[6]

Trelstad and CGV had little interest in voter registration per se. They wanted to register "right thinking" young voters—those with a commitment to the environment. Party voter registration drives often work on the basis of careful targeting by using "bird-dogging" strategies to identify likely supporters before attempting to register them. CGV relied on more subtle targeting strategies. The literature and signs on the registration ta-

bles emphasized environmental concerns drawing environmentally oriented students. Encouraging voter registration among that pool of students increased the likelihood of creating an environmentally oriented
bloc of voters.

Harnessing the youth vote presented a double-barreled challenge.
Young potential voters often fail to go through the rigors of registration.
Once registered, they often fail to cast ballots. Trelstad saw the voting participation record of young voters less as a problem and more as an opportunity. He pointed out that the estimated 14 million college students make
up about 8 percent of the voting-age population. In 1988, only 36 percent of
those between eighteen and twenty-four voted, as compared with 48 percent of those between twenty-five and thirty-four and over 60 percent of
those over thirty-four (see table 11.1). As with all age groups, the critical in-
termediary step to voting is registration. Among voters over twenty-four,
over 70 percent were registered, compared with 48 percent of those between eighteen and twenty-four. Once registered, a person is likely to vote.
Eighty-seven percent of voters over twenty-four who registered actually
voted in 1988. The gap between voting and registering is even greater
among younger potential voters, with only 75 percent of the registered voters voting.[7] The task of activating the youth vote required a two-pronged
strategy: getting them registered and getting them to the polls.

TABLE 11.1
Registration, Voting, and Age, in Percentage

Year	1988	1992	1996	2000
Voter registration				
18 to 24-year-olds	48	54	49	45
All voters	67	68	66	64
Voter turnout				
18–24-year-olds	36	42	32	32
All voters	57	61	54	55
Turnout among registered voters				
18 to 24-year-olds	75	78	65	71
All voters	85	90	82	86
Registration/voting gap*				
18 to 24-year-olds	−12	−12	−17	−15
All voters	−10	−7	−12	−9

Source: Harold W. Stanley and Richard G. Niemi, Vital Statistics on American Politics (Washington, D.C.: Congressional Quarterly, 1995), p. 79; and U.S. Census Bureau, "Voting and
Registration: November 1996." Available at www.census.gov/population/socdemo/voting/
history/co23 and the data available at: www.census.gov/population/socdemo/p20-542/
table1.pdf

*The difference between the percentage registering and the percentage voting.

In 1992, CGV was not working in isolation. Economic conditions scaring young voters about their job prospects primed the pump for political participation. Media efforts such as MTV's Rock the Vote campaign served as the "air war" side of the voter registration campaign, providing a media campaign well beyond the means of CGV and other student groups. CGV carried out the "ground war" at voter registration tables, offering newly motivated participants a practical way of getting involved. In an attempt to share some of the burden and build on varying strengths, CGV formed an informal coalition with MTV, the National Abortion Rights League, and the efforts of a variety of other groups. No one person or program can rightfully take credit for the turnout of the youth vote in 1992. Organizations like CGV clearly contributed. CGV registered 107,704 young voters[8] at 108 schools in twenty-seven states prior to the 1992 election.[9] Overall, registration among eighteen- to twenty-four-year-olds increased from 48 percent in 1988 to 54 percent in 1992. Actual voting increased from 36 percent to 42 percent, resulting in a 78 percent turnout of registered younger voters. Among older age groups of voters, registration in 1992 increased only by 1 percent and turnout by less than 4 percent, compared with the 1988 figures.

During the Reagan/Bush years, young voters registered and voted solidly Republican. College students were somewhat more Democratic, giving Reagan only a five-percentage-point advantage in 1984 and supporting Dukakis over Bush in 1988. In 1992, young voters helped bring the Reagan/Bush era of Republican domination in presidential contests to an end. Young voters gave Clinton 44 percent of their support, compared with 34 percent for Bush and 22 percent for Ross Perot.[10] Although far from monolithic, the youth vote reveals more dramatic swings in support than other age groupings. This is probably due partly to their less fixed attitudes and social conditions and partly to the fact that each presidential election witnesses the influx of a new set of young voters with its own perspectives.

The long-term impact of the increased youth vote of 1992 is less clear. Between 1992 and 1996, two-thirds of those who were eighteen to twenty-four in 1992 moved on to the next higher age grouping to be replaced by a new cadre of eighteen- to twenty-four-year-olds having come of political age. There is little evidence that the new cadre of twenty-five- to twenty-nine-year-olds brought their participatory habits with them. Campus Green Vote claims to have established voter registration programs on 146 campuses and registered over 58,000 new voters for 1996,[11] but the overall figures show little impact resulting from their efforts. In 1996, registration among the new eighteen- to twenty-four-year-olds dropped by over 4 percent, compared with a decline of just over 2 percent for older age groups. Actual voting among young voters declined by over 10 percent, compared with a decline of less than 6 percent for their elders. For young voters, 1996 registrations fell below 1988 levels, and actual participation dropped 32.4 percent. Participation increased somewhat during the close 2000 election contest, but participation of younger voters was 7 percent below 1992 and even below 1988. (See table 11.1.) The 1992 increase in youth voting looks more like a blip than a trend. There seems to be little likelihood that voting registration efforts will increase voting participation of this group to the 50 percent plus figures of the 1960s. The constant influx of new voters into the voting pool seems likely to depress overall participation more and more over the years. Youth registration and turnout drives certainly do not hurt, but they do not seem up to the immense task of permanently reversing the trend toward nonparticipation.

AVOIDING A POSTELECTION LETDOWN

With the election over, CGV needed a broader mandate or it would simply fold. Most of the staff wanted to maintain the momentum they had created. Trelstad convinced NWF that a new student group was needed. NWF provided a three-year, $300,000 grant for a broader-based student activism group based on environmental issues. Campus Green Vote was folded into the Center for Environmental Citizenship (CEC) in the spring of 1993. The new name represented more extensive goals and a realization that the Internal Revenue Service was unlikely to give a group with "vote" in its name tax-exempt status. Trelstad became executive director.

CEC developed a model of regional campus workshops lasting a day and a half to train students in the basics of the political process. They wanted to show students how they could take local issues and raise them on the national level. Rejecting typical political science courses, which they felt lacked real world applicability, their training sessions focused on the steps in the political process, methods of meeting management, coalition building skills, strategies for dealing with the media, voter registration initiatives, and practical lobbying.

Since information is a key power resource, Trelstad helped develop the Shadow Congress project within the CEC. Using an Internet mailing list, he sent out environmental issue briefs targeted to students every week. The direct distribution list reached three hundred students leaders who were encouraged to forward it. CEC estimated an eventual recipient list of 2,000–3,000 environmentally concerned students.

STEPPING INTO THE BREACH

Attempting to ameliorate intractable social problems often gets stymied by the "rule by experts" mode of typical policy making. Many potential activists are dissuaded by the feeling that "if the experts can't fix it, who am I to step in?" Trelstad recognized that he "was as smart as anyone working in the policy world, but it would take me years to catch up to the experts' level of knowledge on my own." He found he could "leapfrog" their expertise by asking lots of questions. He realized that an uninitiated participant could ask questions about basic assumptions and bring a new perspective to bear on a problem while the experts were locked into their traditional ways of thinking. For example, when he found out that Harvard kept monthly energy consumption data, he asked, "Can you compare the energy consumption of individual housing units?" Concerned with simply paying the aggregate bill each month, public works experts did not see the importance of this.

While sitting on the election strategy board of the League of Conservation Voters (LCV), which targeted members of Congress based on environmental votes, Trelstad was constantly asked about how students could help elect or defeat particular candidates. The questions were always premised on the general assumption that this person's record was so good or so bad that environmentally attuned students would surely want to get involved. Using his laptop, some readily available data, and a free weekend, Trelstad created a database of congressional districts ranked by the number of college students. This allowed the LCV to target student potential for influence along with LCV's specific desires to promote the electoral fortunes of specific candidates. Clever nonexperts have the potential for taking existing information and using it for other purposes.

Having access to the financial resources and expert advice of national organizations increased the feasibility of local action. Staff people working for national organizations and networking with other activists offered encouragement and the realization that significant projects were something a student could undertake.

BEYOND VOTING

In the long run, Trelstad's student voting turnout initiatives could be seen as a failure. The 1992 increase in participation by younger voters could be explained by other factors. Even if the 107,000 new-voter figure is accurate, it represents a minuscule proportion of the electorate. The youth vote declined again in 1994 and 1996. The CEC now includes Campus Green Vote and its voter registration and activist training initiatives as one of its components. Although admitting he is "a bit frustrated with the decline in youth voting levels," Trelstad presents a more optimistic and sophisticated analysis of the accomplishments of CGV and its successor organization, CEC:

We needed to move from the macro to micro considerations to assess the impact. Our emphasis on affecting a macro situation like voter turnout was really beyond the control of one small non-profit organization. Economic conditions, public perceptions of societal well-being and the appeal of particular candidates were probably more important in 1992. There is little we can do to change these macro factors. On the micro level, we did assemble a cadre of people and get them to think civic-activism and about working on the environment as a career. We introduced a lot of trained and talented college students to the environmental community.

The CEC created a resume book about its activists, many of whom now work fulltime in the environmental movement. Students trained to man the voter registration tables on college campuses are now sitting behind the research and management desks of numerous environmental organizations. Serving as "matchmakers," organizations such as Campus Green Vote and the Center for Environmental Citizenship continue to bring together environmental groups and environmentally oriented students.

Supporting the environment is not always easy. As Environmental Protection Agency administrator Carol Browner told the 1994 Campus Earth Summit, "You too will meet with resistance; people will tell you that environmental protection and economic progress are incompatible; they'll even call you things like 'Granola Head' and 'Tree-Hugger' and probably some things that are worse. But you must stick to your convictions."[12] Taking his turn in the barrel, Brian Trelstad found creative ways to engage students and empower them to propel the environmental movement forward.

LESSONS

- *New information (or a new way of looking at old information) paves the way for action.* Facts and data have little value until someone organizes them into a useful form. Providing context and structure by putting data "information" empowers the creator to frame issues in a new way.
- *Voter turnout is hard to affect in the long term.* Structured efforts to change behavior pale in comparison to broad attitudinal shifts based on contemporary events. Feelings of "efficacy" (the impression that an act is worthwhile) are difficult to impose from the outside. Personal well-being (or the lack of it) and the nature of the electorate's options serve as far more potent motivating factors for potential voters.
- *National organizations motivate, train, and provide resources for local activists, whereas local activists breathe new life into national causes.* There is a symbiotic relationship between national and local organizations. Each would be lost without the other.

- *Intensive political participation can be habit-forming.* Persons tasked with leadership roles at a young age develop the skills and confidence to apply their energy and expertise to later problems.
- *Political activists are made, not born.* Politics requires a unique set of skills that can be inculcated through drill and practice. Although individuals vary considerably in terms of their native abilities, basic training in political skills allows potential activists to build on their existing strengths.

12

A Taxing and Revolting Job

It did not look like a gathering of revolutionaries: a group of middle-aged to older Americans sitting around a living room table in a modest California house grousing about taxes. Since the founding of the country, death and taxes had been viewed as inevitable and undesirable, the subject of idle conversation. Beginning in the 1960s, conditions were ripe for complaints. The rapid rate of housing inflation in California led to dramatic increases in property taxes. The share of property taxes directly levied on individual homeowners increased from 34 percent in 1970 to 44 percent in 1978. At the same time, the state of California accumulated a surplus approaching $10 billion. State legislators talked about cutting the property tax burden, but talk seemed cheap and action scarce.[1]

Among the twenty neighbors sat sixty-year-old Howard Jarvis, a former publisher and businessman attending his first local antitax meeting. Few at that meeting would have identified him as the leader of a citizen revolt. But they did not know him very well. In the world of talkers and doers, Howard Jarvis had always been a doer. Any project he took on he saw through to the end. He told his early supporters, "If you want me to be the chairman of this organization, I want to tell you something: I'm not a quitter. If I come in here, we're not going to quit."[2] As a former colleague in the tax battle, Paul Gann, put it, "Howard and I both had one disease. If we believed in something completely, we fought for it completely, without holding back anything."[3]

Whereas youth and vigor can provide the energy for activism, age can bring experience and time. Jarvis agreed to write a set of bylaws for the group, putting him in a good position to serve as its leader. That 1962 meeting led to the creation of the United Organization of Taxpayers with Howard Jarvis as its state chairman two years later.[4] Not everyone was willing to stick it out. His organization rapidly expanded to 120,000 members, only to decline to 50,000 a decade later.[5]

Howard Jarvis

LOW TAXATION WITH OR WITHOUT REPRESENTATION

American opposition to taxation runs deep. A key slogan that led directly to the Declaration of Independence was "no taxation without representation." Taxation with representation garners little more support. American tax rates are some of the lowest among developed countries. With income taxes in Scandinavian countries exceeding 60 percent and typical rates for countries such as Great Britain, Canada, France, and Germany in the 40 to 50 percent range, the U.S. combined rate for all levels of government of 33 percent seems quite modest.

Local governments depend on property taxes, which provide a relatively stable yet somewhat inflexible form of taxation. Income taxes rise or fall, depending on one's ability to pay; property taxes impose a fixed burden on property holders even when their disposable income changes. Individuals moving from the ranks of the employed to unemployment or retirement often find property taxes an unbearable burden.

The tax revolts of the 1970s and 1980s were not unique events. In fact, they pale in comparison to a citizen uprising a generation before. Between 1929 and 1932 income fell by over 33 percent. Unemployment soared to over 25 percent. Delinquency rates for property taxes averaged over 25 percent. Public outcry forced political leaders to take drastic steps. In 1932 and 1933, sixteen states and numerous localities enacted property tax limitation. Well-organized tax resistance movements rose up around the country.[6]

Some political battles may net results in a short period of time, but perseverance is often a more faithful ally than perfect timing. Howard Jarvis's success in tax reduction formally began over sixteen years before the passage of Proposition 13. In some ways, Howard Jarvis was a consistent political "loser," easily dismissed as an ineffective political gadfly. In 1962, he ran for the Republican nomination for the U.S. Senate and lost badly. In 1972, his bid for a seat on the State Board of Equalization ended in defeat. In 1977, his entry in the Los Angeles mayoral primary made virtually no political impression.[7] Woven through his personal defeats were a number of unsuccessful attempts to get the tax cut proposal supported by his organization on the ballot.

As in much of life, timing is important. Proposition 13 originated years before but was eventually favored by the fact that tax cuts are particularly popular during times of inflation.[8] The scene for citizen action was set by a state legislature that failed to come to grips with the depth of public consternation over taxes. With tax bills and state surpluses both rising due to inflation, the state legislature had both the motivation and the rationale for a tax cut, but it could not put together a bill acceptable to both chambers. After years of battles to create a strong tax base and make California one of the most progressive states in terms of government services, tax cuts were unprecedented and posed numerous threats—both real and imagined—to legislators who had built their careers on these services. "With the lawmakers failing to deliver, [citizen-initiated action] picked up speed."[9]

TAKING THE LEGAL INITIATIVE

The initiative process provides citizens in about half the states one of the most powerful tools of direct democracy. Twenty-three states provide for initiatives in which citizens place measures directly on the ballot. Twenty-one of those states also allow referenda in which citizens have the right to approve or disapprove of legislation put on the ballots by state legislatures. Three states allow legislature-initiated referenda but not citizen initiatives.[10]

Established by state constitutions, initiative procedures involve acquiring signatures of 5 to 15 percent of the voters to place a proposal on the ballot. Passage of an initiative means placing a new law on the books. Initiatives are not possible for federal legislation, since the U.S. Constitution forbids Congress from delegating its legislative responsibilities.

Not everyone loves the initiative process. Given the hurdles in getting initiative issues on the ballot, the lack of public understanding of the issues at stake, and the fact that over 15 percent of the voters in elections with initiatives fail to vote on the initiative, it is not clear that "the people" are always the ones who are speaking. As political scientist Ted Lascher sees it, "Initiatives are a waste of time and money because they don't produce policies any closer to public opinion than legislatures."[11] Despite the criticism, the romantic notion of citizens taking policy making into their own hands and wresting it away from the special interests and career politicians has significant appeal.

Success rates for the passage of initiatives are relatively low, averaging less than 5 percent.[12] Obtaining enough signatures to place an item on the ballot often proves an insurmountable goal. California law required signatures from 8 percent of the number of voters participating in the last gubernatorial election. That translated into almost 500,000 valid signatures. Signatures could be disqualified for lacking adequate information such as addresses and precinct numbers. To be safe, a petition drive strives for a cushion of half again as many signatures as the number required by law.[13] Thinking about collecting 750,000 signatures is clearly intimidating. It took Jarvis and his supporters five attempts to get their initiative on the ballot.

In the annals of signature gathering, the fight to get Proposition 13 on the ballot deserves a special place. "Fueled by a true voter panic, [it] was qualified for the ballot by thousands of little people volunteering their time and effort; it cost Jarvis about a nickel a signature"[14] at a time when the going rate for using a commercial firm was about a dollar a signature.[15] In 1980, when Jarvis pushed for Proposition 9, there was "no populist revolt . . . [and] Jarvis bought the signatures—at an average of $2.53 each."[16]

Politics often "makes strange bedfellows," but it also strains the egos and identities of competing organizers and organizations. One of Jarvis's key tasks lay in getting the various tax-cutting organizations to work together instead of fighting each other.

On the surface, Proposition 13 sounded pretty simple, limiting property taxes to 1 percent of assessed value and calculating that value only when property is sold rather than on its current market value. The opposition tried a vast array of opposing strategies. In order to discourage individuals from signing the petition, the opposition sent out the false message that they had enough signatures already. Senior citizens were falsely informed that they might lose some tax exemptions and public assistance if the proposition passed. Willie Brown, chairman of the state Assembly Revenue and Taxation Committee, suggested that the legislature might punish cities if their voters approved the proposition.[17] Representing the tendency to personalize politics, the opposition used the fact that Howard Jarvis was picked up for drunk driving during the campaign as an argument against the proposition. Jarvis claimed the charges were trumped up.

During the trial the district attorney admitted that prosecution was "ordered from up above." Jarvis was eventually acquitted.[18]

MAKING IT LESS TAXING ON THE MEDIA

Media coverage results from strategy as much as substance. Jarvis and his supporters learned how to hold press conferences right after someone important held one. Allowing the media to keep their cameras set up in one location made them willing to cover an event they would not travel to attend.[19] Jarvis's personality was a key factor in drawing media attention. His gruff, combative style was good for headlines. Jarvis got media attention the old-fashioned way—he went out and demanded it by making hundreds of speeches up and down the state. In an age of smooth talkers and blow-dried politicians, the media were drawn to Jarvis for what he was not. They described him as "a disheveled, shouting speaker of the William Jennings Bryan school [who] engages in florid oratory studded with four letter words [and who] angers and forgives easily, and seems to enjoy hugely the discomfiture he causes local governments and the news media."[20] Jarvis's political philosophy was as simple as it was revolutionary in the 1960s and 1970s, as government growth became an article of faith: "Our freedom depends on four words: Government must be limited."[21] Such a blunt message from such a blunt messenger was hard for the media to ignore.

The attention Jarvis received from the media was mostly negative, both he and his movement being written off as right-wing crackpots or worse. Accepting the old public relations dictum that "I don't care what they say about me, just so they say something," Jarvis and his followers received a lot of press. Jarvis even credits the negative stories with a positive contribution, concluding that "sometimes the newspaper criticism of 13 was so heavy-handed that I think it helped us more than it hurt us."[22]

The framing of an issue is critical in politics. Jarvis and Gann were successful in defining Proposition 13 as a referendum on unnecessarily high property taxes. Their opponents were unable to convince voters that the issue was maintaining desired public services. "Cutting wasteful taxes" was an easier sell than "undermining government services." Voter surveys prior to the election indicate that Californians were not fed up with government services; in fact, a large majority desired more from the government. Thirty-eight percent of the voters saw Proposition 13 as only attacking waste and inefficiency, and another large percentage anticipated only minor cuts in services.[23]

Opposition to Proposition 13 among the leadership of the state was both deep and broad. Every major liberal leader saw tax reduction as a threat. Opposition crossed typical ideological boundaries, with major business groups arguing that "it was time for the private sector to stand up for principle and fight this measure as financially unsound."[24] When it came down to it, all Jarvis had on his side was the people. Jarvis was able to "mobilize latent antigovernment sentiment into passionate support for [his] cause."[25]

Initially Proposition 13 enjoyed an approval rating of nearly 70 percent among those taking a stand. As the campaign progressed, undecided voters and weak supporters of Proposition 13 began to slip away and the battle became much closer. The slippage was stopped and reversed not by the campaign per se but by the announcement of Los Angeles city officials that new property tax assessment would show a 17.5 percent increase in property value. Since only one-third of the city's property was reassessed each year, the three-year increase would be over 50 percent. Typically, the new assessments were not available until after the June election, but the assessor decided to make them available in May. Property owners flooded the assessor's office, requesting their new rates. For thousands of voters the abstract idea of increased taxes became a clear personal reality as they pored over their new proposed tax bill. A few weeks before the June voting, the Los Angeles board of supervisors bowed to public pressure and rolled back the new assessments, but in the next breath announced that such a freeze would require an increased rate of taxation on the rolled-back assessment. "The furor in Los Angeles was a godsend for Howard Jarvis. The incident concentrated public attention on the specter of rising taxes, crowding out of the news the familiar warnings about the disruption of services."[26]

The property tax scare in Los Angeles galvanized the proponents of Proposition 13, giving them a concrete example of the emotional threat they had been trying to portray. The opponents were driven into a state of "discouraged silence."[27] Public support began to grow in the polls, especially in the Los Angeles area. "The movement to cut property taxes acquired the flavor of an evangelical crusade: an aroused populace was on the march against government."[28]

Pressing toward the home stretch, the tax reduction movement had come a long way from twenty people sitting around a modest living room. The movement had ignited passion and a willingness to fight for change. Jarvis took $180,000 of his contributions for a final paid media push, twice as much as had been budgeted.[29]

The success of Jarvis's media strategy showed in the willingness of voters to take a stand. Just prior to the election an unprecedented 94 percent of the potential voters were aware of Proposition 13, and only 13 percent were undecided.[30] Public awareness is not enough. Voters must care enough to actually make the effort to vote on propositions once they enter the voting booth. Given the complexity of initiative measures, a significant number of voters "drop off," refusing to vote on propositions after choosing among candidates at the top of the ballot. The average drop-off is between 15 percent and 20 percent. Proposition 13 incurred a drop-off of only 3 percent, indicating that voters knew about it and had a strong enough opinion on it to cast a ballot.[31] The tendency to drop off is not randomly distributed throughout the population, with poorer, less-educated individuals more likely to drop off. This bias adds to that caused by lower voting participation among less-educated and poorer citizens in general. Proposition 13 was distinct in the fact that those who voted were representative of the voting population.[32]

When the votes were counted, the people had spoken with a relatively one-sided voice. Almost 65 percent of the voters approved of Proposition 13. In the state legislative races, a large group of Republicans swept into office on the coattails of Proposition 13. These "Proposition 13 babies" were a group of young and aggressive partisans quite different from the moderate Republicans who had dominated the party for decades. Emboldened by hearing the voters speak, they reduced the game of compromise and cooperation in California politics.[33]

AFTER THE VOTES WERE COUNTED

Howard Jarvis's rise from obscurity was astronomical in it dimensions, if not its speed. *Time* magazine characterized him as a "national folk hero" and put him on the cover of its June 19, 1978, issue. The July 17, 1978, edition of *Business Week* characterized the California vote as "the most significant tax revolt of modern times."

Politicians who once scorned him recognized a winner when they saw one. Candidates in every state sought his endorsement, lining up "like damned lemmings," in Jarvis's words.[34] Shortly after the vote, Senator Hayakawa (R-Calif.) invited Jarvis to Washington to meet with his fellow senators. Even Democratic senator Alan Cranston wanted a chance to introduce him around. House Speaker Thomas P. "Tip" O'Neill, an unabashed big government and adequate taxation liberal, agreed to a meeting. He asked Jarvis the rhetorical question, "Do you know how much you have shaken the Congress up?" Never at a loss for words, Jarvis retorted, "I hope so. You've gotten the first trembler, and you're going to get a real shock wave pretty soon."[35] His appeal to politicians breached national boundaries when he was invited to advise British Conservative Party leader Margaret Thatcher on reducing taxes.

Jarvis's personal rewards were psychic, not material. He was proud to point out that "not only did I never receive a nickel for my work, I spent about $100,000 out of my own money" to get Proposition 13 passed.[36]

Proposition 13 had to leap one more hurdle before it could be implemented: the California Supreme Court. In a nearly unanimous decision the court ruled that it was constitutional. In 1982, the California Supreme Court limited the applicability of the Proposition 13 requirement for a two-thirds vote on new taxes to include only governmental entities that assess property taxes.[37]

THE CONTINUING TAX BATTLE

To those interested in tax reductions, Proposition 13 was not so much a victory as an initial shot in a continuing battle. It became a mandate for cutting taxes. It is credited with eventually starting "twenty-seven tax or spending limit movements in nineteen states."[38] "It strains credulity to look upon the near-simultaneous occurrence of tax revolts in 38 states as sheer coincidence."[39]

Proposition 13 reawakened public disgust for the tax system and also reinvigorated the use of ballot initiatives to provide another vehicle for citizen impact on policy and policy makers. The number of state ballot initiatives soared by over 150 percent during the 1980s.[40] The success of ballot initiatives spawned a growing ballot initiative industry and technology. Grassroots armies of volunteers setting up their petition-signing efforts on card tables in shopping centers have often been replaced by consultants paying workers to collect signatures using high technology.[41]

On the national level, Proposition 13 not only "sent shock waves across other states, but it set off a national debate over the whole question of government taxes and spending that had major, long-lasting repercussions in Washington."[42] As governor of California when Proposition 13 was passed, Ronald Reagan had to deal with its initial implications. His link to the proposition helped set the stage for both his election as president and the income tax reduction measures of the Reagan administration. The Republicans and Ronald Reagan made Howard Jarvis's message the centerpiece of their 1980 presidential campaign: eliminating bureaucratic waste would make it possible to cut both taxes and public spending without the loss of valued services, and less government would enhance both the personal freedom and personal finances of citizens.[43] A number of Reagan's campaign ads in 1980 touted that "he could do for America what he has done for California," with tax reduction being a significant part of that record.

Jarvis's key contribution to tax cutting remains the passage of Proposition 13 and the mood it captured. It set into motion both economic and political consequences that went far beyond California and property taxes. Not a bad record for a conversation around a living room table in a modest suburban home and a man who was "mad as hell" about property taxes.

BACK TO THE FUTURE

The debate over Proposition 13 and the state and national discussion of tax cuts were dominated by competing images of the future. Proponents outlined a rosy future marked by increased government efficiency and an economic environment stimulating growth. Opponents pictured a dire atmosphere of degraded government services and mounting deficits. All agreed that the real consequences would take years to become fully known.

The consequences of Proposition 13 for California continue to be colored by the political perspective of the observer:

> One side tells of retirees who hung on to their homes only because of Proposition 13. The other points out that most of the tax cuts have gone not to homeowners, but to large corporations—many of which opposed the measure as fiscally imprudent. One side notes that government, despite campaign rhetoric, did not crumble post-Proposition 13. The other laments the closed libraries, crumbling infrastructure and dramatic falloff in public school spending. Once ahead of the national curve on public education, California by several measurements now scrapes shamefully across the bottom. One side notes that government needed to be humbled. . . . The other will counter that Proposition 13's impact was anything but "populist," that it in fact stole power—and resources—away from town councils and county boards and shifted it to Sacramento [and the state legislature].[44]

In objective terms, property taxes declined to 0.55 percent, compared to 2 to 3 percent prior to its passage. Since property can be reassessed when sold, individuals remaining in the same house since 1979 now pay only about 0.2 percent, whereas new purchases of identical property would pay five times as much (1 percent). Although allowing individuals on fixed incomes to remain in their homes without fear of dramatic increases in property tax burdens, the system also creates a "lock-in" effect that discourages people from moving once they have a guaranteed low rate. Senior citizens and others not desiring to change residences gained, whereas new residents and those hoping to trade up in the real estate market pay a stiffer price.[45]

Moving away from the empirical evidence, opponents of Proposition 13 raise the issue of the diminished range and quality of government services and point out what might have been done with the foregone revenue. The state of California initially allocated some of its surpluses to finance schools and in the process reduce local government control and equalize school funding. Later financial reversals led the state to pull such funding, requiring local governments to seek out new sources of revenue. One of the most lucrative local government sources has been dramatic increases in taxes on new development. A note of caution for conservatives who seek tax reductions while favoring local governmental decision making over state and national decisions: Proposition 13 led to more local government dependence on state government.[46]

The 2003 recall election of California Governor Gray Davis was brought on in part by the California tax shortfalls generated by Proposition 13. Although Jarvis died in 1986, his spectre seemed to have risen from the grave. His tax cut philosophy not only continues to influence California politics but also fueled the tax cut ideology of President George W. Bush. Jarvis's ideas also live on in more concrete terms, since the Howard Jarvis Taxpayer's Association remains an active player in politics.[47]

Jarvis's message to other potential activists is clear: "People can collectively effect change in the public interest, if only they get mad enough, and if their anger is rational and justified. . . . If there is something about government you don't like, get together and do something about it."[48]

LESSONS

- *Public leadership is less about creating issues than getting out in front of issues already on the public mind.* The tax revolt constituency was a movement in search of a leader. Howard Jarvis captured the pent-up demand and channeled it.
- *Media attention is more important than media approval.* A movement that is ignored is doomed to failure. As the old show business public relations cry goes, "I don't care what they say about me, just so they spell my name right." Keeping an issue in the public eye is critical to success. Howard Jarvis served as the butt of media criticism and scorn but in the process became the focal point of the tax revolt, serving as a useful rallying point to stimulate action.
- *Persistence pays.* Howard Jarvis's "instant success" took sixteen years to bear fruit, with numerous failures along the way. After each failure, Jarvis heeded the exhortation in the old song to "pick himself up, dust himself off, and start all over again."
- *The United States is not a closed political system.* The fifty states serve as little laboratories for testing political movements and policies. Jarvis's use of the initiative and his focus on taxes served as examples to activists in other states, providing them with strategic and substantive guidance.
- *The consequences of policy are not always clear.* Observers still disagree over the actual consequences of Proposition 13. To some, Jarvis remains a prophet who helped straighten out an overly accumulative government. To others, his cure was worse than the disease and continues to hamper the necessary role of government. In politics, reasonable people disagree on the definition of problems, the desirability of alternatives, and the evaluation of outcomes.

13

Power Letter Writing: Women in the Military Academies

In 1972, women were regularly called "girls" in the press, the term "Ms." generated ridicule both publicly and especially privately, "women's studies" referred to home economics, and military academies educated only males. Barbara Jo Brimmer of New York and Valerie Schoen of Michigan emerged as unlikely revolutionaries, but their actions foreshadowed the continuing battle for gender equity, paving the way for women to attend military academies and leading to the eventual development of an officer core committed to gender neutrality. Their battle plan included neither bra burning nor street protests, but rather seemingly benign letters to elected officials. They relied on a venerable weapon—the typewriter.

"IF YOU WERE A BOY, YOU COULD BE GOING HERE"

As the daughter of a Naval Academy graduate who rose to the rank of commander and a WW II navy Wave, Barbara Brimmer grew up in Staatsburg, New York, steeped in navy lore. In her own words, "I was raised in the tradition of the navy and I wanted to follow it."[1] On a trip to Florida when Barbara was a senior in high school, Barbara's family stopped in Annapolis, Maryland, to visit a friend attending the Naval Academy. Barbara and the midshipman shared interests and academic backgrounds. Not knowing the course of events he would initiate, the young midshipman naively commented, "If you were a boy, you could be going here." Barbara and her mother looked at each other knowingly and silently agreed "that is not really fair." The car became their war room as they plotted strategies during the remainder of the trip. Barbara's father, born in 1898 and a creature of the old navy, quickly divorced himself from the entire scheme. Barbara re-

Barbara Brimmer   *Valerie Schoen*

members that he did not oppose the project, "he just gulped a bit and let us go on our way."

Relying on her credentials instead of arguing the philosophical points of equal opportunity or the political agenda of feminism, Barbara Brimmer sent letters of interest to her congressman, Hamilton Fish Jr. (R-N.Y.), her two senators, Vice President Agnew, and President Nixon—all of whom could make nominations. She never heard from the president's office. Vice President Agnew and Congressman Fish made inquiries of the Naval Academy and then sent letters of regret. Senators Jacob Javits (R-N.Y.) and James Buckley (R-N.Y.) sent her application packages. Senator Javits was a fortuitous target, since a few years earlier he had fought to appoint the first female, the first black, and the first Hispanic pages for service in the U.S. Senate. She pursued Senator Javits's offer to submit an application and a few weeks later received a summons to New York City for a meeting with Frank Cummings, a Javits aide, and later with Javits himself. Javits and his staff foresaw the considerable media pressure likely to follow and wanted to assess Ms. Brimmer's ability to handle it. Realizing the spotlight would be on her family, Senator Javits wanted to measure her father's support. Family blood clearly emerged as thicker than navy "water." Kenneth Brimmer, USNA class of 1920, committed himself to shaking the foundations of his alma mater!

Weeks later, while returning from the Army-Navy football game in Philadelphia, the reality of what her letter spawned struck home like a lightning bolt. Barbara Brimmer picked up a copy of the *New York Times* to find a brief article mentioning that Senator Javits planned to nominate a woman to the U.S. Naval Academy. The article went on say that the young woman's father was a retired commander. Unable to contain herself, Ms. Brimmer blurted out, "Hey, that's me." Senator Javits and his staff planned a large media event to announce the nomination, but an ambitious reporter who overheard a conversation in Javits's office undercut their plans. As secrecy began to unravel, Barbara received a hasty summons from her classes at Russell Sage University to take the next train to Washington, D.C. She arrived for her fifteen minutes of fame sick with the flu and wearing her mother's old clothes. Little did she know that she would be met by a family friend, Frank Cummings from Javits's office, and a photographer from *Time* magazine. She thus made her media debut with a fever and a borrowed wardrobe. Staying a few days with the family of the midshipman whose comments inspired her nomination, it was clear that he did not want any of his classmates to know the part he and his family had played in this assault on the all-male U.S. Naval Academy.

A few days later, enjoying better health and wearing more comfortable clothes, Barbara appeared at another press conference flanked by Javits, Congressman Fish, and her family to explain her qualifications and motivations for wanting to become a navy doctor. The star of the event, however, was her father. At seventy-four he might have been expected to be hesitant about his daughter's challenge to the navy. When asked by a female reporter for his reaction to the possibility of his daughter changing the U.S. Naval Academy, he shot back, "Young lady, the world is changing. When I went to the Naval Academy, women did not even have the right to vote."

The next few weeks brought radio interviews and television appearances on programs such as the *Today Show* and *Dick Cavett*. Within a month Barbara Brimmer learned that secretary of the navy, John Chafee, had rejected her nomination because it contradicted the Judeo-Christian heritage and there was a lack of toilet facilities. To this day, she chuckles at the combination of shallow arguments and the lack of serious discussion of the issue.

"LISTEN TO YOUR BROTHER"

At seventeen, Valerie Schoen was new to the world of higher education. None of her three older brothers had attended college. Despite sibling rivalry, when her oldest brother, Melvyn, talked, she listened. Fourteen years her senior, Melvyn seemed to possess a different perspective on things. He said she should go to college and she agreed. When he suggested that "it would be really interesting if women got into the military academies," her interest was piqued. When he went one step further, saying, "I think you should try," he had gone too far. Valerie replied, "You've got to be nuts, people don't do things like that."

Valerie chalked it up as the end of an interesting, if outlandish, conversation. Melvyn took her uncommitted response as a challenge. He began visiting recruiting offices describing a potentially great applicant. Carefully avoiding mention of gender, he emphasized academic record, interest in the Russian language, and extensive scouting experience in a marine-oriented troop.

Without warning, Melvyn presented Valerie a full package of information about applications to military academies. After exclaiming, "Melvyn, you're nuts," she studied the materials. When newspapers later wrote that her application started out as a joke, it stung her.[2] In her own words, "It was not a joke in a 'ha, ha' sense, but more of a dare between my brother and me. I just assumed that my application would not be taken seriously."

Avoiding the expected rhetoric or argumentation about a lack of opportunities for women, Valerie's letter of application simply presented a straightforward request for nomination. She wanted her application to stand on its own merits and hoped the letter's recipients would see the value of nominating a woman. She stated her motivation directly: " I did not apply to Annapolis as a woman's liberationist to break down any sex barriers. I want to serve my country."[3]

Schoen's first letters to her U.S. senators from Michigan received polite responses explaining that women are not allowed to attend military academies. Representative Martha Griffith's letter reiterated that refrain but arrived with handwritten words of encouragement: "I can't do anything, but good luck." A few days later without warning, a letter and an application package arrived from Representative Jack McDonald (R-Mich.) After returning the application, Schoen received a physical examination form. A freshman at the University of Michigan, she dashed over to the university health center. While conducting the examination, the doctor, a woman, finally asked, "What is this physical for, anyway?" When told it was for the U.S. Naval Academy, the doctor shook her head and said, "You're kidding." Most likely the doctor believed a mental exam would be a good next step.

Weeks passed in silence. Then one night she returned to her dorm room late only to find a message from a UPI reporter. She returned the call to learn of her appointment as Congressman McDonald's prime nominee. Valerie remembers "that was the day all hell broke loose." No communication with her congressional benefactor or his staff had taken place except for the initial exchange of letters. The next afternoon, following a barrage of media attention, she finally called Representative McDonald's office and was put through to the congressman immediately. In somewhat embarrassed tones, he admitted, "I am sorry. We should really have told you ahead of time." The next four weeks remain a blur. Her roommates began taking the telephone off the hook or wrapping it in a towel to muffle the ring in order to avoid the obtrusive media. Valerie flew around the country, appearing on *Today*, *Phil Donahue*, and *Mike Douglas*. Four weeks later, perhaps apropos of the way she learned about her nomination, she received a call asking if she knew that the navy had rejected her application. "No, not exactly," she stammered.

"BUT WE DON'T DO WOMEN"

The Naval Academy's reaction to the nomination involved a mixture of surprise and reliance on tradition and legal precedence. Opponents outlined concerns regarding facilities, privacy, the distraction women would cause, the navy's need for combat officers, and assertions that women would not thrive in the academy setting.[4] The law under which the academies operated contained no explicit prohibition, but the intent seemed to limit admission to men. The sections of Title 10 of the U.S. Code used the pronouns "he," "him," and "his" throughout. Such pronouns may not be determinative, since other interpretations of the laws in effect at the time indicated that masculine pronouns can mean persons of either sex. A second legal constraint related to the physical standards for appointment. Requirements relating to height, weight, and physical strength assured that few women would qualify. The legal impediments, although a significant constraint, presented a less important challenge than the lack of desire for change. The legal constraints required only a change in the law or administrative rules. The lack of willingness to change this man's world and the old boy network promised a rear guard battle that would take years to overcome.

The navy's first reaction seemed to be, "If we ignore this it will go away." A continuous push from interested members of Congress vitiated that approach. The next step involved the assertion by the secretary of the navy that although the Naval Academy was not the proper place for women, opportunities for women in the Navy Reserve could be expanded. The strategy was clear: "Giving those who seek social change something related to but different from what they have asked for is one way of attempting to quash their drive. . . . If those seeking change are unwilling to accept this "half a loaf," they must assume the burden of showing the respondent's unreasonableness.[5]

Adapting ROTC provisions was not the answer Senator Javits wanted to hear. He then proceeded to draft legislation requiring all four U.S. military academies (army, navy, air force, and coast guard) to admit women. It took four more years for women's rights in this realm to be established. The legislative battle over this issue is a fascinating story in and of itself, but by the time it took place the initial activists were out of the picture.[6]

The coincidence of two women independently choosing the same year to push the issue remains one of those oddities of timing in civil society. Neither woman directly benefited from the changes she initiated. As is often the case in American politics, individual problems stimulate the legislative process, creating changes that impact large blocs of individuals like a rock thrown in a pond. Women first entered U.S. military academies in 1976 after the legislation pushed by Senator Javits and others passed.

With a change in the law, the academies officially reacted to the directive with a "yes, sir, full speed ahead, sir" attitude. But actually changing the institutional culture was more difficult. The first female graduates symbolically threw their hats in the air in 1980. Since that time over 1,200 women have received commissions as naval officers after receiving academy training, with almost equal numbers surviving the rigors of the U.S. Military Academy (army) and the Air Force Academy. A similar percentage (although smaller number) serve in the coast guard. But the changes did not stop there. In the early 1990s, changes in the 1948 "combat exclusion" law allowed women to participate in most combat activities. In the mid-1990s other military training institutions such as the Citadel and the Virginia Military Institute (VMI) found their all-male admission practices challenged. They responded with many of the same arguments used two decades earlier by the federal military academies. With the media sensitized to the issue of gender equity, Shannon Faulkner's battle to attend the Citadel made her name a household word, in stark contrast to the experience of Barbara Brimmer and Valerie Schoen. The media reported each stage in the court battle, her first day, and her resignation a few days later. In 1996, after an unfavorable Supreme Court ruling, the Citadel changed its stance and admitted four women. Although the first year with women at the Citadel involved a very public flap over hazing, the resignation of two women, and the forced resignation of the perpetrator, the die was cast. The class accepted for entrance to the Citadel for the fall of 1997 included twenty-four women. Thus as the twentieth century drew to a close, the age of government-subsidized, single-sex military academies ended as a result of two well-timed and well-directed letters.

BARBARA BRIMMER AND VALERIE SCHOEN: A REPRISE

At times, the story behind the story is as interesting as the story itself. I contacted Barbara Brimmer with some help from her mother. Finally the Barbara Brimmer who existed more as a concept than an individual emerged as a real person on the phone with a distinctive voice, a vivid memory, and motherly concerns about her husband's ability to handle their child's "bath time" while she relived her past.

While her case spurred additional rounds of political battles, Barbara Brimmer went back to her life as a college student after the 1972 confrontation. For the next four years, Senator Javits nominated her every year, but by the time women were accepted she had already graduated from college and was ready to get on with her life.

Barbara Brimmer's contact with the navy continued briefly. She joined a navy nursing program but eventually left for medical reasons. She has worked as a librarian and a business executive, and today she lives with her husband and young daughter in New Jersey. She has no regrets about writing one of two critical letters that changed the face of U.S. military academies. But her life, ironically, changed very little. She does not see herself as a living pioneer with the burden of "I am Barbara Brimmer; do you know what I did in the 1970s?" In fact, her in-laws have never been told the story of their daughter-in-law's premarital political activity. With more than a little pride, she graciously accepts the fact that asking for a nomination was "my claim to fame."

Valerie Schoen's whereabouts proved more elusive. Computer searches initially turned up nothing. Her two-year attendance at the University of Michigan was too short to produce a paper trail through the alumni office. With some coaxing, the registrar's office provided a street address as of 1972. A further computer search confirmed a Norman Schoen still at that address with no telephone listed. Dispatching a letter requesting an interview seemed a bit archaic and anticlimactic in this day and age of computer searches and instant communication. For Valerie Schoen, the written communication created as dramatic a shock as an unanticipated call. When we finally made contact, Valerie exclaimed, "Your letter almost caused an accident."

Unbeknownst to me, her parents could not serve as my conduit. Her father had died a number of years earlier and her mother resided in an assisted living facility. The family residence remained empty. Every few weeks, Valerie drove to the old home to gather the mail. The pile, including my letter, was over a foot high. When she plopped the pile on the passenger seat, letters and brochures began falling onto the floor. The pile stabilized with my letter on top. Starting to back her car into the garage, she glanced over and surprisingly saw a "U.S. Navy" return address. Her first thought was, "What would the navy want with my mother?" Continuing to back in, she glanced over again and saw that the return address was not the U.S. Navy but rather the U.S. Naval Academy. This piqued her interest, since she knew of no reason her mother would have contact with the academy. Craning her neck to read the rest of the envelope, she saw that it was addressed to her in care of her father, and she almost drove into the side of the garage, exclaiming, "Oh my God! I'm forty-two years old and they have just accepted my application to the Naval Academy."

The shock of remembrance was real. After more than a quarter of a century, only occasionally does she think about the Naval Academy and what might have been. However, she can still tell you the date of her nomination—January 18, 1972—and she maintains a scrapbook of her intense, short-lived days of media attention. Valerie wrote a letter to the first woman to graduate at the top of her class, asking, "Do you have any idea how you got this opportunity?" She never mailed it. Valerie Schoen finished her degree in accounting and maintained her interest in Russian. Her current life as a bookkeeper for a landscaping company garners no media attention, but she expresses few regrets. She can always point out, "I was the first official nominee—no one can take that away from me."

Unlike some examples of citizen activity, it is not valid to argue that without the initiatives of Barbara Brimmer and/or Valerie Schoen that military education at federal and/or state funded military academies would have remained all-male. No doubt, someone else would have eventually put the process into motion. This should not demean the fact, however, that they were the first to take action and were ready to accept the consequences.

LESSONS

- *Policy initiators often do not reap personal benefits.* Neither Barbara Brimmer nor Valerie Schoen gained any long-term personal benefit from their actions. The policy process is so slow that those who initially point out problems are no longer in a position to receive the benefits when a solution is finally achieved.
- *Public policy initiatives need vehicles.* Brimmer and Schoen started the ball rolling with their letters to members of Congress and then stood back as events developed. Most of the heavy effort occurred in Congress, with the two initiators giving a human face to abstract policy.
- *Differing motivations can lead to similar behavior.* Although they employed the same strategy—writing a letter—the factors that led to those letters were quite different. Brimmer and Schoen had different goals and expectations, but both saw a letter to their congressman as an effective strategy.
- *Targeting the proper decision makers is important.* Many members of Congress would not have been amenable to an initiative that could be interpreted as an extreme example of women's rights. Senator Javits and Congressman McDonald turned out to be responsive targets, grabbing the issue and pursuing it.
- *One letter can make a difference.* Although not all congressional letters receive the attention or achieve the impact that we have seen in the case of

Brimmer and Schoen, members of Congress use correspondence from constituents to tap into their interests and to justify their own behavior.

- *Policy activism is not necessarily habit-forming.* Neither Brimmer nor Schoen became long-term civic activists. Although there are many activists in search of a cause, integrating the military academies was a cause in search of activists.

14

The Mystery of the Smoking Gun

Fifty-two-year-old former professor Merrell Williams spent most of his life studying drama. Beginning in 1988, he played a leading role in a real-life mystery drama with all the earmarks of a blockbuster. The major elements were in place: deceitful villains, sympathetic victims, and a multifaceted but flawed hero. There was even the hint of a steamy sex scene.

As in any good drama, it was not immediately clear who the villains or the heroes were. Does the audience side with the liar or the thief? Even after the drama unfolded, the public and the players were still taking sides.

SECURING THE SCRIPT

For decades the tobacco companies shielded themselves from blame by arguing that there was no evidence for smoking being either addictive or harmful and that in any event individuals had the right to make their own choices. Over the years, these companies spent millions of dollars on research, trying to disprove any link between smoking and disease and showing that they were studying the issue thoroughly. As the studies and supporting documents began to pile up, they directed their lawyers to classify the findings according to their potential for causing embarrassment. The task was relegated to paralegals who signed a pledge not to disclose their findings to anyone on the outside.

After holding jobs ranging from college professor to car salesman, Merrell Williams was glad to get the $9 per hour paralegal position with the attorneys representing Brown and Williamson Tobacco (B&W), the maker of such popular brands as Kools. He was curious as to why the job interviewer asked him if he smoked.

Merrell Williams

ACT 1: THE THIEF

Merrell Williams first appeared on the stage clutching a "bankers box" of over 4,000 documents that he had surreptitiously copied and spirited out of his workplace. To mask the crinkling sound the documents made under his clothes, Williams walked past the guards loudly crunching potato chips. Like a scene out of a cheap novel, Williams left a strand of hair on remaining documents to make sure no one had touched them and realized that some were missing. He even carried on a brief affair with his supervisor in hopes of allaying any fears she might have about his loyalty.[1]

Williams's motives remain cloudy. He tells of his growing "shock and distress" over discovering a "decades-long conspiracy by the tobacco companies and their law firms to conceal the dangers of smoking."[2] He details his ill-fated attempts at disclosing his findings to the public, only to be rebuffed by reporters covering the tobacco story and federal government officials investigating it.[3] Williams's defenders see him as a "valiant whistle-blower who is courageously challenging the tobacco industry,"[4] whereas B&W lawyers point out that Williams first attempted to use stolen booty to leverage a $2.5 million deal to compensate for his smoking-related heart disease and the stress of his discoveries.[5] If this were an old-fashioned melodrama, Williams might be in line for boos and hisses, since "the whistle-blower loses his shining armor when he tries to use the material for personal gain."[6] Williams had seemingly threatened the confidentiality of a lawyer-client relationship and did so for selfish reasons.

The B&W lawyers rejected what they saw as a tainted deal and secured a restraining order denying Williams the right to reveal any of the information in the documents, even to his lawyer. After the fact, Williams claimed the personal injury suit was a ruse to establish the legitimacy of the documents.[7]

The B&W public relations machine quickly took Williams's measure and publicized his flaws and shortcomings. Twice-divorced, Williams had a checkered career. His stints at university teaching were marred by charges of arrogance and dereliction of duty. His record of employment revealed a series of menial jobs and failed opportunities.[8]

At the end of the first act, Williams is seen as a self-admitted thief who seemed to express a willingness to relinquish the documents and forgo the disclosure of information that he had found so disturbing in exchange for a financial payoff.

ACT 2: SEASONED ACTORS AND AGGRIEVED PARTIES

The tobacco industry reacted to Merrell Williams's larceny with cocky disdain. He was seen as just another ex-smoker trying to eschew personal responsibility and sue a well-established industry responsible for thousands of jobs and known for its charitable largess. Their track record in the legal process engendered confidence. "Tobacco companies [had] never lost a court case, never been assessed a fine, never paid out a dime to a smoker who had sued."[9] They had "always been the king of the mountain, able to beat down plaintiffs one by one."[10]

In the spring of 1994, the House Health and Environment Subcommittee was considering charges that tobacco companies manipulated the nicotine levels in cigarettes to keep smokers addicted and was debating a proposal that the government regulate cigarettes as a drug. Called before the subcommittee, the presidents of the seven largest tobacco companies presented a united front, flatly asserting under oath that cigarettes are not addictive and have not been proven to cause health problems; any attempt to regulate them would run counter to Americans' right of free choice. The stage seemed to be set for another tobacco industry triumph, a victory for free enterprise and personal freedom.

ACT 3: TRUMPING THE LIARS, PRAISING THE THIEF

Merrell Williams was not ready to take his final bow. He was not the typical tobacco health victim with little more to show for his engagement with the cigarette companies than a file of medical bills. He had extensive knowledge about the internal workings of B&W and a set of documents retained as an insurance policy far more potent than the medical variety.

Williams was introduced to Richard Scruggs, a Pascagoula, Mississippi, lawyer who had become wealthy through asbestos suits and was now pursuing tobacco companies to recover costs paid by the state for tobacco-associated health problems.[11] Scruggs verified the explosive nature of Williams's documents as the necessary "smoking gun" in the battle against big tobacco. David, in his battle with Goliath over product liability, "finally got some stones in its sling."[12]

The documents showed that for over thirty years B&W researchers and executives had recognized the addictive nature of tobacco and the link between tobacco and medical conditions such as lung cancer, cardiovascular disorders, and emphysema. Internal reports were so concerned about the cancer link that they referred to it by the code name *zephyr*, concluding that "there is a causal relationship between zephyr and tobacco smoking, particularly cigarette smoking."[13] Addison Yeaman, B&W's chief lawyer, flatly stated in a 1963 memo that the tobacco industry is "in the business of selling nicotine, an addictive drug effective in the release of stress mechanisms."[14] He recommended that they face up to the medical problems and aggressively seek ways to "neutralize" the medical threats while reaping the financial benefits of distributing a medically safe cigarette that would deliver "full flavor—and incidentally—a nice jolt of nicotine."[15] The papers also showed that "chronic intake of nicotine tends to restore the normal physiological function . . . so that ever-increasing dose levels of nicotine are necessary." The tobacco companies were forced to experiment with methods of increasing nicotine delivery by injecting additives.[16] The memos revealed "a consistent pattern of keeping this information outside the United States solely to preserve their ability to deny its existence"[17] and a strategy of funneling documents through their lawyers to place them under the confidentiality of the lawyer-client relationship.[18] The material in Williams's cache was stunning "because it was so frank and because it was so old. The companies apparently had a very good grip on the nature of smoking even in the 1960s."[19] As one prominent lawyer summarized the so-called tobacco papers, "it was the first documented proof that the public saw that the tobacco firms were lying. . . . everyone knew they were liars, but proving it on paper is another thing. . . . When people look back and wonder why the hell anyone smoked in the first place, people will see that this guy Williams could have been responsible for the end of it."[20]

Williams was paranoid about being followed and felt that the tobacco companies would have little hesitation in rubbing him out. From the legal perspective, the documents were stolen and could be traced back to him. The paralegal coders working in his damage control unit initialed every document they examined. At times Williams had been able to spirit away documents handled by others on weekends or left unattended while coders played miniature golf around the office. The cruel fact, though, was that most of the documents had his initials on them.[21]

Things had gone too far to turn back. Williams had been publicly outed as the thief and had little to show for it except for a series of court summonses. The scene shifted to a late-night rendezvous at a quiet Florida airstrip with one of Williams's old college friends who had been keeping a set of the documents. Scruggs, the aggressive lawyer, piloting his own Lear jet financed by earlier asbestos settlements, took possession of the documents. He delivered them to Representative Henry Waxman (D-Calif.), a long-time anti-tobacco activist and chair of the Health and Environment Subcommittee of the House Energy and Commerce Committee, which was investigating the tobacco industry. From there the documents found their way to major newspapers and an antismoking researcher at the University of California, San Francisco, who made them available to the public through the library and on the Internet.[22] Williams had clearly violated the gag order, and the documents were effectively out in the open for public review. This was not the first time members of Congress played a key role in making private documents public. The Pentagon Papers, which revealed misjudgments associated with the Vietnam conflict, reached the public through a member of Congress. Intentional leaking is a way of life in politics and especially on Capitol Hill.

B&W lawyers began pursuing criminal charges against Williams for theft and served subpoenas on Representatives Henry Waxman and Ron Wyden (D-Ore.) demanding that they produce the illegally acquired records. A U.S. district judge denied the B&W motion, harshly criticizing their disregard for constitutional doctrines and their "high-handed course of conduct . . . patently crafted to harass those who would reveal facts concerning B&W's knowledge of health hazards inherent in tobacco."[23] The judge argued that the law protects whistle-blowers trying to bring information to the attention of those responsible for dealing with it.[24] As a parting shot that did little to endear the tobacco companies to Congress, a B&W lawyer charged that this "opinion appears to say Congress is above the law. It's OK for Congress to participate in illegal activities as long as they didn't commit the crimes themselves."[25]

The tide seemed to be turning in Williams's favor. He still faced criminal charges for theft, but observers were increasingly arguing that an individual has a right—even a responsibility—to expose confidential material if hiding it would cause harm to a third party.[26] Even the tobacco industry's defenders agreed that a lawyer was not bound by confidentiality in all cases. For example, if a serial murderer confided in him and provided a list of his future victims, silence would make the lawyer an accomplice.[27] An even broader interpretation asserted that the privileged lawyer-client relationship does not cover evidence of fraud or past crime.[28]

Legal Assistant Today, the professional journal for paralegals, found itself in the unenviable position of recognizing the unscrupulousness of B&W but not wanting to suggest that paralegals have the right to break the principle of lawyer-client confidentiality. Its editorial said that "in the legal system, 'truth' sometimes takes a back seat to system interests, including society's interest in protecting open and trustworthy relationships between lawyers and clients. . . . Two wrongs don't make a right."[29] A few months later Williams was chosen by *Legal Assistant Today* as one of twelve paralegals who "changed the profession" in the 1990s. Although his accomplishments were not seen as positive by all, it is hard to ignore the breadth of the consequences that his actions generated.[30] Increasingly, though, most impartial observers were warming to the justification of Williams's larceny. The public began to perceive big tobacco "as an outlaw industry."[31]

Initial media attention varied by locality. The first stories of Williams's actions appeared in the *Louisville Courier-Journal,* which treated it in terms of the actions of a hometown boy and the reaction of a prominent hometown company. Dependent on B&W for advertising and news, the *Courier-Journal* characterized Williams as a thief who broke two written agreements with his employer and whose personal background made him less than a model citizen. Local journalists sought out former colleagues in the document screening project who described him as a "dishonest, conniving opportunist" with an "ulterior motive for everything he does." His assertions about motivation and the content of the documents were framed as personal "claims," versus verifiable truths.[32] Newspapers with less of a tie to the tobacco industry began portraying Williams as either a victim of big tobacco or a hero who risked his own well-being to protect his fellow citizens.

Just as our emerging hero was about to exit stage right, another flaw in Merrell Williams's behavior surfaced. Shortly after he handed Richard Scruggs the box of potent documents, the wealthy lawyer financed a $109,600 house, two cars, and a sailboat for Williams on little more than a handshake. He also helped him find a $3,000 a month paralegal job that seemed to require little work.[33] Scruggs characterized his act as simple charity in helping out a friend who was down on his luck. B&W lawyers saw it as another example of Williams benefiting from an illegal act.[34]

ACT 4: PLAYING ON THE LARGER STAGE

With the documents out in the public and B&W contemplating whether it would continue to pursue Williams for theft, a series of associated plots developed. Each depended on Williams's whistle-blowing, and each was complex enough for an entirely new play.

A Scene from the States

In the state courts, over eight hundred[35] liability cases, which the cigarette companies won with boring regularity, began to draw on the B&W documents. The familiar routine of characterizing smoking as a personal choice assumed that the choice was informed.

In August 1996, a Florida jury found B&W negligent in the case of a forty-four-year-old smoker who developed cancer. The key difference from previous cases was the stolen tobacco papers.[36] Members of the jury indicated that the shift in the case came during deliberations when the jury foreman suggested they read the B&W documents as a way to break the deadlock. The more they read the angrier they became. The tobacco companies soon had no defenders in the room and the only issue was the size of the settlement. Each juror wrote a dollar figure on a slip of paper. The jury added up the figures and settled on the average of $750,000. The result shocked the tobacco companies and frightened Wall Street. Philip Morris, which wasn't even a defendant, saw its market value drop by $11 billion.[37] This would not be the last bad day for the tobacco industry.

About the same time, lawyers such as Scruggs devised an alternative way of getting around the personal choice argument. They would sue on behalf of each state to recover funds spent on smoking victims' medical bills.[38] Williams's tobacco papers "energized Scruggs and his team. They would not be paid by Mississippi for their work—unless they won. Their percentage of the verdict would make them rich. But if they lost, they'd be ruined. It was a huge gamble. Now they knew their opponent's hole cards."[39] The tobacco papers evened the playing field. State after state began suing tobacco companies, seeing huge settlements as a way of balancing state budgets and reducing smoking. One of the thirty state attorneys general suing the industry admitted that "I cannot tell you how important the Merrell Williams documents are to my case and to every other case pending against Big Tobacco."[40]

The Media Take Center Stage

Although Williams was a little fish, his courage (some would say foolhardiness) emboldened other high-level whistle-blowers who could legitimize his claims, update his historical data, and put a human face on the industry's deceit.[41] Former B&W vice president for research Jeffrey Wigand, clearly a big fish, came forward with information on his former employer after seeing the seven industry presidents lie before a congressional committee. Getting Wigand's story out proved difficult. The news media had become wary of the tobacco industry's power after ABC buckled under pressure and publicly apologized to Philip Morris over a story about controlling the levels of nicotine to keep people smoking. Although many felt ABC had a strong defense, fighting big tobacco in a tobacco state like Virginia looked like too large a risk. Mike Wallace of CBS's *60 Minutes* conducted a wide-ranging interview with Wigand that confirmed most of the charges in the documents. Following a major internal battle, CBS decided not to run the Wigand interview for fear of a lawsuit.[42]

The Wigand story eventually got out and a series of other tobacco company researchers came forward with their own damning evidence.[43] Although B&W could discredit a few dissidents like Williams and Wigand, "it was no longer possible to imagine discrediting every employee who left the company and was willing to describe his or her own work. . . . The operation of the companies now began to be laid bare brick by brick."[44]

The tobacco companies were known for competing in the marketplace but linking arms in perfect unity in court and in public. Seeing the handwriting on the wall, Bennet LeBow, CEO of Liggett and Meyers, the smallest of the tobacco companies, broke ranks. Deciding to cut his company's losses, LeBow admitted that the industry had known for decades about the addictive nature of cigarettes, that they had lied about it, and that they had worked with their lawyers to conceal evidence. Liggett agreed to pay twenty-two states $25 million up front and 25 percent of its profits for the next twenty years.[45] For some, LeBow was a hero protecting his stockholders and telling the truth. For the tobacco industry, he emerged as another turncoat in their ranks.

Congress Attempts to Steal a Scene

At first, Democrats in Congress reacted to being cut into the battle against the tobacco industry with appreciation. Representative Pete Stark (D-Calif.) proposed awarding the Congressional Medal of Appreciation for Public Spirit to the unnamed courageous citizen who leaked the documents to Congress.[46] The proposal died quietly after the Democrats lost their majority.[47] With the Republicans in power after the 1994 election, the tobacco industry's long-term strategy of cultivating key legislators through significant campaign funding seemed to pay off. Using its power of the purse, the House took the unprecedented action of trying to eliminate a specific research grant intended for Dr. Stanton Glantz, a well-respected researcher from the University of California, San Francisco, medical school. Glantz engendered the tobacco industry's ire by receiving a set of Williams's stolen documents, making them public, and writing a series of articles based on their content.[48] The staff director for the Republican majority in the House Appropriations Committee, a former Philip Morris lobbyist, complained that Glantz's work did "not properly fall within the boundaries of the National Cancer Institute portfolio" since it dealt with the politics of the tobacco situation. The action was seen by all as an attempt "to silence a leading critic."[49] Although the Senate failed to go along with the cut, such congressional micromanagement had the potential for creating a chilling effect on anti-tobacco research.[50] Such efforts presaged more successful state-level attempts sponsored by the tobacco industry to specifically disallow funding for such research from state tobacco settlement income.[51]

As the depth of the tobacco industry's deceit emerged, its longtime alliance with Republicans and members from tobacco districts began to unravel. Republican House Speaker Newt Gingrich (R-Ga.) angrily lectured a group of tobacco lobbyists, saying, "You guys have screwed us. The Republican party has been saddled with tobacco. I will not let Bill Clinton get to the left of me on this. We're not going to support anything the industry's for."[52] Lying and misleading enemies was one thing, but doing the same to friends was unforgivable. The $15 million the tobacco industry had given to Republicans over the previous five years had gone up in smoke.[53] The reservoir of political goodwill they thought was bought and paid for evaporated. Virtually everyone in Congress wanted to be part of giving the tobacco industry its comeuppance.

The President Steps In

The scene now shifted briefly to the executive branch. After consulting the leaked documents and polls paid for by Williams's lawyer, Richard Scruggs,[54] President Clinton ordered the Food and Drug Administration to propose classifying tobacco as a drug-delivery device, greatly expanding its potential control over such products. Marching forward with the attempt to regulate tobacco as a drug, the FDA ran into opposition from the courts. In the fall of 1998, a three-judge panel of the 4th U.S. Circuit Court voted 2 to 1 that the FDA lacked the authority for such control. An appeal in the case is currently pending and will probably reach the Supreme Court.

Congress Regains the Stage

Fearful of being out of the loop, Congress found a way to reassert its usefulness in the battle over tobacco. Congress can play a mediator role when different sides all see the utility of a solution without having to agree on the nature of the problem. The tobacco industry saw itself being bled by defeat after defeat on the state level with the threat of an open-ended set of individual personal injury suits. They were looking for a "cease fire with legislators, state prosecutors and . . . antismoking groups."[55] Most importantly, they sought the help of Congress to head off the horde of individual suits by smokers claiming they were harmed by the companies' negligence. Those opposing the tobacco industry wanted to teach corporate America a lesson about ethics and honesty while using fines against the tobacco industry to fund a wide variety of programs, only some related to reducing the dangers of tobacco. Congress's forte lies in brokering compromises between competing sets of values. If a nationwide settlement of significant proportion could be negotiated legislatively, the tobacco industry could go on chastised and punished but economically viable. At the same time, states could recover some of their financial losses and the tobacco companies could be made responsible for discouraging smoking among the young.

EXIT, STAGE RIGHT

As the curtain goes down, the plot has not been entirely resolved. The unprecedented $400 billion tobacco deal brokered by Congress ended without a final agreement. The tobacco companies eventually settled with the states, providing a $246 billion payoff and agreeing to limits on advertising.[56] The more comprehensive national legislation stalled in Congress may well have kept the companies at the state bargaining tables in hopes of thwarting more severe penalties. Unlike in the past, the courts began to approve of large multimillion dollar settlements for individuals claiming harm from tobacco and the Supreme Court refused to overturn them.[57]

Merrell Williams missed his starring entrance in the play he forced on the stage. When *The Insider* told the story of the battle against big tobacco, the star was Jeffrey Wigand, the former Brown and Williams research director, and Williams was never mentioned.[58]

Authors often worry about how their subjects will see their efforts. Williams was one of the few people I was not able to interview before this book was published. When an e-mail with his name arrived a few months after publication, I steeled myself to a tirade on how I had "gotten it wrong." To my pleasure, Williams found the chapter "thoughtful and interesting" and credited it with "assuag[ing] many of the bitter feelings that have lingered during the last ten years."[59] What more could an author ask for?

Williams still struggles with the question of whether he is a hero or a thief and for now answers the question by saying, "You can call me Robin Hood. . . . You can call me a prostitute. But I met my goal. The documents got out."[60] As to being a hero, Williams concludes with the flair of a former drama professor lecturing his students, "I've decided I am an anti-hero."[61] "The 'Cigarette Papers' case offers us a tale of how the giants fall in modern times: tripped by their own big feet—or by little guys who tangle them up in Webs."[62]

LESSONS

- *You can't always tell the actors without a program.* Politics is seldom a game of pure heroes and absolute villains. Flawed heroes and redeemable villains more often populate its scenes. The political process is often forced to choose between the lesser of two evils, with the balance of that choice often not satisfying everyone.

- *Congress plays a number of potential roles in American politics.* At times members of Congress operate largely on the margins, serving as cheerleaders or facilitators. At other times, Congress is in the thick of the decision-making process. The wide variety of interests represented by members of Congress assures a sympathetic ear for a wide range of causes. Members of Congress use their status, political protection, and legal authority to act in ways other public officials might be wary of. Engaging Congress in a political battle usually results in opening the process to broader awareness as Congress and its members seek publicity.

- *There is more than one way to skin a cat.* The tobacco industry could have corrected the errors in its ways privately, by cooperating with the courts, or by agreeing to executive branch oversight. Any one of these actions might have deactivated its opposition. By eschewing these remedies, the industry forced itself onto the congressional agenda. Congress deals with the toughest battles over societal values, which cannot be settled on other levels. Congress seldom receives issues for which there is a "right" answer but rather negotiates compromises.

15

Just What the Doctor Ordered

The words rang through the room and were transported throughout the nation electronically. The young woman in the balcony of the U.S. House of Representatives joined the handful of individuals whom recent presidents have used to put a human face on abstract societal goals and public policy. Adding a little mystery and human pathos to a speech often filled with self-congratulatory rhetoric and complex issues gives the news media a useful hook for a story that was hard to turn into criticism. Presidents have long used the presidency and the annual State of the Union address as a "bully pulpit" to exhort their fellow Americans to strive and reach for new goals. But an increasingly cynical public has made it more and more difficult for that message to stick. The self-admitted gimmick of having the president, who usually deals with kings, queens, heads of state, and major power brokers, give equal time to average citizens is daring enough to garner media attention.

Ever since Ronald Reagan seated Washington bureaucrat Lenny Skutnik, who had dived into the icy Potomac to rescue victims of an Air Florida jet, next to First Lady Nancy Reagan in 1982 and mentioned him in his speech, the ritualistic political theater has become a tradition. President Reagan later honored individuals such as twelve-year-old church choir director Tyrone Ford; Jean Nguyen, a Vietnamese refuge who graduated from West Point; and Sergeant Stephen Trujillo, a participant in the U.S. invasion of Grenada. President Clinton continued the tradition by honoring two students and a teacher from the Illinois school district that won first place in the world science exam, heroes of the Oklahoma City bombing, and the Maryland minister of one of the nation's fastest growing black congregations.

The pattern became established. An average American who has done something very un-average is called, often discreetly, to sit with the presidential family. Scanning the gallery, the television pundits rack their

Dr. Kristen Zarfos

brains to determine who is sitting with the First Lady. At the appropriate time during the speech, the president mentions the name and gestures to the gallery. On cue the cameras turn for the photo op and the person's few minutes of fame begin. The instant analysts from the media try to fill in the story, and the next day's news is filled with speculation about the person's identity and the president's reasons for recognizing him or her.

The young woman mentioned in President Clinton's 1997 speech was a quiet doctor dedicated to her family and patients. A mastectomy patient of hers moved the doctor from being a shy observer to occupying the center of a contentious battle that would pit the economic concerns of big health insurance companies against the doctors and hospitals whose bills they pay. In the middle would be the patients who paid the premiums undergirding the insurance companies' income and the doctors who questioned whether the best interests of their patients were being maintained when economic motivations came into conflict with medical judgment calls. As the argument was boiled down into sound bite proportions, Dr. Kristen Zarfos summarized the problem: "Physicians and surgeons take the blame for complications resulting from early discharge after a mastectomy, patients take the risks, and HMOs (Health Management Organizations) pocket the profits."[1]

JUST WHAT THE DOCTOR ORDERED

Dr. Zarfos sees patients at their most vulnerable time. Diagnosed with cancer, they are confused and bitter, and they often feel helpless. They need their energy in the fight to stay alive and have little energy left to fight economic battles with large bureaucratic health insurance companies or political battles with government agencies.

America's long-term commitment to private, as opposed to public, health insurance exemplifies our commitment to the private enterprise system and the belief that the economic motive will combat the bureaucratic inefficiency and impersonality of large government and business bureaucracies. For-profit entities do a good job of making cost-effective decisions on black-and-white issues such as getting the best price on drugs and equipment, but they serve less well when dealing with human variations in condition or pain tolerance. We all believe in efficiency in the abstract but find it less comforting when gray-area decisions that impact our personal interests are based on speed, efficiency, and/or economic considerations.

Zarfos's entry into the growing battle between physicians and insurance companies began on the abstract level. During a May 1996 chance conversation in the outpatient recovery room at a Middlesex, Connecticut, hospital, another surgeon mentioned that some health plans were adopting new rules making lymph node dissections outpatient surgeries. Zarfos was shocked. Such procedures are painful, require careful monitoring of drains, and typically involve at least an overnight stay in the hospital.[2]

Disbelieving, Zarfos set out to determine the veracity of the purported new guidelines. She discovered that in the high-risk arena of health insurance, companies had turned to medical actuarial firms to determine coverage. Scanning the Milliman and Robertson lymph node guidelines that were scheduled for implementation in a few weeks, Zarfos learned that mastectomies also fell into the category of outpatient surgery.[3] Barring a vigorous challenge by a patient's doctor, health insurance companies using this guideline would not pay for an overnight stay in the hospital after a mastectomy. Coursing through Zarfos's mind were images of the dozens of her patients racked with pain, suffering from nausea and/or faced with clogged drainage tubes after surgery. It was clear that the hospital was the best place for them. Zarfos remembers the moment, feeling that "inherently as a surgeon it was a turning point in my career. I was forty-three years old. I knew I could not do this surgery and send my patients out of the hospital that day. I asked myself if I was going to acquiesce, or was I going to quit surgery."[4]

Doing the right thing is not without its costs. Insurance companies place doctors on approved lists. There was always a danger that too much trouble from one doctor would lead companies to "deselect" her, leaving her patients with the dilemma of choosing between Dr. Zarfos or being reim-

bursed by insurance. The potential hazard "that keeps colleagues quiet is the obvious ability for an HMO to find some pretext for removing them from their list of accepted health care providers."[5]

Before joining the battle, Zarfos decided on a reality check by seeking advice from fellow surgeons and her patients. Five calls to leading breast cancer specialists confirmed that outpatient treatment for mastectomies was very rare and dangerous. National data were clear: outpatient mastectomies occurred in only about 7 percent of the cases.[6] A survey of Zarfos's own patients confirmed the fears of those she knew best. With near unanimity, 225 of her former mastectomy patients indicated they would not have been able to handle the consequences of their surgery at home.[7] The patients expressed anger and outrage over the fear that HMOs would ignore their needs.[8] Zarfos worked with her patients "to organize their experiences and present them as part of a collective voice. This process involved writing letters to patients, informing them of upcoming legislation, and encouraging them to contact their representatives in the state and federal legislatures."[9] Armed with evidence and a base of public support, Zarfos felt confident that she could challenge the impending guidelines. In the end, she "ignited a rebellion" against outpatient mastectomies and unleashed "a national backlash" against managed care. As Connecticut state legislator Edith G. Prague (D-Columbia) phrased it, "Most doctors don't want to put their careers in jeopardy, She stood tall, that little 100-pound doctor. . . . She's given other doctors the permission to be strong and take a stand."[10]

Fearful of "crying wolf" and losing credibility, Zarfos sought to verify the impending threat to her patients. She wrote letters to the eight HMOs serving Connecticut regarding their length of stay policies for mastectomies. Five companies said they did not follow the outpatient guideline, one refused to answer, and two confirmed their acceptance.[11]

HAND ME A SCALPEL, PLEASE

As a surgeon, Zarfos knew the importance of selecting the right instrument and choosing the appropriate place to operate. Zarfos's initial instrument of choice was the telephone. Expressing concern over the impending guidelines to her friend, a gynecologist, she was advised to alert her member of Congress, Rosa DeLauro (D-Conn.). DeLauro proved to be a fortuitous target. As a strong advocate of women's health issues and a survivor of ovarian cancer, she took on the cause with enthusiasm after only one conversation, eventually introducing the Breast Cancer Protection Act of 1997. A call to Zarfos's own state representative led her to the majority leader of the state House of Representatives, Moira K. Lyons, a prime mover behind managed care reform in Connecticut. Lyons further spiked the interest of the Connecticut Breast Cancer Coalition, which in turn tipped off the media.[12] The policy "train" had left the station, but the issue was still largely abstract for Kristen Zarfos.

Abstract concern turned into a real-world crisis a few weeks later. In early August 1996, Zarfos treated a mastectomy patient insured by an HMO that followed the new guidelines. On the Thursday prior to Monday's scheduled surgery, Zarfos herself called to get approval for two nights in the hospital. Over the next day and a half she was on a rollercoaster ride of secretaries, voice mail, reviewers, and mediators. She eventually got through to the HMO's medical director, a family physician. In initially arguing against the request for an overnight stay, the director incorrectly asserted that it was standard procedure in Connecticut to do mastectomies as outpatient procedures and that the pain could be controlled with oral medication. Using her own survey of doctors and personal experience, Zarfos challenged the medical director on each point. In the end, the medical director approved one night in the hospital, not the two days Zarfos preferred.[13] After nine frustrating phone calls over a seven-hour period,[14] Zarfos won a partial victory. But her experience raised the question of what was happening to other patients whose surgeons lacked the knowledge, motivation, or time to fight the insurance guidelines.

THE IMPORTANCE OF READING THE LABELS

Coincidentally, a few days after Zarfos's battle with ConnectiCare, Diane Levick, the journalist Zarfos tipped off in her first round of telephone calls, published her article on the emerging controversy. The substance of the article was important, but the headline, "New Health Care Concern: Drive-Through Mastectomies," created a pejorative label summarizing the problem in widely understandable terms. The thought of a surgeon invading our bodies with a drive-through mentality brings shudders to even the most callous. The story now had all the elements for action—a brave heroine fighting for her patients, a villainous insurance industry putting profits before people, politicians with a popular cause to ride, and an emotion-laden label with only one reasonable interpretation.

This was not an entirely new issue. Only a year before, state and national legislators had faced the issue of insurance companies mandating limited hospital stays for maternity patients. Congress passed the so-called drive-by baby delivery bill legislation requiring the option of covered forty-eight-hour hospital stays for normal deliveries.[15]

Stung by the labels of "drive-by" deliveries and "drive-through" mastectomies, the insurance industry faced an uphill battle to gain acceptance of their more benign label "managed care." Zarfos's disbelief at the new guidelines imposed on her patients had turned into a personal rage with broader implications questioning the right to quality health care. Her cause struck a nerve well beyond mastectomy patients. Zarfos voiced the fears of doctors and patients alike by boldly asserting, "It's a glaring example of the ill that pervades the managed care industry today. The patient-doctor relationship has been destroyed by the imposition of a businessman trying to make health-care decisions."[16]

IS THERE A DOCTOR IN THE HOUSE?

In January 1997, Dr. Kristen Zarfos, a first-generation college graduate from rural Maryland, now practicing medicine in Connecticut, received a call from the White House inviting her to the State of the Union message. She paid her own way and joined the First Lady in the gallery of the House chamber not knowing what to expect. Toward the middle of the speech, President Clinton, whose mother died of breast cancer, picked up the "drive-through mastectomy" characterization and supported her cause to a national audience. Looking to the gallery, he stated:

> Just as we ended drive-through deliveries of babies last year, we must now end the dangerous and demeaning practice of forcing women from the hospital only hours after a mastectomy. I ask your support for bipartisan legislation to guarantee that women can stay in the hospital for forty-eight hours after a mastectomy. With us tonight is Dr. Kristen Zarfos, a Connecticut surgeon whose outrage at this practice spurred a national movement and inspired this legislation. I'd like her to stand so we can thank her for her efforts. Dr. Zarfos, thank you.

Stunned by the magnitude of the attention, Zarfos modestly commented, "I felt incredibly honored as the voice of women with breast cancer. I felt elated that the complex issues they faced were acknowledged [by the president]. . . . This issue needed to be heard."[17]

The shift from the glow of national publicity to the reality of everyday life shows Dr. Zarfos's commitment to her patients. The morning after the State of the Union recognition, she was back in her office treating patients. She caught up on her practice by working until midnight only to be awakened at 3 a.m. to insert a tube in a collapsed lung.[18] With only three hours of sleep in the last thirty-six, the memory of her moment of fame dimmed.

THIS IS THE PRESIDENT CALLING

As chief executive, the president controls the administration of government programs. In the limited realm of Medicare, the government insurance program for the elderly, the president could act unilaterally. Within a week of the State of the Union message, Zarfos returned to Washington for a White House press conference. Using the White House as the setting and the First Lady as the organizer guaranteed press coverage. At that session, Health and Human Services Secretary Donna E. Shalala forbade the 350 care plans treating Medicare patients from requiring outpatient mastectomies. Medicare accounted for only 8,400 mastectomies in 1996, so the ultimate impact of such an executive branch initiative remained minimal.[19] The vast majority of Americans are covered by private health insurance. With over 185,000 women diagnosed with breast cancer each year,[20] the White House hoped that dramatic action on its part would stimulate more sweeping changes emanating from Congress.

The publicity generated by the president did cause the desired ripple effect, encouraging congressional sponsors and increasing public support. Attempting to capitalize on the president's initiative, congressional supporters created a Web site (www.breastcare.shn.com) to put pressure on Congress. Over 9,000 women signed an electronic petition to support the legislation and over 2,200 described their struggle with breast cancer.[21]

Presidential power is limited in the American system. Highlighting drive-through mastectomies and moving the enabling legislation higher on the national agenda increased the likelihood of action but did not guarantee it. Although modern presidents have been called "chief legislators," they must still depend on the 535 members of the House and Senate to join together in two separate majorities to pass legislation. Few legislators publicly opposed the Breast Cancer Patient Protection Act of 1997, but the wisdom of dealing with the details of health care one affliction at a time slowed legislative action. The bill is still pending.

Not all policy making happens at the national level. Zarfos's plea for outlawing drive-through mastectomies first bore fruit at the state level. By the spring of 1997, thirteen states had passed such legislation,[22] with presidential attention providing state lawmakers an additional reason to act.

Not all problems require a legislative remedy. With a shot fired over their bow by the president of the United States and growing public opinion expressing fears that company bureaucrats would overrule doctors,[23] insurance companies began revising their guidelines. The back-to-back flaps over limiting hospital stays, first for childbirth and then for mastectomies, was a public relations disaster for the image of "managed care," which quickly became perceived as limited care. It did little to help that the two health problems affected women directly and that many of the key decisions were made by men. Through a healthy dose of self-regulation, the insurance industry scrambled to assure the public that medical decisions would be in the hands of patients and their doctors. The

American Association of Health Plans adopted a policy statement that "as a matter of practice, physicians should make all medical treatment decisions based on the best available scientific information and the unique characteristics of each patient." As one insurance company spokesperson frankly admitted, "We adopted this policy because it was going to be mandated."[24] The chief medical officer of ConnectiCare, the company that initially denied Zarfos's patient an overnight hospital stay, put his own best spin on the outcome, declaring that Dr. Zarfos has "been a catalyst for a renewed effort on our part to involve doctors in medical management issues."[25]

CONFESSIONS OF A DOCTOR ACTIVIST

Zarfos was never subjected to overt penalties from insurance companies deselecting her from their plans, but political activism did not come without costs. She is quick to point out to colleagues that "advocating for patients at the legislative level does take away physician time from practicing medicine." She also found it more difficult to balance her additional professional demands with carving out time for her husband and seven-year-old son. On the other hand, she proudly asserts that "if physicians do not advocate for patients and stand up for their rights to basic health care, who is left to do so?"[26]

Not everyone saw Zarfos as a heroine. Columnist Charles Krauthammer, himself a doctor, directly chastised the congressional proponents of breast cancer legislation and indirectly took on Kristen Zarfos in a nationally syndicated column. The title of the column in the *Washington Post* stingingly talked of "Playing Doctor on the Hill."[27] The "meek and mild" doctor struck back, saying, "I am not playing doctor—I am a doctor. . . . I brought this problem to Rep. DeLauro's attention and implored her to act. This is the way the legislative process is supposed to work—regular citizens bringing problems they face in their daily lives to the attention of the elected representatives."[28] Nevertheless, Zarfos has grown weary of political activism, pointing out that "I love seeing patients, doing surgery, and helping people through the process. I don't like the deviousness in the political system. I became an advocate because I think it is my responsibility. It is what I said I'd do when I took the Hippocratic oath. To that extent, this work has been incredibly gratifying."[29]

Whatever Zarfos's personal feelings, forced outpatient mastectomies had been thwarted. Whether or not federal legislation is passed, doctors have been emboldened and insurance companies publicly put on notice all because of the efforts of one doctor with a little help from her president.

LESSONS

- *Do your homework.* Kristen Zarfos's quest may well have been a quixotic "tilting at windmills" exercise without adequate evidence. Before beginning her endeavor, she verified the nature of the problem, discovered the false claims of the insurance companies, and tested the waters with her own colleagues and patients.
- *Presidents are popularizers and agenda setters.* Presidents are seldom the ones initially identifying societal problems. Others closer to the situation have an easier time recognizing potential danger. A president's more important role lies in sifting through the thousands of potential problems society might address and focusing public attention on a few. By gaining presidential attention, Kristen Zarfos increased the likelihood that the problem she identified would become part of the national agenda.
- *Presidents don't always get their way.* The Hollywood ending for this story would be a White House bill signing ceremony with Dr. Kristen Zarfos receiving the first pen on behalf of her patients. In reality, the president could order executive branch employees to force action within their narrow realms of influence. More indirectly, the president invigorated a national dialogue on the question of who should make medical decisions and forced the health care industry to develop defensible guidelines to express in that debate. So far, though, the proposed legislation remains stuck in the process.
- *The threat of government action may be as effective as the action itself.* In many ways, self-regulation is the best regulation, since it requires no external monitoring, evaluation, or punishment. Government action serves as a last resort or "safety net" for situations in which no private solution is evident. The combination of going public with the issue and holding out government action as a threat forced health insurance companies to reconsider whether they wanted to face the ire of current and potential customers fearful of lower-quality health care.

16

Unaffirmative Action

Office of Admissions
Diversity University
Dear Mr./Ms. Applicant,
   Congratulations! The admissions committee is impressed with your strong academic record and your extensive list of extracurricular activities.
   The University is committed to providing an excellent education to the widest range of students possible. Our commitment to diversity requires some tough decisions. Unfortunately you made our decision much more difficult by your unlucky choice of parents and grandparents. Although you are fully qualified in every other way, admitting you would not improve the racial and ethnic diversity we seek.
   We are sure you will understand that sacrifices need to be made to compensate for past discrimination. Your spot in this year's freshman class will be given to someone who will contribute to our diversity goals. You can take pride in the fact that by standing aside you are helping erase racially discriminatory policies perpetrated by nameless individuals from your parents' and grandparents' generations.
   We wish you luck as you attempt to pursue higher education at an institution far inferior to your stellar qualifications. If you should succeed and prosper, we hope you will consider financially supporting our institution in the future for allowing you to assuage your guilt and contribute to the greater good.
                              R.U. Worthy, Dean of Admissions

No one would expect to receive such a letter. Reading between the lines of typical university admissions procedures, however, suggests that this letter does represent an honest portrayal of the position taken by many institutions, whether by choice or mandate.

   The debate over affirmative action pits a series of competing values against each other. Although in the abstract, proponents and opponents

Carl Cohen

could simply "agree to disagree," this is impossible when the principle of affirmative action is applied to real-world situations.

A DISCRIMINATING SOCIETY

American laws and practice traditionally favored white citizens for philosophical, practical, and political reasons. Philosophically, whites were deemed morally superior and deserving of an exalted social station. The early settlers and constitutional founders were largely white Anglo-Saxons with much to gain from a discriminatory outlook benefiting their ethnic compatriots. Practically, prior benefits provided whites the skills, experience, and temperament to succeed in the emerging social structure. Politically, whites held the social and political power and could structure decision making to benefit those like themselves. In the middle decades of the twentieth century, "American society turned away from its history of racial and ethnic discrimination."[1] With decisions such as *Brown v. Board of Education* (1954) and the Civil Rights Act of 1964, discrimination on the basis of race, nationality, and other similar categories was banned. Preference based on these categories was banned by law but not necessarily done away with in practice. When a "color-blind," "ethnicity-blind" society failed to result, the courts were called in regularly to help eradicate practices that "although apparently innocuous, sustained entrenched patterns of racial preference"[2]

such as recruitment practices of colleges, business, and industry. The practice of aggressively seeking members of formerly disadvantaged groups and assuring that they would be evaluated for the benefits of society without discrimination was labeled "affirmative action."

In many proponents' minds, the goal of fairness and equal "opportunity" quickly shifted to support for equality of "outcome." Leveling the playing field was not enough to compensate for past patterns of discrimination as some proponents subtly or overtly called for intentional "tilting." They sought a "score" based on explicit counting of minority "winners" in the competition over scarce societal benefits such as positions in college classes or highly sought-after jobs. As Justice Harry Blackmun wrote in the 1978 Bakke case, "In order to treat some people equally, we must treat them differently."[3] Proponents of aggressive affirmative action argued that societal goals, unenforced laws, and/or changed attitudes do no good if the results in people's lives varied little from the past.

This shift to guaranteeing equality of outcome was supported by a complementary shift in the understanding of constitutional rights. Traditionally rights adhered to individuals as opposed to groups. Historically, specific harm to the individual in question must be established to prove an abridgment of rights. The contemporary civil rights movement engineered a change in perspective: if the rights of a group were abridged, amelioration for any member of that group evidenced appropriate corrective action.[4] Although virtually everyone agreed that slavery was wrong, many argued that those most aggrieved could not be compensated and that those responsible were not around to take their punishment. Many civil rights leaders argued that descendants of those aggrieved as defined by their group membership deserved compensation, whether or not any direct link to personal or family mistreatment could be proved. University of Michigan philosophy professor Carl Cohen vocally disagreed:

A remedy for injury may be given justly only to those who have suffered that injury, not to other persons whose skin is of the same color. Wrongs done to some Blacks (and other minorities) cannot be redressed by giving favor to other Blacks, any more than wrongs done by some whites may be punished by penalizing other whites. Rights are possessed by persons, not by skin color groups. Where a remedy is due, it is due to the person damaged, not the group to which that person belongs.[5]

Cohen asserted that racial preferences are based on "the confused conviction that one group has an entitlement, another a debt. . . . [It mistakenly assumes] that racial or sexual groups are the bearers of rights. It is the very blunder that led us, long ago, to the evils flowing from categorization by race, differential treatment by race. It was wrong then and it is wrong

now."[6] "To give favor to males or females, to whites or to blacks or to persons of any color, because of their sex or color, is morally wrong because doing so is intrinsically unfair. . . . The inevitable result is the award of advantages to some who deserve no advantage, and the imposition of burdens upon some who deserve no burden."[7]

Those questioning affirmative action policy argued that it "has come to mean the programs and devices used to insure certain results. . . . The phrase is now a widely accepted euphemism for institutionalized favoritism. . . . Affirmative action has thus been turned completely on its head. What was once the name for active pursuit of equal treatment regardless of race has become the name for instruments designed to give deliberate preference on the basis of race."[8]

Elected officials have "little to gain and much to lose by advocating laws that will effectively ban, and punish, racially preferential practices."[9] Opponents of affirmative action face the danger of being labeled as racist recalcitrants denying opportunities to minorities and women.

Leaders of minority communities also have little to gain by opposing affirmative action. Those who benefit by current preferential treatment under affirmative action programs have a stake in their continuation. Those with doubts face the criticism that they have "abandoned their brothers and sisters and become Uncle Toms."[10] Any hint that a minority leader benefited from affirmative action confronts them with the potential charge of hypocrisy and the comments that "they got theirs and now they want to deny benefits to those who came along afterwards." Supreme Court Justice Clarence Thomas received considerable criticism for disagreeing with affirmative action, even though his career was promoted by it. From a practical perspective, affirmative action has become a "minor industry" in the minority community, with many minority leaders and their constituents professionally engaged in the management of affirmative action programs.[11]

THE FACULTY FOR CHANGE

Pressure for change usually emanates from the outside. Members of institutions under challenge typically close ranks to protect the school, club, or company. "Ratting" on one's own institution is generally seen as both a sign of disloyalty and being dangerous to one's continued internal acceptance. After more than forty years at the University of Michigan, professor of philosophy Carl Cohen seemed unlikely to blow the whistle on the university's "dirty little secret" of intentional discrimination. No "Johnny-come-lately" to this issue, Cohen began waging his lonely campaign to raise the issue of race-based admissions with the university's administration in 1973. Cohen was clear to point out that "there is no institution in the world, save only my family and my country, that I love more than the

University of Michigan."[12] That loyalty was unable to overcome a core issue over which he and the university administration disagreed. Cohen confronted the issue with strong words, charging that the university professes "absolute equal treatment for all races, sexes and ethnic groups. . . . We cheat. We give racial preference knowingly while saying that we do not, but we hide the fact with murky references to 'diversity.' "[13] He firmly asserted that at the University of Michigan, "diversity remains the shield of legitimacy for outright favoritism, the talisman with which institutional preference by race has been justified without . . . apparent fear of constitutional attack."[14] He argues that "my interest is a personal one. I am interested in justice. I want to make the University better, a non-discriminatory place."[15] Cohen supports affirmative action to the degree that it implies better outreach programs to expand the pool of potential applicants and other programs that help prepare racial and ethnic minorities to compete for positions based on relevant academic qualifications, but he opposes establishing or maintaining procedures involving different standards for whites and minorities.[16]

AFFIRMING ACTION

University of Michigan officials saw the situation quite differently, justifying its decade-old "Michigan mandate" as a worthwhile drive to create ethnic-gender proportionalism and "multicultural community," assuring that the university would "look like America."[17] Lee Bollinger, president of the university, described challenges to its admissions process as a "test of character," asserting that

> for almost 200 years, public universities have unlocked the doors to social and economic opportunity to students from many different backgrounds, and we believe it is absolutely essential that they continue to do so. Our mission and core expertise is to create the best educational environment we can. We do this in part through diverse faculty and student body. . . . We use a variety of factors to determine a student's admissibility. . . . No one factor is determinative; our approach utilizes both objective and subjective factors, treating admission of students as both an art and a science.[18]

COURTSIDE GUIDANCE

The Supreme Court's struggle with affirmative action reflected the complexity of the issue. Since the Court first took up the issue, its decisions, with some significant exceptions, have supported the general goal of diversity while imposing sharp limits on preference based solely on race. In general, the Court has ruled that "preference by race is tolerable only where it can

be shown to serve a compelling governmental interest, and even then the preference must be shown to be necessary to achieve that end, and must be narrowly tailored to do so."[19]

Nationwide, the university community received a shock when the Supreme Court explicitly ruled in the *Regents of the University of California v. Bakke* (488 U.S. 265, 1978) that college admissions programs could not use racial quotas to deny access to nonminority students. In writing up his own rationale for the decision, Justice Powell, the swing vote on the nine-person court, refused to completely close the door on racial considerations, asserting the value of diversity in an intellectual environment such as a university. He asserted that race could be "one of a complex of factors involved in the decision to admit or reject." Justice Powell's caveat keeping the door open a crack became the accepted understanding of the Court's view, even though the remainder of the Court did not necessarily accept his position.

Along with many other institutions, Michigan argued that it used race as a "plus" factor in the admissions process but denied that it dominated or predetermined the outcome. Cohen saw admissions processes moving in the opposite direction, arguing that "having been advised that they might weigh race along with other factors to achieve diversity, universities found irresistible the pressure to use race in ways going very far beyond the limits that Powell had drawn."[20]

WHO BLEW IT?

Cohen's views generated considerable outside interest. Cohen possessed a record as a good community "citizen," having chaired key faculty committees. Politically, his affiliations as a past director of the county branch of the American Civil Liberties Union and as a member of the county Democratic party executive committee would typically tag him as a liberal and a supporter of affirmative action. Early in his teaching career, he taught a course on Marxism and found himself monitored by the "Red Squad" of the Michigan State Police charged with keeping track of suspected communists. Clearly an opponent of the status quo, Cohen championed individual acts of civil disobedience such as staging civil rights sit-ins and resisting the draft.[21] One of his early books, entitled *Civil Disobedience,* served as a philosophical justification for antigovernment actions.

Why would such an individual join forces with conservatives, write widely in opposition to affirmative action, and use university documents to embarrass his own administration? Two pieces of the puzzle help in developing an explanation. First, the tenure system protected Cohen from explicit retribution. Second, as a philosopher, Cohen was accustomed to pushing his arguments to their logical extension by starting with bedrock principles and

applying them to real situations. Cohen's commitment to philosophical consistency has been tested a number of times. Despite being Jewish, he supported the ACLU's position affirming the right of American Nazis to march through the predominantly Jewish suburb of Skokie, Illinois.[22] Everyone recognized that the Nazis chose the most offensive location possible to exercise their right of free speech, but that did not vitiate the necessity to protect free speech for all, no matter what their views or venue.

Cohen applauded the goal of providing equality of opportunity but questioned the use of "irrelevant and illegal" factors such as race as inappropriate shortcuts. For Cohen, the driving principle was the equal protection clause of the Fourteenth Amendment, which states that government cannot "deny to any person within its jurisdiction the equal protection of the laws." He viewed the commitment in the 1964 Civil Rights Act that "no person in the United States shall, on the grounds of race, color, or national origin, be excluded from participation in, be denied in the benefits of, or be subject to discrimination under any program or activity receiving federal financial assistance" as a worthy statement of societal goals and acceptable practice. He vividly remembers, as a young ACLU member in 1954, hearing Thurgood Marshall in his pre–Supreme Court days arguing in the *Brown v. Board of Education* case that "all governmentally imposed race distinctions are so odious that a state, bound to afford equal protection of the laws, must not impose them."[23] He admits that "I'm a professor. I use words and words have meaning."[24] He decided to stand up and challenge his institution and its interpretation of some important words.

Cohen's tool was another set of words, the Freedom of Information Act, which guarantees access to most government documents. After he filed numerous requests, the university released internal documents and data on the admissions process. What he found shocked his sensibilities.

THE SMOKING MATRIX

The first clue of preferential treatment lay in aggregate acceptance rates. At the University of Michigan and at most other colleges and universities, acceptance rates for blacks were "significantly higher than acceptance rates for whites."[25] On average, the percentage of blacks accepted was twice as large as the percentage of whites from the same pool of applicants. Such aggregate figures do not necessarily prove a quota system, since black applicants may well outrank others on a variety of other relevant criteria.

The trick in proving a de facto quota system lay in showing that even when other relevant criteria were held constant, blacks continued to be selected at significantly higher rates. Fortunately for Cohen, the University of Michigan had so many applicants that its admissions process needed to rely heavily on empirical data and decision-facilitating shortcuts. The "smoking gun" in the case of Michigan was a matrix. The matrix charted academic achievement (high school grade point average) against intellectual potential (Scholastic Aptitude Test scores) and created 108 cells for different combinations. For each cell, it was possible to indicate University of Michigan acceptance rates for whites and "unrepresented minorities." For example, in the cell for applicants with GPAs between 2.80 and 2.99 and SAT scores between 1200 and 1290, nonminorities were accepted at a 12 percent rate, compared with 100 percent for minorities. In virtually every cell, a significant differential appeared.[26]

The differing acceptance rates in the matrix resulted from a point system applied to applicants. A total of one hundred points on the 150-point scale generally led to admission. A perfect grade point average was worth eighty points, while having a parent who attended Michigan added up to four points. An excellent essay garnered one point. Perhaps the most difficult to explain bonus was reflected in the fact that a perfect SAT score was worth only twelve points, while being a member of an underrepresented minority added twenty points.[27]

WHO PAYS THE PRICE?

The proximate "winners" from affirmative action are those gaining jobs or places in educational institutions at least partially on the basis of their race or gender. In the long run, the beneficiaries are harder to determine. Although affirmative action programs profess to benefit only those who are "qualified," measuring capabilities is often difficult and the pressure to give minority candidates the benefit of the doubt can lead to the uncomfortable situation of admitting or hiring individuals incapable of performing at an adequate level. Little is gained when individuals are set up for failure by being given an opportunity they may not have the skills or capabilities to perform.

Even when those selected possess the requisite capabilities, the perception of special treatment can affect the individual chosen, his or her associates, and eventually the wider society. "By applying lower standards . . . all blacks [or other minorities], not just those given special favor, are injured when everyone (black and white) comes to believe that blacks just don't have it, can't make it on their own. An outstanding minority candidate for a demanding position is now commonly viewed not as the best person for the role, but, cruelly, as 'the best black.' "[28] The 5th Circuit Court of Appeals argued in *Hopwood v. Texas* that using race to promote diversity "exemplifies, encourages and legitimizes the mode of thought and behavior that underlies most prejudice and bigotry in modern America."[29]

Members of favored minorities and those from majority racial groups both recognize the skepticism emerging from affirmative action. A recent poll indicated that 19 percent of black women and 28 percent of black men believe their colleagues "privately questioned your abilities or qualifications because of affirmative action." Similarly, 32 percent of whites thought that "a racial minority where [they] worked got an undeserved job or promotion as a result of affirmative action programs."[30] Cohen argues that with aggressive affirmative action "majorities become resentful while minorities are demeaned. . . . Affirmative action in preferential form postpones the day when all persons, of whatever race, may be judged as persons, on the content of their character."[31]

For most members of targeted minority communities, the potential for personal gain among their friends and family outweigh the larger issue of possible failure, backlash, and societal attitudes. As Cohen sees it, "perhaps worst of all, racial preference does direct and serious harm to the very minorities it was designed to assist. . . . Preference by race is morally indefensible and socially wrong."[32] Minority voices such as Thomas Sowell (who pointed out the possible ancillary gains resulting when minority students rejected at elite institutions end up at lower-ranked colleges where they have a better potential for competing)[33] have trouble being heard. Studies by the Department of Education indicate that the arrival of affirmative action was accompanied by a decline in the percentage of blacks actually receiving college degrees once admitted, indicating a mismatch between the students' abilities and the institutions to which they were admitted.[34]

Proponents of affirmative action assert that the decline in black graduation rates is actually less in the more competitive schools and that blacks do not feel a stigma and that both blacks and whites appreciate the opportunities affirmative action gives for cross-race interaction. The assessment of the impact of affirmative action remains unclear.[35]

Preferences based on affirmative action are more than abstract principles. Individuals and groups seek affirmative action as the only feasible way to achieve scarce opportunities. It is a short step from affirmative action to "reverse discrimination" in which penalties are handed out in as unfair a manner as benefits had been distributed in the past. As liberal columnist Richard Cohen (no relation to Carl Cohen) painfully concluded after years of supporting affirmative action,

> The trouble with affirmative action [is that] sooner or later, we get down to names—the people who were not hired or who were fired on the basis of race. . . . Once, I suppose, the racial situation in this country was so dire that on balance the good that affirmative action did outweighed the bad. This was especially the case when those being helped were precisely the same people that once had been victimized. Now, though, we are usually one or two generations from the actual victims of racist bigotry, making it much harder—if not impossible— to justify what inevitably is victimizing someone on the basis of race.[36]

COURTING A SOLUTION

Carl Cohen could publicize what he saw as wrongdoing and perhaps embarrass the university into reversing its admissions policies, but he had few personal tools for forcing a change in procedures. When intransigent parties fail to agree on common ground, external regulatory institutions often provide direction. With the University of Michigan standing firm, the civil courts were the next option. United States courts do not make advisory decisions, and Carl Cohen could not claim significant personal injury granting him the legal standing to bring a suit. His publication of evidence of an apparent racial quota system caught the attention of four Republican state legislators who encouraged rejected white students to contact them. Politics does make for strange bedfellows. Lifelong Democrat Cohen found himself supported by conservative legislators.

The names garnered by the state legislators were sent to the Center for Individual Rights (CIR), which promised to organize a legal challenge to University of Michigan policies. The CIR cut its legal teeth in the 1996 case of Cheryl Hopwood, a white student denied admission to the University of Texas law school. The Fifth Circuit Court of Appeals challenged the interpretation of Justice Powell's decision that diversity was a compelling interest justifying racial preferences in college admissions. The U.S. Supreme Court allowed the lower court decision to stand by refusing to hear an appeal, indirectly implying its approval.

Previous cases such as *Bakke* and *Hopwood* had focused on graduate schools; the CIR felt it was now time to take on the issue of undergraduate admissions. From the over one hundred rejected students claiming harm, the CIR chose Jennifer Gratz and Patrick Hamacher. Gratz had graduated with a 3.8 grade point average and an ACT score of 25. Her application listed an impressive set of extracurricular activities.[37] Hamacher had a 3.4 grade point average and an ACT of 28, placing him in the top 6 percent of those taking the test. He played in three sports, sang in the choir, and volunteered in a hospice.[38] Based on their objective records and the university's matrix, both would have had a very high probability of admission if they were members of a targeted minority group. Both ended up on a waiting list, eventually receiving rejection letters.

Like many litigants in the past, Gratz and Hamacher became vehicles to provide legal standing to sue. Gratz graduated from the University of Michigan at Dearborn in math and works as a software trainer, not the forensic scientist job she thought a University of Michigan degree would lead to.[39] Hamacher graduated from Michigan State University in East Lansing and works as an accountant for the city of Flint, Michigan.[40]

The University of Michigan mounted a serious legal defense of its admissions procedures costing in the millions. Much of the cost was to be borne by the university's insurance, but Michigan taxpayers paid for the extensive public relations campaign the university carried out in coordination with the suit. The CIR underwrote the case for Gratz and Hamacher using private donations. The Hopwood case, in which the CIR was only one of the actors, involved 3,500 billable hours in legal fees valued at close to $1 million.[41] Serious legal challenges are clearly beyond the resources of most individuals.

To a large degree, Cohen, Gratz, and Hamacher became spectators in a competition that they helped initiate. It was played out by a new set of actors. Cohen's philosophical writings and inside data played a pivotal role in the CIR attempt to make the case that race served as the primary variable in a dual track admissions procedure that they view as contrary to the equal protection guarantees of the Fourteenth Amendment. Looking over their shoulders were future waves of college applicants and a myriad of college administrators eagerly awaiting the precedent the court would establish. Although the specific decision only applies directly to the three parties (Gratz, Hamacher, and the University of Michigan), its implications caused a ripple effect. Colleges and universities will look for clues as to whether to maintain their current practices related to affirmative action or scramble to bring them in line with court interpretation. All colleges fear emerging as the next institution brought under the judicial and media spotlight.

In the course of going through the legal process the University of Michigan became the focal point for determining the limits of affirmative action. The initial case involving undergraduate education (*Gratz v. Bollinger*) focused on the grade/SAT chart, which guaranteed minorities admission for the same scores that denied admission to nonminorities. A related law school case (*Grutter v. Bollinger*) charged that in pursuit of a "critical mass" of minority students the admissions process created a de facto quota system.

State and federal appeals courts reached conflicting rulings on the cases, setting the stage for a Supreme Court appeal. Both sides requested that if the Court decided to hear one case, it should hear both, given their closely related issues. As the cases proceeded, Theodore Shaw, the NAACP (National Association for the Advancement of Colored People) supplied lawyer representing minority students at the University of Michigan, argued that these cases "represent the most significant civil rights cases the Supreme Court will have decided in the last quarter century."[42]

AFFIRMATIVE AMBIGUITY[43]

The Supreme Court split on the Michigan cases, upholding by a 5–4 vote in the law school case the general policy of affirmative action to help achieve a "critical mass" of diversity, but rejecting by a vote of 6–3 the undergraduate admissions procedure of automatically granting points to minority students. The Court viewed the twenty points for being a minority as too mechanistic but allowed race to be a "plus factor" in admissions.[44] To a large degree the Court reflects the split in society, where opinion polls indicate public support for the concept of affirmative action in theory but a wariness of it in practice.[45]

The Court emphasized a subtle shift in its rationale behind supporting affirmative action. Previous rulings have emphasized the need for affirmative action to redress the effects of past discrimination. The rulings in the Michigan cases emphasized the importance of elite education as the route to "effective participation by the members of all racial and ethnic groups in the civic life of our Nation." The majority of the Court saw affirmative action as a short-term (perhaps twenty-five-year) "deviation from the norm of equal treatment" necessary to open top-level positions in society to individuals of all races.[46] Justice O'Connor also emphasized that a critical mass of minority students not only opened opportunities for them, but also facilitated crossracial understanding of nonminorities, helping to break down racial stereotypes.[47]

Proponents of affirmative action saw the thrust of the rulings as affirming affirmative action once and for all. University of Michigan President Mary Sue Coleman characterized it as a "green light to pursue diversity in the college classroom [and] a road map to get us there."[48] Opponents, on the other hand, saw the rulings as cautioning schools on the constraints under which the Court would approve affirmative action in practice. Carl Cohen was frustrated, arguing that "one of the unhappy aspects of this ruling is that the argument that has been raging since 1978 will continue for years to come."[49]

As colleges and universities began adjusting their admissions procedures to avoid another court challenge, opponents of affirmative action became ever more vigilant looking for possible transgressions. While Carl Cohen seeks to have the issue settled once and for all, the multi-round political game of action/challenge/ruling/adjustment that Cohen helped initiate goes on. In the process both the accepted rationales and behaviors have been more clearly defined.

LESSONS

- *Hard data trumps anecdotes and impressions.* In applying abstract principles, the courts attempt to frame specific definitions with associated empirical data.
- *Whistle-blowing makes more noise from the inside.* Critics from within institutions often carry more force and legitimacy than those from the outside.

- *Courts only deal with real situations affecting real people.* Unwilling to give purely advisory decisions, those attempting to prove a point must find an injured party and define the person or institution at fault.
- *Judicial action is a continuous game with numerous rounds.* Different courts serve as a check on each other as losers push unfavorable decisions through the review process. Courts tend to decide cases on the narrowest bases possible, opening the door to additional cases, situations, and questions outside the purview of previous decisions.
- *Contesting issues in court is expensive.* Those on whose behalf cases are filed often lack the personal resources to pursue a judicial decision. Large institutions and organizations often end up underwriting the cost of preparing and presenting cases to the courts.
- *Desirable policy goals often come into conflict in real-world applications.* Policy battles are seldom issues of good versus evil but rather involve tough decisions as to which competing good should prevail. Diversity and fairness are both desireable goals that may not be simultaneously reachable.

17

A Hard Guy to Live With

The dripping intravenous tube is a familiar sight in modern hospitals, where wonder drugs regularly prolong lives. Such tubes are also part of the scene in prisons, where they are used by the state to mete out capital punishment. In either case the antiseptic image of a sterile environment pervades. But there was something very different about this scene. The individual hooked up to the tube had not been convicted of any crime and she was not in a hospital. She was lying in the back of a rusted-out 1968 Volkswagen camper. She herself activated the intravenous tube to provide the lethal injection that ended her journey in this world. At her side stood Dr. Jack Kevorkian, the instigator of this scene, whose wild ride through the judicial system and the court of public opinion was just beginning.

ESTABLISHING A GRAVESIDE MANNER

Retired pathologist Jack Kevorkian had a long fascination with death. He looked into the eyes of terminal patients to try to pinpoint the moment of death and painted gruesome pictures with themes of death.[1] He earned his nickname, Dr. Death, as a twenty-eight-year-old medical resident in Detroit.[2]

The seeds of ethical euthanasia (mercy killing) were implanted early in Jack Kevorkian's mind. During his internship year, he met a middle-aged woman ravaged by cancer. Her immobile body was grotesque and it seemed to him that her sardonic smile expressed a pleading for death and help at the same time. "From that moment on, I was sure that doctor-assisted euthanasia and suicide are and always were ethical, no matter what anyone else says or thinks."[3]

Kevorkian's position on the margins of the medical profession stemmed from regular proposals to perform live human experiments on death row inmates facing capital punishment in order to learn more about human

Jack Kevorkian

death. "It would be a unique privilege in the most emphatic sense to be able to experiment on a doomed human being."[4] As a pathologist in the 1960s, he experimented with blood transfusions from corpses into living human beings without the typical clinical tests on animals to determine safety.[5] His preoccupation with death resulted in forced retirement, as hospitals refused to hire him.[6]

By the late 1980s Jack Kevorkian began focusing his efforts on "death with dignity" through physician-assisted suicide. Downplaying the idea of experimentation, he moved into a realm in which human compassion expanded the base of potential supporters and diminished the perceived stake of the government in protecting individuals from themselves.

KILLING TIME

Those who break the law or attempt to stretch its meaning are often portrayed as reckless. Not so for Jack Kevorkian. He looked for ways to get around the law or to avoid confronting it. In 1987, he traveled to the Netherlands, where doctor-assisted suicide was accepted. Mistakenly assuming it was formally legalized, he hoped to expand his proposal for death row experimentation on willing terminal patients. Dutch doctors showed little interest in his experimentation and assured him it would have negative legal repercussions in the Netherlands. Nevertheless, speaking to doctors having actual experience with aided suicide "spurred Kevorkian to action."[7]

So it was back home for his quest. His resolve strengthened in 1989 when a panel of doctors convened by the Society for the Right to Die submitted a report supporting the morality of physician-assisted suicide. Attempted or successful suicide was no longer a criminally punishable act in the United States. He concluded that making the means of death available did not turn a suicide into a homicide.[8] State laws and traditions were more murky on the culpability of those assisting a suicide. When a doctor was involved, the level of societal anxiety increased. While planning to carry out what many still saw as murder, he "sweated the small stuff" by making sure he could not be charged for minor crimes. He worried about using his apartment or that of his sister because of lease constraints. Kevorkian requires patients to sign releases and uses videotaped requests for help in committing suicide, which he shares with the media.

FIRST RITES

Where can a willing subject for planned death be found? Kevorkian's attempts to find one seem almost humorous in retrospect. Accepting the modern dictum, "it pays to advertise," he took out a series of ads in local Michigan papers offering "death counseling" and help to those desiring "death with dignity." He had business cards printed describing his new practice of "Bioethics and obitiatry, special death counseling, by appointment only."[9] Perhaps it was the outrageousness of the concept, or perhaps it was the public's inability to understand his self-coined word *obitiatry*, that led to no viable leads. There was little need to limit public demand by requiring appointments. No one showed up. Attempts to get oncologists to refer their patients received a cool response. Although the medical profession and potential patients seemed uninterested, the media, with its penchant for the unusual, picked up on this strange aberration. Local stories gave way to national attention on talk shows and publications such as *Newsweek.*[10] With a wider audience, the calls began to come. Initial responses involved unacceptable clients without terminal illnesses or mental competency, but Kevorkian knew that a suitable patient would emerge.

With abstract theory meeting eventual reality, Kevorkian realized he needed a simple mechanism that a patient could activate to provide painless and sure death. Lacking a sophisticated developmental lab or supply closet, he turned to one of his favorite venues, the flea market. He built his "mercitron" from scrap aluminum, a clock motor, and a solenoid. The mechanism would allow a patient to trigger a lethal injection.

Kevorkian's first attempt at physician-assisted suicide was not the image of modern medicine at its best. Bending his previous criteria, the patient was neither immediately terminal nor wracked with pain. When experimental drug treatment to stem the early effects of Alzheimer's disease failed, Jane Adkins contacted Kevorkian in 1990 complaining about the deteriorating quality of her life. It was a tricky medical and legal call, since the closer she came to natural death, the less she was responsible for her own actions. After a one-time dinner conversation, he agreed to help her die. In order to avoid the legal ramifications, Kevorkian set up his "suicide machine" in his 1968 Volkswagen camper parked in a public campground. The case aroused immediate public attention and led to further requests for help.

The Michigan State Board of Medicine suspended Kevorkian's medical license by an 8 to 0 vote in 1991 after he had assisted in his first three suicides.[11] In later court cases that action resulted in charges of "improperly representing himself as a physician," which were added to those directly involving assisting with a suicide.[12]

COURTING A SOLUTION

Kevorkian and his supporters view patient autonomy as a basic human right. It was natural for them to rely on the courts, which in recent years have become inextricably involved in drawing the boundaries of human rights. The U.S. court system neither seeks business to transact nor provides advisory judgments. An individual or organization harmed by some action must explicitly challenge the offending behavior. In the case of physician-assisted suicide, the person subject to the greatest potential harm, the suicide victim, is not around to make the legal challenge. Friends and family often either agree with the decision of the deceased or refuse to second-guess it afterward. The lack of a legal challenge presumes the lack of any harm. By inaction, the courts imply approval of the status quo.

Kevorkian escaped a murder conviction initially when the local court ruled prosecution unconstitutional, since at the time Michigan had no law against assisted suicide. Kevorkian went on to assist in a number of suicides. Stimulated by Kevorkian's actions, the Michigan legislature proceeded to pass legislation specifically outlawing assisted suicide in 1992, only to have the law struck down by the courts on largely technical grounds. Kevorkian was not home free, however. In 1994, the Michigan state supreme court ruled that assisted suicide had always been a "common law crime," based on custom rather than legislation. With the door open for prosecution, he faced a series of jury trials. Juries acquitted Kevorkian in three cases, accepting his argument that his motivation was to relieve suffering and that the patients themselves made the decision to end their lives. The Kevorkian cases helped assert "that individual rights outweigh the state's interest" and helped establish "the critical first step toward complete expansion of patient autonomy."[13]

Court actions affect the individuals involved, serve as precedents for future cases, encourage or discourage additional legal action, and affect other aspects of the political process. On the individual level, Kevorkian's acquittals spared him from prosecution, popularized his cause, and emboldened his activity. Knowing that successful prosecution was unlikely, Kevorkian expanded the pace of his involvement in assisted suicides.

A SUPREME EFFORT

When the Michigan Supreme Court ruled that the Constitution does not protect assisted suicide, Kevorkian challenged their ruling through an appeal to the U.S. Supreme Court. The Supreme Court controls its own schedule by determining which cases it will hear. In 1995 it simply sidestepped the issue by refusing to hear the appeal. In 1996, however, the issue came up again after appeals courts in San Francisco and New York affirmed the right to physician-assisted suicide in cases not directly involving Kevorkian. "What began as a personal crusade by Jack Kevorkian [was] now on the national political agenda."[14] In 1997, the Supreme Court ruled that whereas physician-assisted suicide was not a constitutionally guaranteed right, state laws allowing or forbidding such acts were constitutional. After the politically embarrassing sequence of legal moves and court rebuffs, the state of Michigan took its cue from the Supreme Court and again passed a specific ban on assisted suicide.[15] The issue was clearly not dead yet. Other states will have to consider where they stand. Even in Michigan, Jack Kevorkian vowed to keep his challenge going.

SOCIAL MALADIES AND POLITICAL WOUNDS

Opponents fear that court rulings supporting assisted suicide diminish society's respect for human life and harden the public to the rights of the mentally and physically disabled. By raising the threshold of tolerable quality of life, activists representing the disabled fear reinforcement of "society's acceptance of health care rationing and the denial of adequate funding for assistive technology and personal assistance services."[16]

   The broader political consequences of Kevorkian's legal battles emerged in a number of realms. With physician-assisted suicide firmly on the public agenda, activists in a number of states attempted to thwart further court challenges by enthroning explicit rights or new limitations into law. California voters twice (1988 and 1992) confronted pro-euthanasia initiatives and defeated them. A 1991 Washington State initiative lost by a 54 percent to 46 percent margin. Although Kevorkian's actions helped raise consciousness to get the Washington initiative on the ballot, some argue that his continued highly-publicized application of assisted suicide to nonterminal patients may have provided the Washington opponents enough ammunition to defeat the measure.[17] In Michigan, Kevorkian and his supporters failed to secure enough signatures to qualify their initiative to legalize physician-assisted suicide on the 1994 ballot. In 1998, the Michigan legislature passed legislation banning assisted suicide.[18] Later that year, Michigan voters soundly rejected a physician-assisted suicide referendum along with nipping the gubernatorial aspirations of Kevorkian's lawyer-publicist, who had acquired the Democratic nomination based primarily on the notoriety he had received on the issue.

In 1994, by 51 percent of the vote, Oregon became the first state in modern history to pass a law legalizing physician-assisted suicide for terminally ill patients through lethal prescriptions. The initial passage of Measure 16 was reconfirmed in a second referendum in 1997. The first legal physician-assisted suicide in the United States occurred in March 1998.[19] Staying in the lead on the issue, Oregon also became the first state to cover physician-assisted suicide under Medicaid, the government-paid insurance program.[20] Despite its legality, the demand for assisted suicide in Oregon produced only mild interest. Initial evaluation indicates that empowering terminal patients provides them with more options, lessening some of the trauma of facing certain death.[21]

Public opinion supports euthanasia as an option for the terminally ill, with more limited support at the polls.[22] Two different explanations for this lack of consistency between public opinion and voter actions are possible. Proponents credit election turnout variations between supporters and opponents, arguing that they have a hard time getting their supporters to the polls. Opponents argue that assertions about "death with dignity" sound good in the abstract but lose their glow in the harsh reality of expanded information and actual application.

Attempts to outlaw assisted suicide claimed other political victims. After losing two expensive cases against Kevorkian, Oakland County, Michigan, prosecutor Richard Thompson was soundly defeated in the Republican primary by an opponent who promised not to waste the taxpayer's money "unless the legislature gives me an enforceable law."[23] As the first incumbent to lose the seat in twenty-four years, Thompson blamed the loss on his tough stance against Kevorkian.[24] The signal to other elected prosecutors was clear: Don't enter legal battles you cannot win.

OPERATING IN PUBLIC

Jack Kevorkian engenders strong personal reactions. Blunt, acerbic, and sharp featured, he is far from a public relations director's dream. Proponents of physician-assisted suicide constantly fear Kevorkian becoming the issue. A low-key family doctor type with a deep voice and reassuring manner would serve better as a spokesperson. But causes can seldom choose their spokespersons, and a volatile issue such as assisted suicide is unlikely to be publicly pursued by the ideal advocate chosen by central casting.

Dr. Jack Kevorkian arrived on the scene with a lot of baggage. His record as a pathologist was checkered at best. His bedside manner reflected his acerbic personality, not the reassuring persona most doctors attempt to exude. His previous forays into public policy debates were even more on the fringes than physician-assisted suicide. In a 1992 medical journal, he proposed a pilot program of death clinics to actively facilitate assisted suicide.[25] His professional judgment, medical methods, and personal motivations regularly came under attack.

Kevorkian's willingness to allow nonterminal patients to decide their fate without availing them of all medical remedies stretches the boundary of public acceptance and professional norms of helping fully rational patients in extreme pain to end a hopeless situation. With over a hundred assisted suicides to date, opponents have a range of individual stories questioning whether the specific patient was rational, well-advised on alternatives, and really the one who made the decision. His continued insistence that physician-assisted suicide is only a first step in his goal of human experimentation unnerves many potential supporters. Even pro-euthanasia organizations such as the Hemlock Society keep their distance from Kevorkian.

Assessing Kevorkian's personal motivation remains difficult. If his goal is monetary, he has largely failed. He refuses to charge patients and lives on his Social Security check and a small hospital pension in a house donated by his lawyer.[26] He shows significant ambivalence about publicity, often assiduously avoiding the media. His publicized antics, such as a hunger strike and dressing up in a colonial-style costume at one of his trials to mock the "out of touch legal system,"[27] seem more like feeble attempts to tweak the system than a sophisticated media strategy. In many ways, Kevorkian remains a "political innocent who had never even registered to vote."[28] He views the political system and its institutions with disdain, harboring only slight respect for the jury system that has kept him out of jail.

Despite the questionable morality of his public quest, Kevorkian has brought the issue out in the public for debate. As one physician put it, "Kevorkian has played a positive role in raising the issue and making sure the issue is not going to go away. There is plenty of evidence that some doctors have long 'played God' with terminal patients with little oversight or guidelines. There's no way we can play hide-and-seek any more with physician-assisted suicide thanks to Doctor Death."[29] The counterargument, that some issues should not be discussed, assumes that the behavior those arguments imply represents abstract concepts with no real-world examples. That simply is not the case. Jack Kevorkian was not the first (and will not be the last) doctor to assist in a suicide. Six percent of doctors admit to secretly hastening patient death with lethal injections or prescriptions, and one-third of doctors would do so if the law were changed.[30] The advantage of public debate lies in the sanitizing effect of competing opinions and information. Operating in secret, people can inflict great harm with little or no chance of correction. When they go public, the contours of acceptable behavior become established.

GETTING A SECOND OPINION

Kevorkian serves as a visible target and a sometimes reluctant rallying point on the issue of assisted suicide. He has stimulated a spate of opposing opinions and data points that have helped to invigorate the debate by challenging assumptions, refining definitions, providing alternative interpretations of information, and seeking legitimized government response.

To some, Jack Kevorkian is a lonely Don Quixote tilting against the "windmills" of government and the medical establishment. In reality his efforts have drawn public support from a relatively broad range of supporters. Organizations such as the Hemlock Society and Compassion in Dying support his quest without fully endorsing his tactics. In her nationally syndicated column, Ann Landers expressed support for assisted suicide when life becomes "worthless, useless, unbearable, or excruciatingly painful." This stance caused some editors great discomfort and some papers refused to run the columns.[31] Kevorkian's legitimacy soared when an editorial in the *British Medical Journal* asserted that "Jack Kevorkian is a hero. No one has demonstrated any discernible motive from him except that he believes his work is right. . . . To be a hero does not mean being right. . . . but it does mean being honest with yourself and acting on your own morality. . . . We need the hero to make us uncomfortable. . . . Patients who suffer need their pain to be heard and felt. Those who are dying need our commitment to stay with them through their journey."[32]

In the best tradition of open democratic debate, Kevorkian's extreme position spawned the creation or activation of a number of countervailing groups. Diane Coleman helped form Not Dead Yet, calling euthanasia "the ultimate form of discrimination." Coleman argues, "We can't trust the courts, we can't trust the medical profession. It's time to act before it is too late."[33] Not Dead Yet pushes its agenda through testimony, its web page, and demonstrations. Using Kevorkian as a lightning rod, their first demonstration was in front of his house.

Established medical organizations such as the American Medical Association also weighed in, which maintained its strong stand against physician-assisted suicide at its 1996 national convention.[34] Kevorkian criticizes the AMA and his other opponents in medicine, saying that the "medical profession's single-minded obsession with the longevity of life has blinded it to other special needs of society and spawned the inevitable ethical dilemmas now upon us."[35] Although Kevorkian blames the AMA for the ethical debate, he created the public debate. When dealing with issues such as physician-assisted suicide, which have no universally accepted and demonstrably correct answer, democratic societies establish active debates.

DECIDING WHERE TO OPERATE

The outcome of political battles often depends on the framing of the issue. Kevorkian and his lawyer-publicist Geoffrey Feiger consistently attempt to frame the issue in terms of individual civil rights of patients. They emphasize language, such as the right to "die with dignity." The Hemlock Society calls assisted suicide the "ultimate civil liberty."[36] By taking a human rights position, supporters legitimize court action to protect those rights. Proponents argue that the "right" to physician-assisted suicide says nothing about its desirability in specific cases. It only broadens the legitimate options available to patients.

Opponents emphasize the potential incapacity of patients to make such judgments and the extensive power that the approval of doctor-assisted suicide gives to the medical profession. They also point out the broader dangers of supporting radical individualism that "elevates personal autonomy above all other cultural values" and can lead to "social anarchy that asphyxiates true freedom."[37] In their view, society has the responsibility to care enough to protect individuals from themselves during times of trial and despair. They worry that the legal right to assisted suicide too easily morphs into the "duty" of a patient—or the patient's doctor—to relieve society of his or her burden.

POLLED TO DEATH

Democracies pay considerable attention to public opinion. Kevorkian pushes the envelope, forcing a redefinition of acceptable grounds for euthanasia. The "court" of public opinion is relatively one-sided in support of doctor-assisted suicide for terminal patients. The national Opinion Research Center general social survey annually asks, "When a person has a disease that cannot be cured, do you think doctors should be allowed, by law, to end the patient's life by some painless means if the patient and his family requests it?" In 1977, 60 percent of their national sample agreed, with the percentage increasing to 72 percent in 1991 before declining back into the 60 percent range by the late 1990s. Although most Americans support the right to assisted suicide, the public debate has tempered approval. "As theory becomes reality, the percentage of those approving the procedure has fallen."[38]

Kevorkian goes beyond assisting terminal patients to include those who are in constant pain, are physically disabled, or suffer from mental degeneration. Shortly after he assisted a patient in the early stages of Alzheimer's disease, a *New York Times* survey asked, "If a person has a disease that ultimately destroys that person's mind or body and the person wants to take his own life, should a doctor be allowed to assist in this?" Fifty-three percent of the respondents replied "yes."[39] Kevorkian's threshold for intolerable quality of life is quite low, establishing a bottom line of acceptable tolerance for assisted suicide against which American society must measure its own preferences.

THE UNFINISHED OPERATION

Without endorsing or challenging Kevorkian's medical actions, we must give him credit for forcing the issue onto the policy agenda by openly challenging societal values and public policies. Prior to his initial assisted suicide, he expressed the modest goal of "help[ing] clarify the law"[40] on assisted suicide. Later, he stated his goal in typically immodest fashion as implementing "a rational policy of planned death for the entire civilized world."[41] Most other doctors assisting with suicide do so in private, to protect the patient, and leave no trail of legal responsibility. Kevorkian's "in your face" approach forces a democratic society to define what is acceptable and what is not. "Every movement needs a pioneer like Dr. Kevorkian to focus public attention and expose the pros and cons of the issue. . . . If it had not been for Dr. Kevorkian and his strong convictions . . . physician assisted death might still be on the periphery."[42]

The final outcome of America's public debate over physician-assisted suicide has not been realized. Inspired by Kevorkian's blatant involvement in over 130 assisted suicides, Michigan passed a law making assisted suicide a crime. Shortly thereafter Kevorkian taunted the authorities by videotaping himself injecting a lethal dose of barbiturates into a terminal patient with Lou Gehrig's disease and then providing the tape to CBS's *60 Minutes* for broadcast. Kevorkian was charged with murder and insisted on defending himself in court. During the trial Kevorkian clearly attempted to secure a ruling that physician-assisted suicide was not a crime by asking the jurors to look at him, saying, "Honestly now, do you see a criminal? Do you see a murderer? . . . If you do, then you must convict."[43] The jury took him up on the challenge, convicting him of second degree murder for which he received a 10-to-25-year term. Faced with life, and possible death, in prison the ailing Kevorkian appealed to the state courts, which rejected his claim that he had been improperly represented. The U.S. Supreme Court, which had earlier ruled there was no constitutional right to assisted suicide, refused to review his case. Taking another approach

Kevorkian attempted to get out of jail on bond based on his poor health. He killed his own chances by saying, when asked if he might assist in more suicides if released, "I'll always help a suffering patient, and if that keeps me in jail for life, then let it happen."[44]

In 1997, Oregon voters approved the Death with Dignity Act, making it the first state to legalize physician-assisted suicide. With the approval of two doctors, mentally competent terminally ill patients with less than six months to live can secure lethal medication. An average of twenty-five patients a year have taken advantage of the law to end their lives.[45] U.S. Attorney General John Ashcroft has taken an active role in challenging the Oregon law but has so far been unsuccessful in the courts.

Public opinion is divided on the issue. When asked if physician-assisted suicide is "morally wrong," 49 percent respond "yes." On the other hand, when asked, "When a person has a disease that cannot be cured, do you think doctors should be allowed to end the patient's life by some painless means if the patient and his family request it?" 72 percent of the public say "yes."[46]

The issue of physician-assisted suicide is unlikely to die. While Jack Kevorkian is a moral crusader to some and an outrageous outlaw to others, he deserves credit for stimulating a public debate on an important issue. Democracies should never be afraid of ideas and should take pride in the fact that tough issues can be debated and decided upon in the public forum.

LESSONS

- *Judicial procedures and politics are closely intertwined.* Political forces help set the agenda of the courts as competing interest groups attempt to use cases to legitimize their point of view. Strong assertions by one group in society often spawn the emergence of countervailing interests. Although not required to follow public opinion, court officials (prosecutors, judges, etc.) realize they must take it into account. When the law and public opinion are at odds, strict enforcement of the letter of the law falters.
- *The judicial system is selective.* Not all criminals are apprehended or prosecuted. It is possible to literally "get away with murder" if the law lacks clarity or public support. Elected prosecutors choose their cases carefully, since too many losses imply incompetence and inefficiency punishable at the polls. The Supreme Court's right to control its own agenda leads to certain issues never receiving its final adjudication.
- *Abstract rights and principles often conflict with acceptable applications.* It is one thing to agree in the abstract that individuals have a right to die with dignity; it is another to see people (especially friends and family) exercise that right. Most of us have complete confidence in our ability to use available rights in a responsible manner. We are often less comfort-

able in granting those rights to others. Public opinion captures the same ambivalence policy makers face in dealing with issues such as assisted suicide.

- *The personality and actions of advocates can overwhelm issues.* Jack Kevorkian became a magnet for media attention given his willingness to push the boundaries. In the process he turned off some potential supporters who saw his actions as an undignified way of promoting death with dignity.
- *The court system seldom decides issues once and for all.* In what seems like a giant chess game involving action and reaction, a succession of court decisions tends to constrain areas of ambiguity and invite additional legislative action. The definition of public policy takes a series of incremental steps, often involving one step backward for every two steps forward.

The Bureaucracy

18

If You Can't Lick 'Em, Enjoin 'Em

COMING TO AID

Little did Jean Anne Hlavacek know that a stop in New York City to see an old girlfriend as a respite from a long trip would change her life. Jean Anne's friend and her husband lived with his parents, and Jean Anne felt hesitant about intruding. Much to her surprise, she "walked into a giant welcome mat." As an early riser, Jean Anne began a routine of sunrise conversations over a cup of coffee with her friend's father-in-law. At some point the conversation turned to health, and he confided in Jean Anne, telling her of his AIDS. As a critical care nurse, Jean Anne confronted illness and death every day, but AIDS remained largely an abstraction. Before now she had never known anyone suffering with AIDS. Suddenly the disease had a personal face, and it disturbed her.

Months later, in August 1987, Jean Anne Hlavacek opened her *Newsweek* magazine to read its cover story, "The Faces of AIDS." Among the pictures of victims, the image of her friend's father-in-law jumped out at her. A flood of memories of "a wonderful caring, urbane, and talented scientist" washed over her like a wave. She did not want him forgotten, nor others stricken. Jean Anne Hlavacek immediately committed herself to doing something. Raising money was a possibility, but raising consciousness seemed more productive and far-reaching. Jean Anne began with only a commitment to act.

PUTTING HER STAMP ON PUBLIC CONSCIOUSNESS

The chosen vehicle seems obvious in retrospect. It flooded into her apartment day after day on a myriad of envelopes and packages. The lowly postage stamp could serve as a miniature billboard blanketing the country and appearing in millions of homes and offices daily.

Jean Anne Hlavacek

Not knowing how to begin the process, Jean Anne wrote to her congressman. Surely the institution that can outlaw cigarette advertising and raise taxes could order the U.S. Postal Service to issue a stamp. Not satisfied with half measures, she proceeded to write all 535 members of the House and Senate. The crucial response emanated not from her own Madison representative nor from one of her Wisconsin senators. A distant senator politely informed Jean Anne of the misdirection of her letters. Senator Lloyd Bentsen of Texas explained that stamp issues fell under the control of the Citizen's Stamp Advisory Committee (CSAC), not the Congress. Annually, this group of private citizens reviews 30,000 to 40,000 suggestions, recommending about thirty new issues to the U.S. Postal Service.

With undiminished fervor and a more appropriate target, Jean Anne redirected her proposal to the CSAC. Her initial letter to the committee's administrative offices generated a "very bureaucratic response indicating the criteria for new stamps, the procedure for approval and a listing of CSAC members." With the names in hand, she began searching for personal addresses of the committee's members at the homes, businesses, and/or university departments.

Not wanting to miss any bets, nurse Jean Anne Hlavacek became multifaceted social activist Jean Anne Hlavacek, approaching the CSAC on many levels. A daughter of the populist soil of Wisconsin, she knew the advantage of harnessing the power of the "little guys." She began setting up a table at the Madison farmers' market each week, getting signatures on a petition and passing out information on how to contact the CSAC.

Using her own proposed stamp design (the international "stop" symbol—
a red circle with a line through it—over the word AIDS surrounded by the
words "prevention," "research," "education," and "compassion") as a
backdrop, she presented a visual image of the awareness message she
hoped to spread. The experience of facing her neighbors with her crusade
revealed a great deal about public attitudes and ignorance. Many people
passed by quickly, whispering "she must have AIDS or something." She
remembers "feeling a little bit like a leper," with some individuals fearing
their signature would endorse an "irresponsible lifestyle" or make them
more likely to get the disease. Increasingly, though, people stopped and
letters and petitions began to flow. Jean Anne set up her rickety card table
when the AIDS quilt came to Madison, but the emotion of all the lives lost
was too much for Jean Anne and she packed up her one-person lobbying
effort in tears.

Persistence paid off in terms of spreading the word. Local media began
writing stories about her efforts. In each printed story and oral interview
Jean Anne made sure the mailing address of the CSAC appeared.

Not all strategies panned out. Turning her efforts to the various health
and lifestyle organizations concerned with AIDS led to disappointment.
Most failed to respond. Those who did respond revealed a greater interest
in getting her support for their efforts than vice versa. No bandwagon fueled by well-endowed organized groups emerged. It became clear that
Jean Anne was on her own.

Jean Anne's populist respect for the average citizen coexisted with mid-
western modesty, recognizing that many political decision are controlled
by the "big guys." She began a successful initiative to "get people with
some clout to contact the CSAC." She believes that letters from individuals like former surgeon general C. Everett Koop, dozens of governors, Vice
President Bush, and scores of congressmen and senators kept the issue
alive. Her favorite response probably had little to do directly with the
progress of the proposal, but it certainly lifted her spirits and reinforced
her resolve. In her favorite movie, *It's a Wonderful Life,* Jimmy Stewart
shows that success goes to those who improve the lives of others. In response to Jean Anne's letter, Jimmy Stewart wrote, "I think it's great work
you are doing and I wish you every good wish and I hope you have a wonderful life. God Bless you."

With growing support and renewed enthusiasm, Jean Anne trudged forward. In the pre-personal computer age, generating letters was not easy. At
one point, her old electric typewriter broke down and she traded the use of
her paint sprayer for the use of a neighbor's manual typewriter. A few
friends helped address envelopes, but she sometimes resorted to photocopying letters and adding personal addresses. Despite everything, the
CSAC seemed unmoved.

LITTLE AID FROM THOSE WHO MUST GIVE
THE STAMP OF APPROVAL

The CSAC deliberates in secret. The idea of government in "sunshine" that has pervaded many executive branch decision-making bodies has not crept into the stamp design process. Jean Anne found it difficult to learn when and where meetings would be held or what would show up on the agenda. Despite the secrecy, word filtered out that the issue of an AIDS stamp had been brought up and rejected at least eight times. Jean Anne had a few advocates within the CSAC who surreptitiously kept her abreast of the process. The hesitancy of the CSAC stemmed more from economic than ideological concerns.

No one has linked licking a stamp—even an AIDS stamp—to getting the disease. Yet the U.S. Postal Service expressed great hesitancy to adopt disease-related stamps out of fear that association with disease would dampen the public's interest in using them. The CSAC was well aware of the Postal Service's hesitancy and of the financial disaster connected with the 1981 alcoholism stamp, which languished on the shelf for months only to be destroyed by the truckload. Few people showed any willingness to confront their friends with the message, "Alcoholism/You can beat it!" Postmaster General Anthony Frank weighed in on the AIDS stamp, saying, "It just wouldn't work. . . . People may be reluctant to purchase and use it."[1]

Proponents of dreaded disease stamps face a dilemma. They promote such stamps as a symbolic way to increase public awareness of the target disease. The public, however, may well cringe at sending an unwanted or unintended message on their mail. Who wants to spoil the joy of a birthday card with a subliminal message about the medical dangers lurking ahead? Does the use of an AIDS stamp imply sympathy for a redirection of government funding or condone a particular lifestyle? Should the public be forced to use its letters as a billboard for depressing issues? Who cares?

Interestingly, a lot of people must care. Adopting a new stamp design involves groups and individuals wishing to have their favorite person, symbol, or cause immortalized on a stamp; the Citizen Stamp Advisory Commission, charged with screening new stamp ideas; and the U.S. Postal Service, which must evaluate the costs and benefits of a new issue. At times these regular players find themselves joined by other political actors in the White House or on Capitol Hill who see political advantage in joining the fray. In the case of the AIDS stamp, all these players were involved. Most of them were stimulated to take action by the 10,000 letters sent out by one Jean Ann Hlavacek.

Determining what broke the AIDS stamp logjam is unclear. Certainly public attitudes and awareness changed dramatically between 1987 and 1992 with the death of Ryan White, Arthur Ashe, Rock Hudson, and a variety of other well-known individuals. The mounting death toll indicated that AIDS was no longer limited to particular segments of the population. Over time, urging compassion for AIDS sufferers and launching government efforts had become politically correct and politically beneficial. And Jean Anne Hlavacek continued to keep the issue before the CSAC. On December 18, 1992, CSAC member Mary Ann Owens, a longtime supporter, brought up the issue of an AIDS stamp one more time. The CSAC gave tentative approval, based on the ability to create a design that was "altogether positive in nature."[2]

Jean Anne Hlavacek received word unofficially after the meeting and declared it "a wonderful Christmas present." The CSAC acted just in time without being superseded. With the change of administrations, it became clear that the newly appointed postmaster general, Marvin T. Runyon, was going to issue an AIDS stamp with or without CSAC approval.

UNDESIGNING WOMAN

With a decision to issue the stamp having been reached, the effort turned to the design. Jean Anne Hlavacek's design carried a comprehensive message, "prevention-research-education-compassion." The commission opted for a more symbolic and less controversial red ribbon and the words "AIDS awareness." During the 1970s yellow ribbons came to symbolize U.S. hostages in Iran. The image pervaded the public consciousness in Tony Orlando's 1973 hit song "Tie a Yellow Ribbon Round the Old Oak Tree," originally about a prisoner returning from jail to his ever faithful girlfriend. Since that time ribbons of different colors had come to represent a variety of concerns.

"Recognizing the controversial nature of an AIDS stamp among both the population and postal workers, the U.S. Postal Service issued a long memo to all postmasters explaining the rationale behind the stamp and offered suggested responses to critics."[3] The AIDS stamp was launched on December 1, 1993, with a print run of 350 million. Considerable effort was made to issue the stamp simultaneously at all U.S. Post Offices on the first day of issue—a rare strategy.

There are many ways to mark time and effort. Jean Anne Hlavacek's idea for an AIDS stamp took six calendar years to reach fruition. In 1987 no country in the world issued AIDS stamps, and the United States was one of the first to begin the process. By the time the idea had completed its bureaucratic course in the United States, over forty other countries had beaten the U.S. Postal Service to the punch by issuing their own AIDS stamps. When Jean Anne began her campaign, first-class postage stood at twenty-two cents. When issued, the AIDS stamp carried the then current twenty-nine-cent postal rate. She could count her time and effort in terms of the 10,000 letters she wrote, the $7,000 of her own money she expended (over $3,000 of it in postage alone), or the weeks of vacation time she donated to the effort. Was it worth it? For Jean Anne, the answer is an unqualified "yes." Would she do it again? This time the answer is a bit less forceful. On the one hand, she points out that "it took much longer than I ever considered at the outset. I will never do that much volunteer work again. . . . It is sometimes a good thing we don't know everything. If I had known how much time and effort this would take, I would never have attempted it." She remembers thinking at the beginning, "This isn't a very big task. I can knock this puppy out by Christmas." Despite the frustration, she found that "many fellow Americans feel their voices go unheard. I feel it is essential to take the risk that someone just might listen. You can make a difference if you believe in what you are doing and work hard."[4]

LICKING ANOTHER DISEASE

About the time Jean Anne Hlavacek celebrated political victory, a more somber personal revelation emerged thousands of miles away. Again the reality of disease and death would generate the pressure for new public policy. Careful of her health, Diane Sackett Nannery of Long Island, New York, regularly sought medical advice. When Diane faced a diagnosis of breast cancer, the shock, fear, and self-pity were palpable. But she quickly decided to bypass victimhood and treat her condition as a challenge.

Diane initially focused her efforts inward in an attempt to save her own life. She attacked the library with a vengeance, reading every current medical report she could find. Her approach was like the wise consumer who reads every article in *Consumer Reports* before buying a car rather than rely on the car salesman. Within a few months, she could have held her own on a panel of experts on the disease and modes of treatment. She was able to discuss her condition with her doctor more as a colleague than as a helpless patient. She recognized that "knowledge gave me control over an otherwise uncontrollable situation."

Above and beyond professional medical literature, Diane read every personal story she could. She found solace in their common feelings and coping mechanisms but also recognized that many of their stories did not have a happy ending. With her successful surgery behind her, she began to look outward, seeking a way to pay tribute to the women and men who did not survive breast cancer. She sought a visible symbol that would remind others of the tragedy of the disease and would validate its epidemic proportions.

Because she was a longtime postal worker, the idea of a stamp naturally came to mind. She knew a little about the process of choosing new stamp designs. Her position, however, would not provide an inside track; her suggestion would compete with that of every other citizen promoting a stamp idea.

Undaunted, Diane began a one-person national campaign. Again turn-

Diane Sackett Nannery

ing to the library for empowering information, she looked up the name and address of a daily and weekly newspaper in every state and began writing letters to the editor. Her simple letter introduced her as a breast cancer survivor, suggested the breast cancer stamp, and asked readers to send supporting letters to the CSAC. She lurked around grocery store checkout counters copying down the names and addresses of editors of every magazine she could find. Initially focusing on women's magazines, she eventually became less selective: "I even wrote to gun magazines, assuming that some women cleaning up the coffee table might just see my letter there." She asked every breast cancer group she knew to send petitions to the CSAC. "Hundreds of thousands of individual letters and petitions emerged." The media loved her one-woman campaign, leading to appearances on national television promoting her idea, which in turn generated new waves of support.

Initially Diane stayed away from politicians because she did not want the breast cancer stamp to become a partisan issue. Perhaps showing East Coast brassiness, she avoided the "big guys" and relied on average citizens rather than focus on known players, as did Jean Anne Hlavacek. As public support began to grow, the politicians came to her, asking what they could do. Long Island congressman Pete King (R-N.Y.) agreed to send a petition. She remembers that when his aide called a few days later, saying they had twenty names. "I was not very impressed, until she told me these were members of Congress." Eventually Congressman King's congressional petition included 102 names. After hearing Diane speak, Senator Alphonse D'Amato (R-N.Y.) included comments of support in the *Congressional Record* and personally took a petition door-to-door among his colleagues, getting all one hundred to sign in a single day.

As momentum increased, concern turned to the design of the stamp. A pink ribbon already carried the status of a national breast cancer symbol. As Diane went around speaking about breast cancer and the stamp initiative at schools and community groups, she thought, "Why not turn the design into a class project?" She was amazed at the cool reception from teachers and school administrators, who expressed a disturbing level of cynicism. She tried to preach the idea that "everything good in public life has happened because someone had a good idea" (which comes out "idear" in her Long Island accent), with few takers among those who are molding the next generation of citizens.

Although she was frustrated with the cynicism she saw and heard from educators, her experience with the stamp project was disproving the assertions of cynics that little could be done. She had written her first letter to the editor in February 1994. A year and a half later, in July 1995, the stamp was approved and eleven months later, on June 15, 1996, the stamp became a reality with an initial printing of 100 million. With no great influx of money, no national organization, and no paid staff, Diane Sackett Nannery beat the odds, both in terms of her personal battle with breast cancer and her initiative to strike a blow for breast cancer awareness through a U.S. stamp.

The story might have ended there as a good example of success in citizen activism, but success had turned Diane into a medical policy activist. Despite accolades for her efforts, she willingly admits, "it was really not that hard." Her bywords became "hell, why stop now?" She gets irritated with those who doubt that one person can do anything. She reacts, "Don't bitch if you have not tried to change things."

Diane Nannery spends much of her spare time traveling around the country sharing her expertise and experience. Still a full-time U.S. Postal Service employee, her volunteer civic activities "have taken on a life of their own." She preaches the gospel, "Don't let anyone tell you that making a difference is impossible until you have tried it." She is greatly honored by the letters that fill her mailbox from people who were inspired to launch their own civic initiatives based on her example and experience.

No one wants a cancer diagnosis, but Diane expresses no regrets that a life-threatening event forced her to refocus her life efforts. She is not sure she would have wanted it any other way. She points out that "when I look at life, I no longer feel that I just passed through. When someone asks me 'what can one person do?' I am quick to reply, 'plenty.' "

STAMP OUT

Contrary to postal service concerns, the AIDS and breast cancer stamps performed well economically. Little hesitancy to buy or use the stamps emerged. Breast cancer and AIDS remain significant health problems. No one can prove that lives were saved, consciousness raised, or government funds redirected because of the stamps, but they certainly did no harm. For at least two individuals, the journey from an initial creative flash to fruition changed their lives. The two advocates who traveled parallel roads have never met. But both Jean Anne Hlavacek and Diane Nannery share the proof positive that one person can make a difference.

LESSONS

- *Know the appropriate target. Not all policy is made by elected officials.* It is important to know who to target with your initiative. Finding the right sect of decision makers may be more difficult than convincing them of what you want.
- *Numbers still make a difference.* Individuals may initiate action, but broadening the base of support is always a good idea, even when confronting unelected decision makers.
- *Persistence pays off.* In politics a "no" may well not be the final answer. Although it is clearly less risky to get the decision you want initially, constant pressure may reverse initial decisions.
- *Expand the network.* Although elected officials may not be willing to take the first step, they are often useful for increasing the pressure once an issue has built up its own momentum.

Kids in Action

19

Kidizen Democracy

"Go away little kid, don't bother me."

"He who shall teach a child to doubt
The rotting grave shall ne'er get out."

William Blake, *Auguries of Innocence*

"Grownups never understand anything for themselves, and it is tiresome for children to be always and forever explaining things to them."

Antoine de Saint-Exupery, *The Little Prince*, chap. 1

"The gods visit the sins of the fathers upon the children."

Euripides, *Prixus*, fragment, 970

"Children should be seen and not heard."

"And a little child shall lead them."

Isaiah 11:6

Modern society sends mixed signals about the role of children. Children's fables (*The Emperor's New Clothes, Little Red Riding Hood,* etc.), modern literature (*Annie, Harry Potter,* etc.), and contemporary entertainment (*The Simpsons, Home Alone, Spy Kids,* etc.) regularly feature children taking the lead, often acting more like adults than the adults around them.

As the following stories reveal, there is virtually no minimum age limit on recognizing injustice or pointing out public policy failures. As soon as a child connects with family and society through language they begin asking why things are done the way they are. Bedtime stories, classroom readings, and social studies portray an idealized world where right usually prevails, good deeds are supposed to be rewarded, and right and wrong are portrayed in broad black and white strokes. It was no surprise that it was a child who pointed out that the emperor had no clothes. Between the ages of early innocence and the "cool" cynicism that descends on many teenagers, there is a richer pool of potential activists than among any other age group. Hampered by limited resources and experience, they can make up for it by enthusiasm unbridled by past frustration.

Many of the triumphs of younger citizens affect only local policy. The world for children often ends at the busy street they are not allowed to cross or the limits of endurance for walking. While local initiatives are extremely important to the lives of those affected and their stories deserve to be told, they do not fit the basic criterion of this book that they must have significant national implications.[1] The stories that follow were chosen because they profile young activists whose efforts affected a realm broader than a local community and deal with a variety of strategies and political institutions. These stories are shorter than others in the book, not because they are less important, but rather to allow telling more of them.

FROM PEER PRESSURE TO POLITICAL PRESSURE

It is a familiar scene. In the woods beside the playground or in the back alley, a pre-teen pulls out a pack of cigarettes and encourages his or her gathered friends to take one. It is a right of passage, but one with dangerous consequences. More Americans die every year from smoking-related diseases than from car accidents, murders, AIDS, suicides, and fires *combined*.[2] Smoking serves as a "gateway drug" to alcohol and marijuana.[3] While the overwhelming evidence showing the link between smoking and numerous medical problems has resulted in dramatic declines in smoking among adults, teen and pre-teen smoking rates have increased in recent years.[4]

Peer pressure is not a one-way street. Peers can discourage smoking as well as encourage it. Anti-smoking initiatives led by young people themselves have spontaneously sprung up around the country. Marked by creative strategies, these organizations impacted local, state, and national regulations and legislation.

Sniffing Out the Source

In 1990, six-year-old Morgan Lesko and his nine-year-old brother Max conducted their first cigarette vending machine "sting" operation in Montgomery County, Maryland, to show just how easy it was for young people to obtain cigarettes. Urged on by their parents, the two brothers decided to attack the problem head on.[5] After bringing their message to the Montgomery County Council, cigarette machines were banned in the county.

The brothers became spokespersons for the effort to ban cigarette machines, testifying before the Maryland State Legislature, speaking at conferences, and being featured in the media. In 1996, they became active leaders in a countywide student-led group, Students-Oppose-Smoking (SOS).[6]

About the same time, fourteen-year-old Anna Santiago from Highland Park, Illinois, participated in her own series of sting operations and led her classmates in successfully lobbying the city council to prohibit the sale of tobacco products to minors. Expanding her efforts, Anna testified before state and national legislators and in 1996 was selected for the Campaign for Tobacco-Free Kids Advocate of the Year Award.[7]

Making a Federal Case Out of It

Winning the battle to make cigarettes less accessible one jurisdiction at a time is a slow and inefficient process. Publicity generated by local initiatives led to pressure for national action. Based on their local success, the Lesko brothers were invited to the Oval Office to meet President Clinton in 1995 to discuss Federal Drug Administration (FDA) proposals to curb tobacco use. President Clinton called them the "cigarette vending machine killers."[8] They saw the ravages of cigarettes firsthand when they were allowed to sit in on the president's radio address in which he introduced Victor Crawford, a former Tobacco Institute lobbyist who was dying of throat and lung cancer. It was one of the tobacco industry's worst nightmares—one of its "hired guns" joining the opposition. Crawford's message was dramatic. In his raspy voice he implored:

Kids, cigarettes are bad for you, and they're killers. I know. I used to work for the industry that makes them. I was part of a well-organized machine that depends on young people like you believing that cigarettes are okay. Some of the smartest people in America work at just one thing—figuring out how to get you to smoke. As tobacco kills off people like me, they need kids like you to replace me. . . . It's too late for me, but it's not too late for you. Use your brain. Don't let anybody fool you. Don't smoke.[9]

The regulatory process involves publicly announcing proposed regulations and then allowing for a comment period before their enactment. The rule-making process dealing with children and tobacco resulted in the largest outpouring of public response in the history of the FDA. Over 95,000 individuals submitted original comments, while over 600,000 more sent in form letters.[10]

The Lesko brothers and Anna Santiago stood with President Clinton in August 1996 when he announced the new FDA regulations. The president paid "special tribute to the children of America who have joined this crusade, who have organized and led a massive grass roots movement through-out America to educate and inform people about the dangers of tobacco smoking for children."[11]

The youth advocates were back at the White House in 1997 when the final regulations were scheduled to take effect. Among other things, the regulations:

- Banned cigarette vending machines in most places except nightclubs and bars;
- Forbade free tobacco samples and the sale of single cigarettes (the so-called "loosies" sold to children for a few cents);
- Limited advertising in publications with over 15 percent youth reader-ship, on billboards near schools, and on buses and subways;
- Banned tobacco product sales to anyone under eighteen; and
- Required identification for age verification for any purchaser under twenty-seven.[12]

Stomping Out the Remaining Fires

It is one thing to pass new federal regulations and another to enforce them. Anti-smoking activists viewed the age identification as the key to re-duce the supply of tobacco. It is impossible for government officials to oversee every transaction. Enforcement would depend on the public be-coming the eyes and ears of government. The term *informer* has a negative connotation from authoritarian regimes where individuals informed on their neighbors *to* government. In democratic societies, citizens can play a more positive role by informing *on* government. It became important to determine the degree to which tobacco regulations were actually working.

With the regulation on the books, the Lesko brothers and their SOS friends began a new round of sting operations to determine how difficult it was to buy or steal cigarettes. In one round of efforts, ten of twelve clerks were ready to sell cigarettes without any proof of age. Similar patterns were evident around the country.[13] The resulting media attention, in-creased activity by the FDA, and the threat of fines helped put some teeth into the law.

Young people willing to break the law by smoking are also more likely to steal what they cannot buy. The SOS activists tested availability with a series of "steal stings." In order not to break any laws, they brought with them their own mock cigarette packages, placed them on the cigarette racks, and then "stole" them back. In almost every case, placement of cig-arette racks and inattentive clerks made it very easy. As Andrew Tingley, one of the sting activists, put it, "A lot of times they'd put them [cigarettes] right next to the candy and the school supplies. . . . Some stores were so easy that we could have just walked up there with a wheelbarrow and put in cigarettes."[14]

The battle goes on with SOS remaining an active participant despite the departure of many of its early founders for college and careers. In 1999 they received a $10,000 grant to use carbon monoxide machines to assess the damage smoking has done to young smokers' lungs. They conducted a massive survey of tobacco use by Maryland students and helped get a county law passed requiring tobacco products be placed behind the counter to make them more difficult to steal. No one believes that changed attitudes or laws will eliminate youth smoking completely, but the efforts of Anna, Max, Morgan, Andrew, and hundreds of other young people have led to significant steps to reduce the temptation and made access to tobacco products more difficult.

Lessons

- *National laws are important, but the impact of government is more likely to be felt one transaction at a time on the local level.*
- *Creativity counts.* Sting operations have a mystique about them and garner more attention than sterile statistics or well-meaning platitudes.
- *Parents are often indispensable silent (or perhaps not so silent) partners when kids get involved.*
- *Juxtaposition is a powerful weapon.* Having the former tobacco apologist, cancer-racked and dying Victor Clifford, appear next to idealistic and vibrant young people near the beginning of their lives sent a dramatic message.
- *Advocates must have staying power.* Max Lesko was only six when he first got involved. He is still fighting the battle while in college.

A MONUMENTAL DREAM

As the speaker intoned, the audience had little idea that he and they were making history on that 1963 day. On the steps of the monument to Abraham Lincoln, the Great Emancipator, the descendant of slaves laid out his innermost hopes. In the cadence of the black church, this minister turned activist expounded,

> I have a dream that one day this nation will rise up and live out the true meaning of its creed . . . "that all men are created equal." . . . I have a dream that my four little children will one day live in a nation where they will not be judged by the color of their skin but by the content of their character. I have a dream.

The image of Martin Luther King became the staple of textbooks and documentaries fleshing out the hopes of the civil rights movement and

*The "Scottsdale Six": Heidi Sherman, Jaime Lewis, Carol Bien-Willner,
Lizz Cohen, Carol Mack, and Ilene Mass*

guaranteeing him a place in history. While Reverend King captured a significant symbolic place in history, the physical place of his historic utterance remained largely unknown. Thousands of tourists stopped on the front steps of the Lincoln memorial dredging their minds for images of that speech and trying to remember where King might have been standing.

In reality, it took over thirty-five years before a concrete reminder of King's speech stood anywhere near the Lincoln Memorial. Memorials are designed to refresh the memory of visitors and stimulate their rededication to the principles of the individuals memorialized. Increasingly, King's presence at the Lincoln Memorial seemed more like a vague apparition than a real event.

Changing the Field Trip Playing Field

School field trips are designed to educate but are often remembered more for high jinks than for history. No one expects a field trip to change lives and revise curricula. Those consequences began their trip to reality when Saguaro High School history teacher John Calvin brought his students to the Lincoln Memorial in 1989 as he had done for numerous years. As in the past students were surprised by the lack of any indication about where King's speech had been given. In fact there was no suggestion anywhere that history had been made on this spot. Unlike past classes, this one decided to do something about the omission. Encouraged by their teacher, but told they would have to do it on their own, this class of high schoolers launched an effort to erect a plaque where Dr. King had stood. The plaque would be made from pennies sent in by school children. The class leaders, dubbed the "Scottsdale Six," began raising awareness and funds. While enthusiastically supported by students and many policy makers, the effort seemed to come to a grinding halt when the students were told that the federal Commemorative Works Act forbids piggybacking memorials.[15]

Shifting gears, the "Scottsdale Six" took another tack. After discovering the National Park Service planned to improve visitor facilities at the monument, they asked to be part of the planning committee while simultaneously continuing their "Pennies Can Make a Monumental Difference" fundraising campaign. Securing help from the American Federation of Teachers, the Close-Up Foundation, local business leaders, and members of Congress, the students parleyed the $62,000 they raised in pennies and a supplemental appropriation of over $250,000 from Congress into a new basement visitor's center that not only reminds visitors of Lincoln's legacy to freedom, but also highlights the monument as a symbolic gathering place for political activists trying to fulfill that legacy, such as Dr. Martin Luther King.[16]

For the students, success taught an important lesson they would carry with them throughout their lives. As Lizz Cohen, one of the original organizers, put it, "If you are not involved, you'll never make a change."[17] For Saguaro High School the field trip led to the creation of the National Youth Leadership Center and a four-year, award-winning, service learning curriculum.[18]

Field Tripped Up

Imbuing a site with symbolism can be tricky. Not everyone was enamored with the symbolism emphasized. Almost a decade after its installation a controversy arose over the visuals of protest marches used in a video in the museum. Conservative opponents argued that visuals of gay and pro-abortion placards implied that Lincoln would have supported abortion and homosexual rights, while supporters of the video argued that it merely represented the kinds of groups who have congregated at the memorial to promote their causes.[19]

A group called ConservativePetitions.com used the web to secure over six thousand supporters to have the video modified.[20] Borrowing a strategy from the original student proponents, the opponents of the video used quotes from students on field trips who found the video to be offensive and sending the wrong message.[21] After extensive review by a National Park Service advisory panel, it was decided "to modify the video in order to 'give adequate representation' to all political views."[22] Citizen activism gave the policy wheel another spin, but the saga was not over. It is a minor but insightful reminder of former Secretary of State George Schultz's complaint about Washington, that "nothing ever gets settled in this town. [It's] a seething debating society in which the debate never stops, in which people never give up—including me."[23]

And a Little Child Shall Lead Them

A simple memorial with significant references to King tucked away below the Lincoln memorial was one thing, but it still did not commemorate the actual spot. The omission stood out starkly to Louisville lawyer Tom Williams during a 1997 visit to the memorial. In his first-ever letter to his member of Congress, Williams requested that Representative Anne M. Northrup (R-KY) pursue having a marker placed on the steps. Northrup succeeded in getting Public Law 106–365 passed in October 2000 authorizing the secretary of the interior to "install a plaque in the area of the Lincoln Memorial."[24]

In typical bureaucratic fashion, the National Park Service initially opposed identifying the actual spot with the plaque since its location in the middle of the entry steps would "distract visitors as they approached the

Lincoln statue."[25] Efficiency and crowd control threatened to trump historical accuracy until Representative Northrup and King's widow fought to commemorate the actual spot. The carving was completed during the summer of 2003, the fortieth anniversary of the speech, with visitors now able to stop on the actual step and read:

I HAVE A DREAM
MARTIN LUTHER KING, JR
THE MARCH ON WASHINGTON
FOR JOBS AND FREEDOM
AUGUST 28, 1963

Lessons

- *Individual citizens who often observe obvious omissions are the eyes and ears of democracy.* The decision makers in Washington had all probably visited the memorial more than once and many would have thought about M. L. King's speech without considering the value of a memorial or marker.
- *The policy process involves a series of rounds.* Policies are seldom settled "once and for all."
- *Persistence and flexibility pay.* The Scottsdale Six had to redirect their efforts and achieved success in an unintended realm. Failure to mark the spot of King's address their first time did not doom it to failure forever. Today's "no" could be tomorrow's "yes."
- *One letter can make a difference.*
- *Public officials sometimes just "don't get it," allowing the mundane to override the important.* Bureaucrats are not necessarily venal or stupid, only blinded by narrow goals. Left to the Park Service, the marker and its placement would have had little value for the purpose it was intended.

NIMBY, NOT NAMBY-PAMBY

Major battles are often won one skirmish at a time. Lacking a comprehensive national plan for the disposal of hazardous waste, companies with waste to dispose of seek locations with the least likely organized opposition. The NIMBY (Not In My Back Yard) phenomenon generates considerable opposition in communities with supportive skills, resources, and positive experiences with government officials. Poor communities often lack the resources to fight back. Out of necessity, economically disadvantaged areas often trade the promise of jobs for the price of living near potential danger. Since American political jurisdictions have permeable boundaries, toxic waste is often shipped across state borders for disposal where the opposition will be muted or nonexistent.

Dump, Dump, Dump—Dumb

After Kory Arvizu Johnson's sister died of a heart ailment assumed to be related to contaminated well water, the eight-year-old joined a bereavement group and discovered her poor Mexican American and Native American community was a cancer cluster. In clusters, cancer rates are higher than would be normally expected. Such clusters most often appear in areas of high pollution. Her anger rose when the governor of Arizona announced plans to build three hazardous waste incinerators and dumps in her community to handle waste from both Arizona and adjoining states. She formed Children for a Safe Environment (CSE) to fight the plan. Her efforts stemmed from the principle that "young people everywhere are entitle[d] to environmental justice, no matter what their color or socioeconomic status."[26]

Kory's strategy began with organizing her friends, holding public rallies, writing letters, and sponsoring environmental art projects with the goal of educating the public about environmental dangers. Her organization grew to over three hundred volunteers. The work often was not glamorous. On Thanksgiving, after folding and affixing postage to 2,500 fliers, she and her mother claimed that even "the turkey tasked like stamps."[27] Greenpeace, an international environmental lobby organization, literally moved its local operations into her family's house and she had to climb over sleeping volunteers camping out in the living room.[28]

Kory and her friends quickly found out that kids taking action draws media attention, especially with a cute gimmick. At one press conference they received considerable press by pointing out that the incinerator company planning to build the plant had a poor track record in other states and had actually misspelled the word *environmental* on its company logo.[29]

Not everyone was enamored with Kory's efforts. Friends whose parents worked for polluting companies forbade their children to play with her. The mayor of her town could not understand why she was upset after receiving an award for getting the city to stop using Styrofoam cups—her award plaque came mounted on styroboard.[30] One of her teachers drew her aside and said, "If you keep this up, there's not going to be a college that's going to accept you. . . . You're going to have a radical record."[31]

The Challenge of Success

Kory Johnson's initial success came in 1991 when the governor of Arizona cancelled the incinerator plan citing public pressure as the main reason. He went a step further, pointing out that, "If I hadn't done that, my kids wouldn't have let me come home."[32]

Victory in one battle does not guarantee victory in the war. The toxic waste still exists and needs disposal. While the disposal industry should be applauded for working to reduce potential dangers, realistic environmentalists feel the industry should not be in the driver's seat when it comes to determining acceptable risk for a community. Kory did not want the toxic waste simply foisted on another uninvolved community without their informed consent. With her initial efforts, a lifelong environmentalist had been born, and she began advising other communities how to avoid the musical chairs game of having companies shop around their toxic waste disposal problem until the music stops and a clueless community ends up losing.

Johnson continues her environmental efforts, speaking to groups around the country and taking on new issues. She exemplifies the environmental message, "think globally, act locally," seeking broad-based solutions to national and international problems that are now often fought out one community at a time. Her personal plea is clear. "No one is too young to get busy on issues they care about, and if one person takes a stand, other people will follow. If I sing, everybody will sing. Just get going. Stand up for what you believe in."[33]

By the way, her teacher was dead wrong. Johnson attended the University of California at Berkeley, helped along by winning the prestigious Goldman Environmental prize of $100,000.[34]

Lessons

- *American politics is not a closed system.* Problems generated somewhere else can land, almost literally, on your doorstep.
- *Political activism is not all excitement and glory.* For every press conference and award there are many more hours of "grunt work," stuffing envelopes, cooling one's heels outside decision makers' offices, and gathering information.
- *Don't accept all the advice or information of well-meaning teachers, relatives, or friends.* Advice is free, and often worth no more than you paid for it. Education (both formal and informal) gives one the tools to question and evaluate outside input.
- *Don't assume a personal benefit.* For every Kory Johnson with her $100,000 prize there are thousands of unsung heroes who either failed in their initial quest or succeeded and never received proper recognition after paying a significant personal cost.

RESOURCES FOR KIDIZENS

KIDS CAN MAKE A DIFFERENCE provides on-line resources for young activists and examples of success stories; *www.kids.maine.org.*

NATIONAL YOUTH DEVELOPMENT INFORMATION CENTER
serves as a gateway to sites dealing with youth development. Special emphasis is given to the proposed Younger Americans Act which requires
communities to more fully prepare youth to become effective citizens;
www.nydic.org.

PROJECT CITIZEN is a portfolio-based civic education project for middle
school students supported by the Center for Civic Education and the National Conference of State Legislatures. Its curriculum materials guide students through a process of problem identification, solution framing, and
presentation. Groups are encouraged to present their materials in a competitive poster session. Although designed as a learning module, a number
of the projects have led to actual policy changes. The Center for Civic Education also runs a team-oriented "We the People" competition focusing on
student understanding of the Constitution and CIVITAS, an international
citizenship initiative; *www.civiced.org/project_citizen.html.*

THE PUBLIC ACHIEVEMENT PROGRAM of the Hubert H. Humphrey
Institute of Public Affairs provides teaching materials for civic activism
projects; *www.publicwork.org/2_1_pa.html.*

EARTH FORCE provides guidance for student community projects dealing with the environment; *www.earthforce.org/welcome.htm.*

YOUTH ACTIVISM PROJECT serves as a clearinghouse for resources
and success stories for youth activists and the adults who support them.
They offer seminars and publish an excellent guide to youth activism
(*Youth! The 26% Solution*); *www.youthactivism.com.*

Conclusion

Lessons for Nascent Citizens

The vignettes in this collection do not represent a random sample of citizen initiatives from which statistical generalizations naturally flow. They virtually ignore failures, historical examples, and initiatives not focusing on national public policy. The vignettes do cover a wide range of success stories played out in a variety of institutions using a multiplicity of strategies. The desire to go beyond the details of each case study requires looking for patterns.

This discussion began with the assertion that growing cynicism has thinned the ranks of potential players seeking to impact the political game, leaving the playing field open to those with the willingness and skill to get involved. Politics, like nature, abhors a vacuum. Diminished participation by some does not guarantee lack of involvement by others. A key question is, "Who will step up to the plate and attempt a hit?" Although individual citizens could simply retreat to the stands and leave the policy process to paid professionals, that has not been the case. Individual citizens still make a difference, and part of this inquiry has focused on *who the citizen activist players are*. But describing them tells only part of the story. We also want to know *how they accomplished what they did*. What strategies and resources emerge as significant? Finally, it is important to assess *who wins and who loses* in the policy process. To what degree is the political game stacked and who benefits from it?

WHO ARE THE PLAYERS?

Virtually every subject in these vignettes could be described as an *unlikely activist*. No one would have picked a shy housewife like Lois Gibbs out of the crowd of Love Canal residents to challenge governments to redefine responsibility for pollution. Jean Anne Hlavacek certainly looked more comfortable in her nurse's uniform than drumming up support for an

AIDS stamp. The typical demographic descriptors of age, race, and social status do not produce any particular pattern. The activists look like the public as a whole. Few of them were very poor or very rich, with most coming from the broad and inclusive middle class. Women not working outside the home or not fully committed to family responsibilities are somewhat more common as citizen activists, since they can (often at some sacrifice) make the time to get involved.

Citizen activists are made, not born. Personal experiences more than abstract principles move individuals from disinterest to action. Only a few of the activists credit following a role model set by activist parents or spouses, whereas many surprised both themselves and their families with their initiatives. For some, a dramatic event spurred an action; for others, it was a slow accumulation of experiences, none of which alone would have been enough to make a difference. **Victimhood provides a powerful motivation to act** but is no guarantee of action. The vast majority of victims suffer in silence. The activists profiled in the vignettes are **refreshingly human,** not paragons of virtue. Many are "type A" compulsive personalities. Gregory Watson could not take credit for the Twenty-Seventh Amendment nor would Howard Jarvis be remembered as the "father of Proposition 13" if it were not for their dogged determination. Not all the activists are entirely pleasant people. For every pleasant, self-effacing activist, there is an abrasive Jack Kevorkian. Many of the successful activists are driven. Activists reflect no more consistency in their attitudes and actions than the public as a whole. At times their personal shortcomings have come into focus and have undermined their accomplishments.

There are **few "typical activists."** They come in all shapes and sizes. Age is not a barrier, as is clear from the "Kidizen" activists profiled. Activism is neither a liberal nor conservative domain, but rather a strategy available to supporters of causes across the political spectrum.

Political participation **may or may not become habit-forming.** Many of the activists profiled perceived a wrong in society that they wanted to correct, they acted, and then they retreated from the playing field. Others, such as Lois Gibbs, Kory Johnson, Candy Lightner, and Bernice Sandler found a calling in politics, redirecting their lives into new endeavors. Few of the activists were the same after their experience.

ACTIVIST STRATEGIES:
HOW DID THEY ACCOMPLISH WHAT THEY DID?

Strategy trumps resources. Knowing what to do and how to do it stand out as more important than beginning the process with money, fame, or following. **Organization trumps random action.** Although individuals count as instigators, most of the effective activists relied on the organized support of others.

In politics, **a little knowledge goes a long way.** Information is a key power resource. Knowing where a decision will be made, when it is scheduled to be made, and who will make it often spells the difference between success and failure. Many activists spin their wheels by focusing all their efforts on the wrong target. Attempting to change the minds of those with neither the interest nor responsibility for the desired policy wastes energy and turns one into a nuisance. Once the women proposing the AIDS and breast cancer stamps began targeting the actual decision makers on the CSAC, they were halfway home. Changing the minds of appropriate decision makers is often less difficult than determining their identity. Relevant information is a rare commodity in politics. Providing new information or packaging it in a new way can tilt the playing field dramatically. Brian Trelstad used existing data in a new way to challenge his fellow students to save energy. Hard, empirical data usually trumps soft, impressionistic data. Carl Cohen helped redefine the affirmative action debate by uncovering stark data running counter to verbal assertions. **Cleverly presented data usually trump data that are difficult to understand and interpret.** Current data usually trump stale data. The anti-smoking children might only have been cute advocates if they had not gathered irrefutable hard data through sting operations. Although most political decisions are made on the basis of values rather than facts, decision makers seek supportive facts to rationalize the decisions they want to make. At times, the facts are so overwhelming that they force changes despite the preexisting values of decision makers. After seeing the "cigarette papers," even strong supporters of the tobacco industry could not deny that the tobacco companies had lied and covered up.

Charges of **inconsistency provide a powerful rationale for reassessing existing policy.** Martha McSally and Bernice Sandler forced change by revealing inconsistent treatment.

In real estate the three most important factors are "location, location, and location." In public policy the three most important factors are **timing, timing, and timing.** Riding the crest of public opinion, using a self-defined impending crisis, or effectively using the political calendar all increase the potential for success. Gregory Watson's quest to limit congressional salary increases proved more effective than Madison's attempt almost two hundred years earlier, given the contemporary public frustration with Congress. Pushing policies before the public and their political representatives are ready results in active opposition or disinterest. "Striking while the iron is hot" after a widely publicized event often helps coalesce public opinion and create a responsive environment.

In politics as in life, "everything has a season." It takes an activist to plant an idea at the right time. Good ideas promoted at the wrong time have less likelihood of success than bad ideas put forward at the right time. The "art" in politics often revolves around the realization that there are few good milestones for identifying optimal times to act. Political success often involves resetting the political clock and convincing others that "now is the time."

The various institutions of American politics serve different purposes at different times. At times the president is an agenda setter, at times a decision maker, and at times the one who must react to decisions made by others. President George W. Bush helped set the agenda to promote the Amber Alert legislation as President Bill Clinton had earlier helped popularize Meagan's law. The ability of Congress to pass new legislation is not the only measure of its effectiveness. At times the *threat* of government action proves as effective as action itself. Dr. Kristin Zarfos was not successful in obtaining national legislation outlawing drive-by mastectomies nor has a national tobacco settlement emerged, yet the consideration of laws encouraged insurance providers to allow longer hospital stays and pushed tobacco companies to settle with the states. Many of the **effective strategies are institution specific.** What works with Congress may not work with the presidency or the courts.

It is tempting to simply conclude that **persistence counts.** Many of the activists accepted (and in reality lived) the childhood dictum that "if at first you don't succeed, try, try again." Few were successful the first time. Howard Jarvis's efforts to cut taxes took numerous attempts. Many overcame rebuffs, frustration, and exhaustion as they passed by numerous critical junctures where many would have simply thrown up their hands and quit. Politicians use continuing involvement as a measure of personal commitment and the likelihood that the issue at hand will make a difference in the petitioner's political behavior. "Flash in the pan" activism has little potential for success. **Politics is a continuous game** with numerous rounds. The result of the last round affects but does not determine the next round. Persistence does not guarantee success, but lack of persistence almost always dooms the effort to failure.

WHO WINS AND WHO LOSES?

Perhaps the most basic lesson of the vignettes is that **you can't win if you don't play.** Politics is a not a spectator sport. Participation trumps apathy. Sitting back and wishing for change in public policy is about as effective as sitting back and wishing for a change in the weather. Effective promoters of change attempt to activate, guide, and direct the nature of public policy.

In a democracy, proposed public policy is justified by its ability to garner public support. **Numbers count** in making a case. The larger the number of individuals who sign the petition, show up at the rally, and communicate with the decision maker, the greater their potential for success. Successful activists either harness existing public opinion by framing the issue in an appealing way or they work to create favorable public opinion. Although some of the activists worked behind the scenes, most used the media to legitimize their concerns and attract the support of others. In most cases, **media attention is more important than media approval.** The ability to legitimately assert that "most Americans want . . ." is a powerful political resource. Over a century ago, Abraham Lincoln recognized the strategic importance of public opinion: "Public sentiment is everything. With public sentiment, nothing can fail; without it nothing can succeed."[1]

Concrete policy options with a **personal face** have a greater likelihood of success than abstract goals, no matter how worthy. Proposals like Megan's law, Amber Alert programs, or the Clery Act that are linked to particular individuals humanize the policy process and add pathos (feelings) to logos (rationality). Better informing students or notifying people when a convicted sex offender moves into the neighborhood may be good public policy but could be lost in the policy process unless decision makers can translate words into actions that could save a child or compensate for past errors. Doing the right thing for an identifiable someone has more potency than simply doing the right thing.

New messengers and/or new messaging techniques draw attention to issues. Politicians hearing from a newly activated group are likely to say, "They must really be concerned about this issue and I had better respond." Politicians equate activism with concern and concern with the probability of future action. In politics, **"the squeaky wheel gets the grease."**[2] Those who speak up tend to get a response. New techniques of communication have the potential for turning up the volume and/or increasing the speed at which an activist's "squeak" is heard. The use of a new technology may result in a "halo effect" in which form influences substance. The policy maker unmoved by a stack of letters may well initially scramble to respond to a much smaller set of e-mails because of their uniqueness. As recipients Internet activists such as Shabbir Safdar and Jonah Seiger give contemporary meaning to Marshall McLuhan's argument that "the medium is the message." In the long run, though, familiarity with technology allows recipients to understand the effort required to communicate and reassess the degree they allow messges in alternative formats to influence them.

Despite the best laid plans, policy victories have **unanticipated consequences.** The potential impact of Title IX on athletes never entered the consciousness of either its opponents or proponents.

Successful policy activists often pay a **personal price and may not reap the benefits** of the change they initiate. Change implies upsetting the status quo, an act almost guaranteed to engender antagonism and opposition from those benefiting from the current state of affairs. Political lines often harden into competing camps of "friends" and "enemies," with attempts to vilify one's enemies recognized as an acceptable strategy. Redirecting attention to the personal style or background of the activists by questioning the messenger rather than the message undermines personal privacy. Merrell Williams had his rather checkered career splashed across the front pages of newspapers by the tobacco companies. Lois Gibbs's marriage foundered under the pressure of her activism, and Candy Lightner acrimoniously parted ways with the organization she helped found. The time required for activism holds the danger of alienating one from friends and family who find their claims to time and attention attenuated. The price of activism in some cases was failed marriages, lost jobs, and diminished resources. Even when successful, policy correctives may not apply to the activist initiating them. The clock cannot be turned back to erase one's victimhood or to make one eligible for a previously denied benefit.

WHO WILL WRITE THE NEXT CHAPTERS?

In a democracy **politics is not a spectator sport**. All people need to ask themselves, How can I affect the outcome of the game? The corrective for misguided policies and broken policy processes is more citizen activism, not less. Inviting others to join the political game always carries the danger that those promoting "wrong" solutions will out-organize and overwhelm those promoting the "right" policies. The rightness or wrongness of policies is, of course, defined by unprovable personal values. The risk of allowing wrongheaded activists to prevail is balanced by the opportunity for right-thinking citizens to make their mark.

Democracy is the recurrent belief that more than half of the activist citizens are right more than half of the time. In practical terms, "good" public policies are those the participating majority agrees to at any one point in time. The ray of hope for those dissatisfied with current policy is the fact that the policy book is never closed. All policy decisions are tentative. As long as the policy process is relatively open to new ideas, the proof that a policy is acceptable is the fact that no effective opposition has arisen to challenge it. The vignettes included in this book give little credence to the assertion that the American policy process is heavily stacked toward any particular ideological set of policies or type of activist. Proponents of the status quo, whether on the left or the right, do not always win. Civic activism in a democracy is not a liberal thing or a conservative thing—it is a strategy open to all. These activists have won against government inactivity and have overcome active government opposition. They have humbled big business interests, big government, and big education. They have won the attention of those currently in power, enlisting their aid or calling their political bluff.

The successful activists described in these pages overcame the debilitating curse of cynicism and used thoughtful skepticism to develop realistic strategies. Many began with no blueprint but took things one step at a time. What separated the policy winners from the policy losers was their **willingness to act, more than the nature of their cause** or the character of their initial supporters. Truly, "the only thing necessary for the triumph of evil is for good persons to do nothing."[3]

For better or worse, the individuals profiled herein did something. They provided the energy that breathes life into a democracy. They recognized that in a democracy the constitutional rights of free speech, association, and "petitioning government for the redress of one's grievances" remain sterile ideals, fragile and archaic as the parchment on which they were written, unless acted on. For those who take offense at their words, find their associations abhorrent, and remain unmoved by their chosen grievances, the challenge is:

Find your own words.

Organize potential supporters.

Propose your own solutions to the grievances you abhor.

Promote your solutions with creativity, diligence, and persistence.

Don't take "no" for an answer, but be willing to accept a reasonable compromise that moves the process forward.

Help write the next set of chapters on citizen activism.

If *you* are not ready to act, make room for those who are.

Notes

INTRODUCTION

1. Michael Nelson, "Why Americans Hate Politics and Politicians," *PS: Political Science*, March 1995, p. 72.

2. President Jimmy Carter, "Energy Problems: The Erosion of Confidence" (speech delivered to the nation, July 15, 1979). Reprinted in *Vital Speeches of the Day* 45, no. 21 (1979).

3. George W. Bush, quoted in White House News Briefing, Federal News Service, September 17, 2002, LEXIS-NEXIS database.

4. See Joseph S. Nie Jr., Philip D. Zelikow, and David C. King, *Why People Don't Trust Government* (Cambridge, Mass.: Harvard University Press, 1997), p. 81; and Michele Ingrassia, "The Age of Apathy," *Newsday*, July 23, 1990, p. 16.

5. More than 150 national polls by the Roper organization conducted over the last twenty years indicate that attending political meetings has declined from over 15 percent to 12 percent and writing letters to public officials has declined from over 20 percent to below 15 percent. See the RPOLL file of the LEXIS-NEXIS database.

6. Robert D. Putnam, "Bowling Alone: America's Declining Social Capital," *Journal of Democracy*, January 1995, pp. 64–78. Putnam expanded his article into a book, *Bowling Alone: The Collapse and Revival of American Community* (New York: Simon and Schuster, 2000).

7. David S. Broder, "Civic Life and Civility," *Washington Post*, January 1, 1995, p. C7.

8. Richard Stengel, "Bowling Together," *Time*, July 22, 1996, p. 35.

9. Robert D. Putnam, "Tuning In, Tuning Out: The Strange Disappearance of Social Capital in America," *PS: Political Science and Politics*, December 1995, pp. 664–83. Also published in shorter form as "The Strange Disappearance of Civic America," *American Prospect*, Winter 1996, pp. 34–48.

10. See Stephen Frantzich, *Cyberage Politics 101: Mobility, Technology and Democracy* (New York: Peter Lang, 2002).

11. Quoted in David Mathews, *Politics for People: Find a Responsible Public Voice* (Urbana: University of Illinois Press, 1994), p. 131.

12. David Broder, "Frustrated Clinton Assails Falwell and Limbaugh," *Los Angeles Times*, June 25, 1994, p. A21.

13. The phrase "the squeaky wheel gets the grease" means relatively little to most contemporary automobile owners who practice preventive maintenance and have all the wheels greased. To the pioneers crossing the country in covered wagons, the bear grease they used on the axles was too expensive to use so wastefully. They waited until one of the wheels made noise before apply some of such a dear commodity.

14. Attributed to Edmund Burke; quoted in Suzy Platt, *Respectfully Quoted* (Washington, D.C.: Library of Congress, 1988).

15. William Scranton, former governor of Pennsylvania, quoted in Platt, *Respectfully Quoted* (Washington, D.C.: Library of Congress, 1988).

16. John F. Kennedy, 1961 inaugural address, as borrowed from Kahlil Gibran. In Platt, *Respectfully Quoted* (Washington, D.C.: Library of Congress, 1988).

17. Theodore Roosevelt, "Citizenship in a Republic," in *The Strenuous Life*, vol. 13 of *The Works of Theodore Roosevelt* (New York: Scribner's, 1926), p. 510.

18. Attributed to Voltaire. John Bartlett, *Familiar Quotations* (Boston: Little, Brown and Company, 1980), p. 344.

CHAPTER 1

1. Paige St. John, "Student Revives Debate on 199-Year-Old Amendment," *Los Angeles Times*, May 29, 1988, p. A27.

2. *Origins and Development of Congress* (Washington, D.C.: Congressional Quarterly, 1976), p. 46.

3. For a good summary of the pay controversy, see Congressional Quarterly's *Guide to Congress*, 4th ed. (Washington, D.C.: Congressional Quarterly, 1991).

4. John Vile, "Just Say No to 'Stealth' Amendment," *National Law Journal*, June 22, 1992, p. 15.

5. Ibid.

6. Don Phillips, "Proposed Amendment, Age 200, Showing Life—Constitutional Scholars, Congress Troubled," *Washington Post*, May 29, 1989. Reprinted in the *Congressional Record*, September 25, 1989, p. E3157.

7. Frank J. Murray, "Ghost of Madison Stalks Hill Pay Raise," *Washington Times*, June 25, 1990, p. A5.

8. See John R. Hibbing and Elizabeth Thiess-Morse, *Congress as Public Enemy* (Cambridge, UK: Cambridge University Press, 1995).

9. See Gallup Poll, March 1992 (USGALNEW.205100); CBS/New York Times Poll, September 1990 (USCBSNYT.090309); and Washington Post Poll, January 1989 (USWASHP.89803E) in RPOLL database of LEXIS-NEXIS.

10. Tom Tiede, "Lost Amendment May Keep Congress from Raises," *Daily Register* (Gainesville, Tex.), September 16, 1991. Reprinted in the *Congressional Record*, December 18, 1991, p. E4255.

11. Bob Drummond, "Texan Wants to Limit Lawmakers' Pay Raises," *Dallas Times Herald*, February 3, 1987. Reprinted in the *Congressional Record*, March 24, 1987, p. E1102.

12. Kenneth Cole, "Michigan Adopts Constitutional Amendment on Congressional Pay," *Detroit News*, May 8, 1992.

13. Paul Barton, "Political Observers See Bright Future of Boehner," Gannet News Service, February 28, 1995.

14. Siva Vaidyanathan, "Texan Helped Keep Pay-Raise Issue Alive," *Houston Chronicle,* May 31, 1992.

15. *Austin American-Statesman,* May 20, 1992, p. A1.

16. Vaidyanathan, "Texan Helped."

17. "It Takes 203 Years, but Pay Amendment Finally Gets Ratified," *Star Tribune* (Minneapolis), May 8, 1992, p. 1A.

18. Quoted in Richard B. Bernstein and Jerome Angel, *Amending America* (New York: Random House/Times Books, 1993), p. 257.

19. Richard B. Bernstein, "The Sleeper Wakes: The History and Legacy of the Twenty-seventh Amendment," *Fordham Law Review,* December 1992, pp. 540–41.

20. Quoted in Vaidyanathan, "Texan Helped," p. 3.

CHAPTER 2

1. U.S. Congress, House Committee on Education and Labor, Subcommittee on Postsecondary Education, "Statement of Howard K. Clery, Jr.," March 14, 1990, p. 60.

2. Eleanor Randolph, "Students Say Colleges Use Law to Hide Bad News," *Washington Post,* November 30, 1989, p. A22.

3. Bonnie Fisher, "Crime and Fear on Campus," *Annals of the American Academy of Political and Social Science,* May 1995, p. 91.

4. Jan Hoffman, "New Law Is Urged on Freed Sex Offenders," *New York Times,* August 4, 1994, p. B1.

5. "Dealing with Sex Offenders," *New York Times,* August 15, 1994.

6. "Couple Battles for Safer Campuses," *Trial,* July 1989, p. 131.

7. Charles Laurence, "The Murder That Led to Megan's Law," *Daily Telegraph,* January 30, 1997, p. 17.

8. "Couple Battles for Safer Campuses," *Trial,* July 1989, p. 131.

9. Kelly Richmond, "Heartfelt Persuasion; Citizens Turn Loss into Laws," *Bergen Record,* May 15, 1995, p. A1.

10. Rich Miller, "Mother Uses Faith to Deal with Life after Megan," *Plain Dealer,* August 3, 1997, p. 11.

11. Political scientist Ronald Shaiko, quoted in "Political Acts Often Salve for Grief," *Chicago Tribune,* December 27, 1996, p. 16.

12. Denise Kalette, "Campus-crime Fighters," *USA Today,* November 12, 1990, p. 1D.

13. Ken Gross and Andrea Fine, "After Their Daughter Is Murdered at College, Her Grieving Parents Mount a Crusade for Campus Safety," *People,* February 19, 1990, p. 113.

14. Quoted in John J. Goldman, "Trial to Open in Case that Inspired Megan's Law," *Los Angeles Times,* May 5, 1997, p. A21.

15. "Family of Raped 7-year-old Decries Death Penalty," *Legal Intelligencer,* August 5, 1994, p. 6.

16. Midge Decter, "Megan's Law and the *New York Times,*" *Commentary,* October 1994, p. 61.

17. Charles Laurence, "Megan's Legacy Languishes in Courts," *Daily Telegraph,* October 17, 1997, p. 4.

18. Jerry Gray, "Sex Offender Legislation Passes in the Senate," *New York Times,* October 4, 1994, p. B6.

19. "Couple Battles for Safer Campuses," *Trial,* July 1989, p. 131.

20. Gross and Fine, "After Their Daughter Is Murdered," p. 113.

21. Kalette, "Campus-crime Fighters," p. 1D.

22. Lisa Anderson, " 'Megan's Law' Draws Support, Raises Questions," *Times-Picayune,* August 21, 1994, p. A36.

23. Bonnie S. Fisher and John J. Sloan, *Campus Crime: Legal and Social Perspectives* (Springfield, Ill.: C. C. Thomas, 1995), p. 4.

24. Anderson, "Megan's Law," p. A36.

25. "Whitman Latest to Urge Laws on Notice of Sex Offenders," *New York Times,* August 6, 1994, p. 24.

26. Anderson, "Megan's Law," p. A36.

27. Senator Slade Gorton (R-Wash.) quoted in Anderson, "Megan's Law," p. A36.

28. Kalette, "Campus-crime Fighters," p. 1D.

29. Chet Lunner, "Senate OKs Bill Requiring Campus Crime Reports," Gannet News Service (LEXIS-NEXIS database), September 14, 1990.

30. Anthony Flint, "Bill OK'd Requiring Campus Crime Statistics," *Boston Globe,* October 25, 1990, p. 1.

31. "Demand Accurate Crime Statistics from Colleges in Return for Funds" (editorial), *Sun-Sentinel* (Fort Lauderdale, Fla.), April 10, 1998, p. 22A.

32. Informally called the "Jacob Wetterling act," after the victim who was never found. "Political Acts Often Salve for Grief," *Chicago Tribune,* December 27, 1996, p. 16.

33. Dale Russakoff, "States Search for Fairness in Implementing Megan's Law," *Washington Post,* March 7, 1998, p. A3.

34. Mary Zahn, "Watching the Offenders," *Milwaukee Journal Sentinel,* March 29, 1998, p. 1.

35. William Claiborn, "At the Los Angeles County Fair, 'Outing' Sex Offenders," *Washington Post,* September 20, 1997, p. A1.

36. Russakoff, "States Search," p. A3.

37. Mary Zahn, "Notification Law on Sex Offenders Puts Strain on Residents, Police," *Milwaukee Journal-Sentinel,* March 29, 1998, p. 1.

38. "Bogus Fliers Label School Counselor a Sex Offender," *Chicago Tribune,* March 20, 1998, p. 29.

39. "Suicide Is Recalled as Maine Revisits Megan's Law," *Washington Post,* February 17, 1998, p. A2.

40. Dorina Lazo, "Colleges Accused of Hiding Crime," *Chicago Tribune,* June 18, 1997, p. 13.

41. "Parents Jump into Legal Fray over Megan's Law," *Legal Intelligencer,* January 18, 1995. See also Cindy Goldberg, "Study Says Colleges Don't Report Rape Stats," *University Wire,* October 29, 2002.

42. Joan Biskupic, "High Court Rejects Challenge to New Jersey's 'Megan's Law,' " *Washington Post,* February 24, 1998, p. A2. See also Martin Schwartz,

"Supreme Court Rejects Megan's Law Challenges, Key Issues Remain," *New York Law Journal*, April 15, 2003, p. 3.

43. "Home of Accused Killer Is Torn Down to Build a Memorial to Victim, 7," *Chicago Tribune*, December 21, 1994, p. 2.

44. Gross and Fine, "After Their Daughter Is Murdered," p. 113.

45. Richmond, "Heartfelt Persuasion," p. A1.

46. Jay Jorden, "Alert System Helped Save Teens," *Toronto Star*, August 2, 2002, p. A14.

47. See October 2, 2002, press release at www.missingkids.com.

48. "Bush Signs Amber Alert Bill," *Newsday*, May 1, 2003, p. A8.

49. Diane Feinstein, "Why U.S. Needs AMBER Alert System," *San Diego Union-Tribune*, March 14, 2003, p. B9.

50. *Newsday*, May 1, 2003, p. A8.

51. Quoted in Deb Reichman, "Amber Alert Bill Will Mean More Eyes Looking for Kidnapped Children Nationwide," The Associated Press State and Local Wire, April 30, 2003, LEXIS-NEXIS database.

52. Quoted in Todd J. Gillman, "A Bittersweet Moment for Amber's Family," Knight Ridder/ Tribune News Service, *Dallas Morning News*, May 1, 2003., LEXIS-NEXIS database.

CHAPTER 3

1. Even Martin Luther King Jr. uses the term in his book about the Montgomery experience. See Martin Luther King Jr., *Stride toward Freedom: The Montgomery Story* (New York: Harper and Row), 1958.

2. George Metcalf, *Black Profiles* (New York: McGraw-Hill, 1968), p. 256.

3. Janet Stevenson, "Rosa Parks Wouldn't Budge," *American Heritage Magazine*, February 1972, p. 56.

4. Stevenson, "Rosa Parks," p. 57.

5. The law was not entirely clear. Alabama state law did require clearly segregated white and Negro sections, but the Montgomery city code had a provision that no passenger could be required to give up a seat if another was not available. Previous legal opinions indicated that within the city limits the city code took precedence. Stevenson, "Rosa Parks," p. 57.

6. Metcalf, *Black Profiles*, p. 261.

7. Stevenson, "Rosa Parks," p. 56. Not all accounts, including Rosa Parks's autobiography, repeat the offensive "n" word. Contemporary accounts, probably desiring "political correctness," report the request as, "Let me have those front seats" (Metcalf, *Black Profiles*, p. 262), but such sanitized versions minimize the degradation of the era.

8. Vincent F. A. Golphin, "Taking a Seat for Justice," *Christianity Today*, April 24, 1995, p. 10.

9. Stevenson, "Rosa Parks," p. 56.

10. Jo Ann Robinson Gibson, *The Montgomery Bus Boycott and the Women Who Started It* (Knoxville: University of Tennessee Press, 1987), p. 45.

11. Stewart Burns, ed., *Daybreak of Freedom* (Chapel Hill: University of North Carolina Press, 1997), p. 9.

12. Hans J. Masssaquoi, "Rosa Parks: Still a Rebel with a Cause at 83," *Ebony*, March 1996, p. 102.

13. The term *Jim Crow* came from a nineteenth-century Negro vaudeville character. It refers to laws that segregated the races and discriminated against the voting rights of Negroes.

14. "Rosa Parks Lauded on 40th Anniversary of Refusal to Give up Bus Seat in Alabama," *Jet*, December 18, 1995, p. 16.

15. Martin Luther King Jr., *Stride toward Freedom: The Montgomery Story* (New York: Harper and Row), 1958, p. 44.

16. Masssaquoi, "Rosa Parks," p. 104.

17. Stevenson, "Rosa Parks," p. 58.

18. Gibson, *Montgomery Bus Boycott*, p. 50.

19. Burns, *Daybreak of Freedom*, p. 8.

20. Gibson, *Montgomery Bus Boycott*, p. 53.

21. Stevenson, "Rosa Parks," p. 59.

22. Ibid.

23. King, *Stride toward Freedom*, p. 55.

24. Paul Hendrickson, "The Ladies Before Rosa," *Washington Post*, April 12, 1998, p. F1.

25. King, *Stride toward Freedom*, pp. 61–63.

26. Stevenson, "Rosa Parks," p. 62.

27. Metcalf, *Black Profiles*, p. 271.

28. Gayle J. Hardy, *American Women Civil Rights Activists* (Jefferson, N.C.: McFarland, 1993), p. 306.

29. Metcalf, *Black Profiles*, p. 277.

30. As one member of a later audience put it, "Rosa Parks does not enjoy giving speeches, and as a result she does not give them well." Don Covill Skinner, "A Visit from Rosa Parks: Power of the Ordinary," *Christian Century*, April 1, 1987, p. 300.

31. Harry C. Boyte, *CommonWealth: A Return to Citizen Politics* (New York: Free Press, 1989), p. 65.

32. Burns, *Daybreak of Freedom*, p. 188.

33. Stevenson, "Rosa Parks," p. 85.

34. Hardy, *Women Civil Rights Activists*, p. 306.

35. King, *Stride toward Freedom*, p. 69.

36. Metcalf, *Black Profiles*, p. 262.

37. Rhoda Lois Blumberg, *Civil Rights: The 1960s Freedom Struggle* (Boston: Twayne, 1984), p. 41.

38. Skinner, "Visit from Rosa Parks," p. 300.

39. Masssaquoi, "Rosa Parks," p. 102.

40. Ibid., p. 104.

41. Josh Grossberg, "Rosa Parks Trumps 'Rosa Parks'," *www.eonline.com/News/Items/0,1,11783.html*.

42. Shawn Windsor, "Restored Rosa Parks Bus Heads for Its New Home," www.centredaily.com/mid/centredaily/news/5065116.htm.

43. "The Name Game," *www.snopes.com/inboxes/outrager/rosapark.htm*.

44. Journalist Edward P. Morgan, quoted in Metcalf, *Black Profiles*, p. 269.

CHAPTER 4

1. *www.bernicesandler.com/id2_m.htm*
2. Ibid.
3. Ibid.
4. Ibid.
5. Sheila Tobias, *Faces of Feminism* (Boulder, Colo.: Westview Press, 1997), p. 105.
6. www.bernicesandler.com/id2_m.htm
7. Ibid.
8. *www.bernicesandler.com/id44_m.htm*
9. Ibid.
10. Ibid.
11. Joyce Gelb and Marian Lief Palley, *Women and Public Policies* (Charlottesville: University Press of Virginia, 1996), p. 99.
12. Ibid.
13. Ibid., p. 94.
14. Bill Pennington, "Colleges: More Men's Teams Benched as Colleges Level the Field," *New York Times*, May 9, 2002, A1.
15. From "Self Reliance," quoted in Suzy Platt, *Respectfully Quoted* (Washington, D.C.: Library of Congress, 1988), p. 227.
16. Gelb and Palley, *Women*, p. 101.
17. Pennington, "Colleges," p. A1.
18. Ibid.
19. Tobias, *Faces*, p. 123.
20. Gelb and Palley, *Women*, pp. 96–97.
21. Ibid., p. 108.
22. Ibid., p. 109.
23. Ibid., pp. 115, 117.
24. Ibid., p. 120.
25. Tobias, *Faces*, pp. 125, 291.
26. Pennington, "Colleges," p. A1.
27. Ibid.
28. Jake Curtis, "Coming on Strong and Making History," *San Francisco Chronicle*, June 23, 2002, p. B15.
29. Valerie Strauss and Liz Clarke, "Sex Bias Ban Upheld for School Athletics," *Washington Post*, July 12, 2003, p. A7.
30. Lillian Thomas, "Title IX Tug of War," *Pittsburgh Post-Gazette*, October 6, 2002, p. E1.
31. Elizabeth Spaid, "Sizing Up Woman's Rights on Campus," *Christian Science Monitor*, January 19, 1993, p. 14.
32. Thomas, "Title IX."
33. Ibid.

CHAPTER 5

1. David Grogan et al., "Unimpressed by the Freedom to Burn Old Glory, Joey Johnson Still Wants a Revolution," *People*, July 10, 1989, p. 98.
2. Robert Justin Goldstein, *Burning the Flag* (Kent, Ohio: Kent State University Press, 1996), p. 35.

3. Ibid.

4. Ibid.

5. Glen Elsasser, "High Court to Rule on Flag-Burning Case," *Chicago Tribune,* October 18, 1988, p. 16.

6. Goldstein, *Burning the Flag,* p. 39.

7. David G. Savage, "Justices Will Rule If Flag-Burning Is Permissible," *Los Angeles Times,* October 18, 1988, p. 23

8. Goldstein, *Burning the Flag,* p. 34.

9. Ibid., p. 35.

10. Ibid., p. 34.

11. Ibid.

12. Colman McCarthy, "Flag Desecrations and Flag Ostentation," *Washington Post,* July 9, 1989, p. F2.

13. Goldstein, *Burning the Flag,* p. 39.

14. Ibid., p. 40.

15. Scott LaFee, "The Burning Issue," *San Diego Union-Tribune,* July 1, 1989, p. E1.

16. Goldstein, *Burning the Flag,* pp. 49, 53.

17. Ibid., p. 63.

18. Ibid., p. 87.

19. Ibid., pp. 77–87.

20. Linda P. Campbell, "William Brennan and the First Amendment," *Fort Worth Star-Telegram,* August 3, 1997, p. 1.

21. "Excerpts: The Flag Will Be Strengthened . . . Not Weakened," *Los Angeles Times,* June 22, 1989, p. 19.

22. Campbell, "William Brennan," p. 1.

23. "Excerpts: The Flag Will Be Strengthened . . . Not Weakened."

24. Newsweek poll reported in John Dillin, "Bush's Call Sparks Ardent Debate," *Christian Science Monitor,* July 6, 1989, p. 8.

25. Mike Robinson, "Bush to Allow Flag-Burning Ban to Become Law," Associated Press (LEXIS-NEXIS database), October 13, 1989.

26. Robinson, "Bush to Allow Flag-Burning Ban."

27. Goldstein, *Burning the Flag,* p. 235.

28. "Charges Filed in First Court Test of New Flag Desecration Law," *St. Petersburg Times,* November 1, 1989, p. 4A.

29. *Congressional Record,* June 20, 1990, p. H4087.

30. Dillin, "Bush's Call Sparks Ardent Debate," p. 8.

31. John Conyers Jr., "Burning the Bill of Rights," *Connecticut Law Tribune,* June 30, 1997.

32. White House press conference, June 12, 1990, C-SPAN video.

33. "The Flag Burning Page," available at *www.indirect.com/www/warren/flag/ johnson.html.*

34. lawweb.usc.edu/news/releases/Johnson.htm

35. www.cfa-inc.org/latest_news/cfanr72.htm

36. Although the exact wording and specific source is questioned, experts attribute the thought to Voltaire. John Bartlett, *Bartlett's Familiar Quotations* (New York: Little, Brown, 1980), p. 344.

37. *United States v. Schwimmer* (279 U.S. 644) (1929).

38. Conyers, "Burning the Bill of Rights."

CHAPTER 6

1. Quoted in Lionel Van Deerlin, "An American Air Force Officer and Saudi Custom," *The San Diego Union-Tribune*, December 19, 2001, p. B7.

2. "A Female Right Stuffer Takes on the Pentagon," *U.S. News and World Report*, December 10, 2001, p. 3.

3. Vin Suprynowicz, "Show the Colors," *The Libertarian*, December 14, 2001.

4. Ibid.

5. "Window of Opportunity," *The San Francisco Chronicle*, December 19, 2001, p. A26.

6. Ann Gerhart, "The Air Force Flier in the Ointment," *Washington Post*, January 7, 2002, p. C1.

7. Ibid.

8. Ibid.

9. Ibid.

10. Ibid.

11. Quoted in Suprynowicz, "Show the Colors."

12. "Dress Blues: Fighter Pilot Martha McSally Battles to Liberate U.S. Servicewomen in Saudi Arabia for a Confining Cloak," *People Weekly*, February 11, 2002, p. 71.

13. Elaine Sciolino, "Servicewomen Win, Doffing Veils in Saudi Arabia," *The New York Times*, January 25, 2002, p. A6.

14. James Dao, "Pentagon Drops Rule on Women in Cars," *The New York Times*, March 2, 2002, p. A13.

15. "Women's-rights Activist to Speak at Graduation," *Providence Journal-Bulletin*, April 25, 2002, p. B-6.

16. "Servicewomen in Saudi Arabia," *The Buffalo News*, May 17, 2002, p. B4.

17. *www.rutherford.org/articles_db/press_release.asp?article_id=314*

CHAPTER 7

1. Vic Sussman, "A New Precinct: Cyberspace," *U.S. News and World Report*, February 19, 1996, p. 58.

2. M. J. Zuckerman, "How the Internet Became a Rumor Central," *USA Today*, September 18, 1996.

3. A list-serve is a distribution list for targeted messages. Individuals join a list-serve and receive messages submitted by other list-serve members. Most list-serves deal with a specific subject matter area. List-serves are usually "moderated," with the editor determining what is appropriate for distribution and what is not.

4. Matthew MacAllester, "Censorship on the Net," *Newsday*, November 3, 1996, p. A61.

5. Matthew MacAllester, "Web Spreads News of Serb Conflict," *Newsday*, December 28, 1996, p. A6.

6. Ibid.

7. Ibid.

8. John Carey, "Virtually Kissing Babies," *Business Week,* March 25, 1996, p. 70.

9. Michelle Slatalla, "Hi-Tech Soapbox," *Newsday,* March 14, 1995, p. A13.

10. Graeme Browning, "Net Effects," *National Journal,* June 3, 1995.

11. Slatalla, "Hi-Tech Soapbox," p. A13.

12. Leslie Miller, "Pair of Activists Demonstrate Their Views in Net," *USA Today,* March 5, 1997, p. 11D.

13. Browning, "Net Effects." See also Joan Biskupic, "Suddenly, It's Standing Room Only at Supreme Court," *Washington Post,* January 26, 1997, p. A6.

14. Graeme Browning, *Electronic Democracy* (Wilton, Conn.: Berton, 1996), p. 53.

15. "Teclo Offer Made on Media Ownership Concentration," *National Journal's CongressDaily* (LEXIS-NEXIS database), December 13, 1995. See also Michelle Rafter, "Groups Protest Communications Decency Act," Reuter Business Report (LEXIS-NEXIS database), December 13, 1955.

16. Over 60 percent of adults with an opinion favored restrictions in general, with over 80 percent favoring restrictions on child pornography and 67 percent favoring restrictions on X-rated material. (National polls conducted by Princeton Survey Research Associates for the Pew Research Center, LEXIS-NEXIS database, 1996, 1997.)

17. Genny Wilkinson, "Rep. Klug Says Telecom Bill Will Empower Consumers," *Capital Times* (Madison, Wis.), February 9, 1996, p. 7C.

18. Miller, "Pair of Activists," p. 11D.

19. Hall Straus, "Publishers Changing Own Pages to Protest Communications Act," *Atlanta Journal and Constitution,* February 8, 1996, p. 3D. See also Linda Dailey Paulson, "Cyberspace Protest Darkens Internet," UPI (LEXIS-NEXIS database), February 8, 1996.

20. "Proposed Ban on Indecent Speech on the Internet," *ABC World News Tonight* (LEXIS-NEXIS database), February 8, 1996.

21. Heather Newman, "The Page Is Black, the Rage Is White-Hot," *The Tennessean,* February 8, 1996, p. 1A.

22. Lou Dolinar, "New 'Cybersensor' Law Protested," *Newsday,* February 10, 1996, p. A8.

23. Peter H. Lewis, "Protest, Cyberspace-Style," *New York Times,* February 8, 1996, p. A16.

24. Seiger and Safdar quoted in Brock N. Meeks, "Noted Net Lobbyists Form For-Profit Firm," MSNBC. Available at www.msnbc.com/news/129054.asp.

25. Jeannine Aversa, "Telcom Bill's Anti-Smut Provision Ignites Protest in Cyberspace," Associated Press (LEXIS-NEXIS database), February 7, 1996.

26. "Government Says Decency Issues Won't Go Away, May Appeal," *Media Daily,* June 12, 1996.

27. Elizabeth Weise, "Word of Court Victory Spreads Fast on Internet," Associated Press (LEXIS-NEXIS database), June 12, 1996.

28. Ibid.

29. Leslie Miller, "Decency Ruling to Storm the Web," *USA Today,* June 24, 1997, p. 2D.

30. Maria Seminaerio, "CDA Ruling: Magna Carta for the Internet," *PC Week,* June 30, 1997, p. 16.

31. Mark Rockwell, "Decency Withers under Court Scrutiny," *Communications Week,* July 7, 1997, p. T9.

32. Tony Mauro, "Scenes from a Historic Week," *Legal Times,* June 30, 1997, p. 8; Richard Carelli, "Supreme Court Notebook," Associated Press (LEXIS-NEXIS database), July 7, 1997.

33. Carelli, "Supreme Court Notebook."

34. Jon Katz, "The Digital Citizen," *Wired,* December 1997. Also available at *www.hotwired.com/special/citizen.survey/survey.html.*

35. John Defterios and Steve Young, "Politics and the Web," CNN Financial (LEXIS-NEXIS transcript), February 6, 1998.

36. Aaron Pressman, "Congress Look to Internet to Reach Voters," Reuters World Service (LEXIS-NEXIS database), March 11, 1997.

37. Rex Nutting, "Net Organizers Learn from CDA Debacle," TechWire (LEXIS-NEXIS database), March 17, 1997.

38. Michelle V. Rafter, "Community Groups, Activists Slowly Getting Wired," Reuter Business Report (LEXIS-NEXIS database), August 6, 1996.

39. Graeme Browning, "Some in Congress Get with the Net," *National Journal,* July 13, 1996; Jackson Bond, "D.C. Area News," *Computer Shopper,* November 1996, p. D12; Graeme Browning, "Soon There'll Be No Escape," *National Journal,* October 12, 1996, p. 2182.

40. Rebecca Vessely, "Democracy.net Brings Congress to Your Monitor," *Wired News,* March 14, 1997. *www.wired.com/news/politics/story/2575.html*

41. Leslie Miller, "Pair of Activists Demonstrate Their Views in Net," *USA Today,* March 5, 1997, p. 11D.

42. Deirdre Shesgreen, "Clinton Lobbyists Jumping Ship," *Legal Times,* December 15, 1997, p. 4.

43. Defterios and Young, "Politics and the Web."

CHAPTER 8

1. Katherine Griffin, "No Longer MADD," *San Francisco Chronicle,* August 7, 1994, p. 6/Z1.

2. Candy Lightner and Nancy Hathaway, *Giving Sorrow Words* (New York: Warner Books, 1990), p. 1.

3. Ibid., p. 8. The driver of the car that killed Cari Lightner, Clarence Busch, eventually served twenty-one months in jail for his actions. Otto Friedrich, "Seven Who Succeeded," *Time,* January 7, 1985, p. 41.

4. Katherine Griffin, "MADD Again," *Health,* July–August 1994, p. 62.

5. Craig Reinarman, "The Social Construction of an Alcohol Problem," *Theory and Society,* January 1988, p. 97.

6. Friedrich, "Seven Who Succeeded," p. 41.

7. "MADD Founder Candy Lightner Still Crusades against Drunken Driving," UPI, May 6, 1985.

8. Friedrich, "Seven Who Succeeded," p. 9.

9. Lightner and Hathaway, *Giving Sorrow Words*, p. 228.

10. Friedrich, "Seven Who Succeeded," p. 12.

11. Ibid., p. 11.

12. Tamar Lewin, "Founder of Anti-Drunk-Driving Group Now Lobbies for Breweries," *New York Times*, January 15, 1994, p. 7.

13. Lightner and Hathaway, *Giving Sorrow Words*, p. 12.

14. Kristin Lopez Eastlick, "MADD Agenda Goes Mad with Neo-prohibitionism," *Atlanta Journal-Constitution*, March 25, 2002, p. 14A.

15. Doug Bandow, "Targeting the Most Dangerous Drunk Drivers," *Washington Times*, January 28, 1994, p. A23.

16. Griffin, "MADD Again," p. 64.

17. Ibid., p. 63.

18. "How Effective are MADD's Efforts?" *USA Today*, April 7, 1992, p. 4.

19. Friedrich, "Seven Who Succeeded," p. 41.

CHAPTER 9

1. Lois Gibbs, *Love Canal: My Story* (Albany: State University of New York Press, 1981), p. xii.

2. Greg Mitchell, *Truth . . . and Consequences: Seven Who Would Not Be Silenced* (New York: Dember Books, 1981), p. 184.

3. Gibbs, *Love Canal*, pp. 3–4.

4. Andrew J. Hoffman, "An Uneasy Rebirth at Love Canal, New York," *Environment*, March 1995, p. 4.

5. Adeline Gordon Levine, *Love Canal: Science, Politics, and People* (Lexington, Mass.: Lexington Books, 1982), p. 194.

6. Gibbs, *Love Canal*, pp. 3–4.

7. Ibid., p. 12.

8. Levine, *Love Canal*, p. 31.

9. Gibbs, *Love Canal*, pp. 26, 47.

10. Mitchell, *Truth . . . and Consequences*, p. 177.

11. Gibbs, *Love Canal*, p. 27.

12. Levine, *Love Canal*, p. 29.

13. Gibbs, *Love Canal*, p. 30.

14. Ibid., p. 51.

15. See Luke 16:10, Luke 19:17.

16. Gibbs, *Love Canal*, p. 2.

17. Mitchell, *Truth . . . and Consequences*, p. 195.

18. Levine, *Love Canal*, p. 198.

19. Gibbs, *Love Canal*, p. 200.

20. Quoted in Levine, *Love Canal*, p. 194.

21. Gibbs, *Love Canal*, p. 76.

22. Ibid., p. 96.

23. Levine, *Love Canal*, p. 191.

24. Mitchell, *Truth . . . and Consequences*, p. 216.

25. Gibbs, *Love Canal*, p. 78.
26. Ibid., p. 102.
27. Levine, *Love Canal*, p. 196.
28. Gibbs, *Love Canal*, p. 93.
29. Mitchell, *Truth . . . and Consequences*, p. 170.
30. Gibbs, *Love Canal*, pp. 148–49.
31. Levine, *Love Canal*, p. 149; Mitchell, *Truth . . . and Consequences*, p. 171.
32. Quoted in Levine, *Love Canal*, p. 150.
33. Gibbs, *Love Canal*, p. 144.
34. Ibid., p. 79.
35. Levine, *Love Canal*, pp. 200, 208.
36. Mitchell, *Truth . . . and Consequences*, p. 217.
37. *www.intac.com/PubService/hu . . ._CANAL_MEXICO_U_S_POLUTION_ ENVIRON*
38. *www.medaccess.com/newsletter/n10415/cchw_fact.htm*
39. Booth Gunter, "The Cost of the Superfund," *Tampa Tribune*, July 23, 1995, p. 1.
40. See Jack Plano and Milton Greenberg, *The American Political Dictionary* (Fort Worth, Tex.: Harcourt Brace, 1997), pp. 501–502.
41. Gunter, "Cost," p. 1.
42. Gibbs, *Love Canal*, p. xv.
43. Ibid., p. 2.
44. Ibid., p. 65.
45. *www.intac.com/PubService/hu . . ._CANAL_MEXICO_U_S_POLUTION_ ENVIRON*; Hoffman, "An Uneasy Rebirth at Love Canal," p. 14.
46. Levine, *Love Canal*, p. xi.
47. Ibid., pp. 208–209.
48. Levine, *Love Canal*, p. 209.

CHAPTER 10

1. American National Election Study, 1994 Postelection Survey, Center for Political Studies, University of Michigan. National survey of 1,795 adults, available at ICPSR Web site *www.umich.edu/~nes/resources/studies/94study.htm*.
2. New York Times poll of 1,432 adults, December 8, 1996, LEXIS-NEXIS database.
3. Everett Carll Ladd and Karlyn H. Bowen, *What's Wrong?* (Washington, D.C.: AEI Press/Roper Center for Public Opinion Research, 1998), pp. 55, 58.
4. Richard A. Cloward and Frances Fox Piven, "Toward a Class-Based Realignment of American Politics: A Movement Strategy," *Social Policy*, Winter 1983, p. 3.
5. Frances Fox Piven and Richard A. Cloward, *Why Americans Don't Vote* (New York: Pantheon, 1988), p. 9.
6. Cloward and Piven, "Toward a Class-Based Realignment," p. 4.
7. Ibid.
8. Piven and Cloward, *Why Americans Don't Vote*, p. 13.

9. Richard A. Cloward and Frances Fox Piven, "Trying to Break Down the Barriers," _The Nation,_ November 5, 1985, p. 433.

10. Ibid.

11. Senator Malcolm Wallop (R-Wyo.), "Capitol Research Center," 137 _Congressional Record,_ November 21, 1991, p. S17424.

12. Ibid., p. S17425.

13. Jordan Moss, "Motor Voter: From Movement to Legislation," _Social Policy,_ Winter 1993, p. 14.

14. Richard A. Cloward and Frances Fox Piven, "How to Get Out the Vote in 1988," _The Nation,_ November 23, 1985, pp. 547–48.

15. Cloward and Piven, "How to Get Out the Vote," p. 548.

16. Cloward and Piven, "Trying to Break Down the Barriers," p. 434.

17. Ibid., p. 435.

18. Piven and Cloward, _Why Americans Don't Vote,_ p. 17.

19. Cloward and Piven, "Trying to Break Down the Barriers," p. 436.

20. Wallop, "Capitol Research Center," p. S17424.

21. Piven and Cloward, _Why Americans Don't Vote._

22. See Senator Paul Wellstone (D-Minn.), "National Voter Registration Act of 1992," 138 _Congressional Record,_ September 21, 1992, p. S14202; and Wallop, "Capitol Research Center," p. S17424.

23. See Murray Edelman, _Politics as Symbolic Action_ (New Haven, Conn.: Yale University Press, 1971); and Ted Robert Gurr, "A Causal Model of Civil Strife," _American Political Science Review_ 61 (December 1968).

24. Piven and Cloward, _Why Americans Don't Vote,_ p. xiv.

25. Frances Fox Piven and Richard A. Cloward, "Government Statistics and Conflicting Explanations of Nonvoting," _P.S.: Political Science and Politics,_ September 1989, p. 580.

26. Piven and Cloward, _Why Americans Don't Vote,_ p. 19.

27. Walter Dean Burnham, "Theory and Voting Research: Some Comments on Converse's 'Change in the American Electorate,' " _American Political Science Review,_ September 1974, p. 1019.

28. Wallop, "Capitol Research Center," p. S17426.

29. Jordan Moss, "Motor Voter: From Movement to Legislation," _Social Policy,_ Winter 1993, p. 27.

30. Ibid.

31. Wallop, "Capitol Research Center," p. S17426.

32. See "Recent Action in Congress," _Congressional Digest,_ March 1993, p. 96; and Staci L. Rhine, "Registration Reform and Turnout Change in the American States," _American Politics Quarterly,_ October 1995, p. 409.

33. Staci L. Rhine, "Registration Reform and Turnout Change in the American States," _American Politics Quarterly,_ October 1995, p. 409.

34. Stephen Knack, "Does 'Motor Voter' Work? Evidence from State-Level Data," _Journal of Politics,_ August 1995, p. 796.

35. Stephen B. Fawcett, Tom Seekins, and Louise Silber, "Low-Income Voter Registration: A Small-Scale Evaluation of an Agency-Based Registration Strategy," _American Journal of Community Psychology_ 16, no. 5 (1988); also reprinted in 136 _Congressional Record,_ February 28, 1990, p. E445.

36. See Richard Sammon, "Deal May Speed Up 'Motor Voter,' " *Congressional Quarterly Weekly Report*, May 1, 1993, p. 1080; Richard Sammon, "House OKs 'Motor Voter' for Final Senate Vote," *Congressional Quarterly Weekly Report*, May 8, 1993, p. 1144; "Should the Congress Pass the National Voter Registration Act?" *Congressional Digest*, March 1993, p. 78.

37. Sammon, "Deal," p. 1080; Sammon, "House Oks," p. 1144; "Should the Congress Pass the National Voter Registration Act?" p. 78.

38. See the Human SERVE Web site at *www.igc.org/humanserve/summary.html*.

39. The court was reacting to a California case, *Wilson v. Voting Rights Coalition*. The Ninth Circuit Court had already ruled that the election power in Article 1 of the Constitution allowed such federal action. See *www.igc.org/humanserve/supreme.html*.

40. Marshall Ganz, "Motor Voter or Motivated Voter?" *American Prospect*, September–October 1996, pp. 43–44.

41. Lynne M. Casper and Loretta Bass, "Voting and Registration in the Election of November 1996," *Current Population Reports*, U.S. Census Bureau, *www.census.gov/population/www/socdemo/voting.html*.

42. Paul Leavett, "Election Boosts Chances for Patients' Rights Bill," *USA Today*, November 6, 1998, p. 7a.

43. Harold W. Stanley and Richard G. Niemi, *Vital Statistics on American Politics* (Washington, D.C.: *Congressional Quarterly*, 1995), p. 79; and U.S. Census Bureau, 4 "Voting and Registration: November 1996." Available at *www.census.gov/population/socdemo/voting/history/co23 and the 2000 data available at www.census.gov/population/socdemo/p20–542/table1.pdf*

44. Benjamin Highton and Raymond Wolfinger, "Anticipating the Effects of the National Voter Registration Act of 1993," reported in Ganz, "Motor Voter or Motivated Voter?" p. 47. See also Daniel P. Franklin and Eric E. Grier, "Effects of Motor Voter Legislation: Voter Turnout, Registration, and Partisan Advantage in the 1992 Presidential Election," *American Politics Quarterly*, January 1997, p. 113.

45. See Stephen E. Frantzich, *Cyberage Politics 101: Mobility, Technology and Democracy* (New York: Peter Lang, 2002).

46. Ganz, "Motor Voter," pp. 43–44.

CHAPTER 11

1. "Campus Life: Harvard; House by House, An 'Olympics' in Conservation," *New York Times*, December 16, 1990, p. A60.

2. Ibid.

3. "Students Plan Ways for Colleges to Act on Environmentalism," *New York Times*, February 21, 1994, p. B4.

4. Barbara Ruben, "Greening the Ivory Tower," *Environmental Action Magazine*, January 1993, p. 15.

5. Ibid.

6. "Robert Redford Urges 18–29 Year Olds to Be 'Swing Vote,' " U.S. Newswire (LEXIS-NEXIS database), October 29, 1992.

7. Registration and turnout figures are based on "reported behavior," which undoubtedly inflates the figures. This analysis assumes that inflation is consistent

across age groupings. The data come from the U.S. Bureau of the Census, *Current Population Reports: Voting and Registration in the Election of*—; available in Harold Stanley and Richard Niemi, *Vital Statistics on American Politics* (Washington, D.C.: *Congressional Quarterly*, 1995), p. 79. Also available at *www.census.gov/org/population/socdemo/voting/history/vot02.txt.*

8. Trelstad modestly admits that there may have been some double counting.

9. Brad L. Graham, "Talkin' 'Bout My Generation," *St. Louis Post-Dispatch*, Everyday Magazine, p. 1F.

10. Paul Rogat Loeb, *Generation at the Crossroads* (New Brunswick, N.J.: Rutgers University Press, 1994), p. 379.

11. "CEC's Recent Accomplishments," *www.cgv.org/cgv/cec.html.*

12. "Students Plan Ways for Colleges to Act on Environmentalism."

CHAPTER 12

1. Arthur O'Sullivan, Terri A. Sexton, and Steven M. Sheffrin, *Property Taxes and Tax Revolts: The Legacy of Proposition 13* (Cambridge, UK: Cambridge University Press, 1995), p. 3.

2. Howard Jarvis, *I'm Mad as Hell* (New York: Times Books, 1979), p. 18.

3. "Howard Jarvis, 82, Led Proposition 13 Battle," *Chicago Tribune*, August 13, 1986, p. 7.

4. Jarvis, *Mad as Hell*, p. 17.

5. Ibid., p. 25.

6. O'Sullivan et al., *Property Taxes*, p. 1.

7. David O. Sears and Jack Citrin, *Tax Revolt: Something for Nothing in California* (Cambridge, Mass.: Harvard University Press, 1985), p. 26.

8. David B. Magelby, *Direct Legislation* (Baltimore: Johns Hopkins University Press, 1984), p. 148.

9. Jim Schultz, "Major Firms Gained Most with Prop 13," *Sacramento Bee*, September 7, 1997, p. F1.

10. Magelby, *Direct Legislation*, p. 36.

11. Jake Henshaw, Gannett News Service (LEXIS-NEXIS database), October 31, 1996.

12. Jarvis, *Mad as Hell*, p. 9.

13. Ibid., p. 32.

14. Robert Kuttner, *Revolt of the Haves: Tax Rebellions and Hard Times* (New York: Simon and Schuster, 1980), p. 22.

15. Magelby, *Direct Legislation*, p. 64.

16. Kuttner, *Revolt of the Haves*, p. 22.

17. Jarvis, *Mad as Hell*, p. 61.

18. Ibid., p. 80.

19. Ibid., p. 48.

20. Lou Cannon, "1978: The Year the States Cut Taxes," *Washington Post*, April 17, 1978, p. A1.

21. Robert Lindsey, "Howard Jarvis, 82, Tax Rebel, Is Dead," *New York Times*, August 14, 1986, p. D23.

22. Jarvis, *Mad as Hell*, p. 94.

23. O'Sullivan et al., *Property Taxes*, p. 3.

24. Schultz, "Major Firms," p. F1.

25. Sears and Citrin, *Tax Revolt*, p. 8.

26. Ibid., pp. 19–30.

27. Ibid., p. 30.

28. Ibid., p. 31.

29. Jarvis, *Mad as Hell*, p. 125.

30. Based on a statewide Mervin Field poll reported in Sara Fitzgerald and Patricia Meisol, "The 'Taxpayers' Revolt' Takes to the States," *National Journal*, June 3, 1978, p. 873.

31. Magelby, *Direct Legislation*, p. 125.

32. Ibid., p. 145.

33. Jim Schultz, *The Initiative Cookbook* (San Francisco: Democracy Center, 1996), p. 2.

34. Bill Gardner, "TODAY's TOPIC: Jarvis Talks, Politicians Listen," Associated Press, November 3, 1978.

35. Jarvis, *Mad as Hell*, p. 134.

36. Ibid., p. 23.

37. Magelby, *Direct Legislation*, p. 53.

38. Ibid., p. 5.

39. David Lowery and Lee Sigelman, "Understanding the Tax Revolt: Eight Explanations," *American Political Science Review* 75 (1981), p. 971.

40. Bill Lambrecht, "Voters Try to Bypass Politicians: Initiatives Are on Ballots in Near-Record Numbers," *St. Louis Dispatch*, November 3, 1996, p. 18.

41. Kent Mulligan of the Free Congress Foundation, quoted in Joyce Price, "Ballot Initiatives Abound," *Washington Times*, October 19, 1996, p. A4.

42. Donald R. Wolfensberger, "Congress and the Threat to Direct Democracy" (paper prepared for delivery at the 1997 annual meeting of the American Political Science Association, Washington, D.C.), p. 18.

43. Sears and Citrin, *Tax Revolt*, p. 2.

44. Peter H. King, "On California," *Los Angeles Times*, November 12, 1997, p. A3.

45. O'Sullivan et al., *Property Taxes*, pp. 137–38.

46. Ibid., pp. 139–40.

47. John Lancaster, "In Different Eras, Two Big Tax Plans," *Washington Post*, May 20, 2001, p. A5.

48. Jarvis, *Mad as Hell*, p. 12.

CHAPTER 13

1. "Notes on People: Shaping Up for Naval Academy," *New York Times*, January 25, 1972, p. 28.

2. "Women: Tradition Aweigh," Nimitz Library, U.S. Naval Academy clipping archives.

3. "Navy to Keep Its Academy All Male," *New York Times*, February 9, 1972.

4. For example, see "Academies' Sex Bias Attacked," *News American*, March 28,

1972; "Comment from Afar on Co-eds at Academy," *Evening Capital* (Annapolis), February 1, 1972; and "No Girls for Academy," *Evening Capital*, February 9, 1972.

5. Judith Hicks Stiehm, *Bring Me Men and Women* (Berkeley: University of California Press, 1981), p. 11.

6. For a detailed discussion of this battle, see Stiehm, *Bring Me Men and Women*, 1981.

CHAPTER 14

1. David Barstow, "The Thief and the Third Wave," *St. Petersburg Times*, April 6, 1997, p. 1A.

2. Andrew Wolfson, "Judge Will Try to Clear Smoke Surrounding Stolen Legal Papers," *Courier-Journal* (Louisville, Ky.), December 1, 1993, p. 1A.

3. Michael Orey, "A Mole's Tale," *American Lawyer*, July–August 1995, p. 86.

4. Wolfson, "Judge Will Try to Clear Smoke," p. 1A.

5. Myron Levin, "The Unlikely Figure Who Rocked the U.S. Tobacco Industry," *Los Angeles Times*, June 23, 1996, p. D1.

6. Wolfson, "Judge Will Try to Clear Smoke," p. 1A.

7. Barstow, "The Thief and the Third Wave," p. 1A.

8. Levin, "Unlikely Figure," p. D1.

9. Mark Curridan, "The War against Cigarettes," *Atlanta Journal and Constitution*, April 17, 1994, p. A1.

10. Ibid.

11. Orey, "A Mole's Tale," p. 86.

12. John Schwartz, "For Tobacco, a Turning Point Looms," *Washington Post*, May 14, 1994, p. A1.

13. Philip J. Hilts, "Health Risks Reportedly Known to Tobacco Firm," *Dallas Morning News*, June 16, 1994, p. 1A.

14. Myron Levin, "Tobacco Firm Lawyers Try to Smoke Out Possible Mole," *Los Angeles Times*, May 17, 1994, p. A1.

15. Schwartz, "Tobacco," p. A1.

16. Barstow, "The Thief and the Third Wave," p. 1A.

17. Schwartz, "Tobacco," p. A1.

18. Peter Pringle, "Stealing the Truth," *The Independent* (London), October 27, 1996, p. 4.

19. Philip J. Hilts, *Smokescreen* (Reading, Mass.: Addison-Wesley, 1996), p. 138.

20. Levin, "Unlikely Figure," p. D1.

21. Barstow, "The Thief and the Third Wave," p. 1A.

22. The Web site is *www.libracy.ucsf.edu/tobacco*. For a fascinating story of the disclosure, see Jon Wiener, "The Cigarette Papers," *The Nation*, January 1, 1996, and Carrick Mollenkamp et al., *The People vs. Big Tobacco* (Princeton, N.J.: Bloomberg, 1998), p. 47.

23. Mike Brown, "Judge Protects Congressmen from Giving Up Tobacco Papers," *The Courier-Journal* (Louisville, Ky.), June 7, 1994, p. 1A.

24. Bloomberg Business News, "Smoke Clouds Lawyer-Client Privilege," *Sun-Sentinel* (Fort Lauderdale), July 4, 1994, p. 8.

25. Brown, "Judge Protects Congressmen," p. 1A.

26. Andrew Wolfson, "B&W," *The Courier-Journal* (Louisville, Ky.), May 24, 1994, p. 1A.

27. Bloomberg Business News, "Smoke," p. 8.

28. Maya Bell, "Who Can Use the Stolen Tobacco Records?" *The Orlando Sentinel,* February 1, 1997, p. D1.

29. Laurie L. Levenson, "It May Be Moral, But Is It Ethical?" *Legal Assistant Today,* May–June 1997, p. 5.

30. Robert Sperber and Gina Gladwell, "Profiles: Legal Assistants Who Have Made a Difference," *Legal Assistant Today,* September–October 1997, p. 72.

31. Hunt Helm, "Blowing the Whistle on Big Tobacco," *Courier-Journal* (Louisville, Ky.), May 25, 1997, p. 1A.

32. Wolfson, "B&W," p. 1A.

33. David Barstow, "Can This Man Tame Tobacco?" *St. Petersburg Times,* April 7, 1997, p. 1A.

34. Orey, "Mole's Tale," p. 86.

35. Barstow, "Can This Man Tame Tobacco?" p. 1A.

36. "Tobacco Company Held Liable," *Dallas Morning News,* August 10, 1996, p. 1F.

37. Barstow, "Can This Man Tame Tobacco?" p. 1A.

38. Ibid.

39. Ibid.

40. Mark Curridan, "Tobacco Informant Draws Praise," *Dallas Morning News,* June 1, 1997, p. 1H.

41. Helm, "Blowing the Whistle," p. 1A.

42. Mike Wallace, "Cigarettes; CBS Says No to Interview Regarding Tobacco Industry Due to Possible Lawsuit," *60 Minutes,* November 12, 1995. LEXIS-NEXIS transcript.

43. Barstow, "Can This Man Tame Tobacco?" p. 1A.

44. Hilts, *Smokescreen,* p. 204.

45. "Williams on the Liggett Deal," *Legal Assistant Today,* May–June 1997, p. 5.

46. Hilts, *Smokescreen,* p. 141.

47. Richard Leiby, "Smoking Gun," *Washington Post,* June 23, 1996, p. F1.

48. Wallace, "Cigarettes."

49. Jon Wiener, "The Cigarette Papers," *The Nation,* January 1, 1996.

50. Sheryl Stolberg, "Activist's Battles Highlight Cigarette Firms' Power," *Los Angeles Times,* April 14, 1996, p. A1.

51. Mike Dorning, "Rush Puts Meigs Proposal on GAO's Radar," *Chicago Tribune,* July 7, 1996, p. 2.

52. Ceci Connolly and John Mintz, "For Cigarette Industry, a Future without GOP Support," *Washington Post,* March 29, 1998, p. A1.

53. Connolly and Mintz, "Cigarette Industry," p. A1.

54. Matthew Cooper, "Tolls on the Tobacco Road," *Newsweek,* June 22, 1998, p. 27.

55. John Berlau, "Fighting the Tobacco Wars," *Insight on the News,* June 16, 1997, p. 8.

56. Saundra Torry and John Schwartz, "Big Tobacco, State Officials Reach $206 Billion Deal," *Washington Post,* November 14, 1998, p. A1. See also Jeremy Laurance,

"The Tobacco Barons: It's Payback Time for the Biggest Lie," *The Independent* (London), March 12, 2000, p. 18.

57. Robert Lusetich, "Packet of Trouble for Big Tobacco," *The Australian,* July 10, 2001, p. 17.

58. Ibid.

59. Personal communication, April 18, 2001.

60. Myron Levin, "Smoking Gun," *Los Angeles Times,* June 23, 1996, p. D1.

61. Leiby, "Smoking Gun," p. F1.

62. Marjorie Kelly, "Cigarette Company Is Caught Holding the 'Smoking Gun,' " *Star Tribune* (Minneapolis), January 15, 1996, p. 3D.

CHAPTER 15

1. Kristen Zarfos, "Point/Counterpoint," *Physician's Weekly,* January 20, 1997. Also available at *www.physweekly.com/archive/97/01_20_97/pc.html.*

2. Joe Lang, "The Surgeon Who Said No," *Hartford Courant,* October 19, 1997, p. 27.

3. Ibid.

4. Ibid.

5. Bill Slocum, "A Surgeon's Fight with H.M.O.s," *New York Times,* April 20, 1997, sec. 13CN, p. 1.

6. Nancy Henderson, "How One Physician Can Make a Difference," *Medical Economics,* June 28, 1997, p. 64.

7. Lang, "Surgeon Who Said No," p. 27.

8. Judy Mann, "A Champion of Breast Cancer Patients," *Washington Post,* February 7, 1997, p. E3.

9. Kristen A. Zarfos, "The Legislative Arena: Physician Advocacy for Patients' Rights," Medscape, *www.medscape.com/ACCC/OncIssues/1997/v12.n04.oi1204 .zarfos.html.*

10. Lang, "Surgeon Who Said No," p. 27.

11. Henderson, "One Physician," p. 64.

12. Lang, "Surgeon Who Said No," p. 27.

13. Ibid.

14. Zarfos, "Legislative Arena."

15. Charlotte Huff, "The Only Recourse," *Las Vegas Review-Journal,* February 9, 1997, p. 1B.

16. Slocum, "Surgeon's Fight," p. 1.

17. Mann, "Champion," p. E3.

18. Lang, "Surgeon Who Said No," p. 27.

19. Amy Goldstein, "Under the Scalpel and Then Out the Door," *Washington Post,* November 19, 1997, p. A1.

20. John A. MacDonald, "Women Tell Their Stories to Get Breast Cancer Law," *Hartford Courant,* November 3, 1997, p. B9.

21. MacDonald, "Women Tell Their Stories," p. B9. See also "Nearly 10,000 Sign First Internet Petition to Improve Breast Cancer Care," *Business Wire,* March 11, 1998.

22. Goldstein, "Under the Scalpel," p. A1.

23. Peter T. Kilborn, "Trend toward Managed Care Is Unpopular," *New York Times*, September 28, 1997, p. 25.

24. Henderson, "One Physician," p. 64.

25. Stacy Wong, "Surgeon's Fight for One Patient Becomes a Catalyst for Change," *Hartford Courant*, January 27, 1997, p. A1.

26. Zarfos, "Legislative Arena."

27. Newspaper editors create their own headlines for syndicated columns. Zarfos reacted to a column printed in the *Washington Post* (Charles Krauthammer, "Playing Doctor on the Hill," February 14, 1997). The *Tampa Tribune* ran the same column under the title "Washington Plays Favorites with Patients" (February 16, 1997, p. 2). Even without the provocative *Post* headline, the message that government should not get involved in medicine came through clearly.

28. Kristen Zarfos, "I Am Not Playing Doctor, I Am a Doctor," *Washington Post*, February 27, 1997, p. A20.

29. Henderson, "One Physician," p. 64.

CHAPTER 16

1. Carl Cohen, *Naked Racial Preference: The Case against Affirmative Action* (Lanham, Md.: Madison Books, 1995), p. 1.

2. Cohen, *Naked Racial Preference*, p. 2.

3. *Regents of the University of California v. Bakke*, 438 U.S. 265 (1978).

4. Douglas A. Jeffrey and Brian T. Kennedy, "A Citizen's Guide to the Affirmative Action Debate," *www.townhall.com/claremont/citguide_affirm.html*.

5. Carl Cohen, "Race in the University of Michigan Admissions," *University Record*, February 25, 1997, *www.umich.edu/~aaupum/affirm06.htm*.

6. Carl Cohen, "Let Us Mark the End of Racial Preferences with the Beginning of Equal Opportunity," *www.nationalcenter.org/Cohen.html*.

7. Cohen, "Let Us Mark the End."

8. Cohen, *Naked Racial Preference*, pp. 3–4.

9. Ibid., p. 230.

10. Originating in Harriet Beecher Stowe's 1852 novel, *Uncle Tom's Cabin*, the term *Uncle Tom* refers to a subservient member of the minority community lacking the militant attitude needed to bring about change. The original Uncle Tom was portrayed as "long-suffering but heroic," but the negative emphasis has overwhelmed that characterization. See William Safire, *The New Language of Politics* (New York: Collier Books, 1972), p. 696.

11. Cohen, *Naked Racial Preference*, p. 230.

12. Cohen, "Race."

13. Katie Wong, "Profs Debate Affirmative Action," *Michigan Daily*, March 27, 1999, *www.pub.umich.edu/daily/1966/mar/03–27–96/news/affirmact.html*.

14. Carl Cohen, "Race, Lies, and Hopwood," *Commentary*, June 1996, p. 39.

15. Quoted in Rusty Hoover, "Race and Reconciliation," *Detroit News*, June 22, 1997, p. A1.

16. Adam Cohen, "The Next Great Battle over Affirmative Action," *Time*, November 10, 1997, p. 52.

17. Frederick R. Lynch, "Commentary: Mending the Michigan Mandate," *Detroit News*, March 30, 1997, p. B4.

18. "Lawsuit Targets U. Admissions Policy," *Michigan Today*, Fall 1997, *www .umich.edu/~newsinfo/MT/07/Fa97/mt7f97.html*.

19. Cohen, *Naked Racial Preference*, p. 232.

20. Cohen, "Race, Lies," p. 39.

21. Eve Silberman, "Outspoken, Outraged, and Outrageous," *Michigan Today*, Fall 1997. Available at *www.umich.edu/~newsinfo/MT/97/Fal97/mt10f97.html*.

22. Ibid.

23. Jessica Gavora, "The Quote Czars," *Journal of American Citizenship Policy Review*, May–June 1997, p. 22.

24. George Cantor, "Would Polices at U. of Mich. Make the Perfect Test Case on Affirmative Action?" *Gannet News Service*, July 13, 1996, p. S12.

25. See "News and Views: The Progress of Admissions of Black Students to the Nation's Highest-Ranked Colleges and Universities," *Journal of Blacks in Higher Education*, September 30, 1995, p. 6.

26. Cohen, "Race, Lies," p. 39.

27. Anne Hull, "A Dream Denied Leads Woman to Center of Suit," *Washington Post*, February 23, 1003, p. A17.

28. Cohen, *Naked Racial Preference*, p. 231.

29. *Hopwood v. State of Texas*, 78 F 3d 932 (Fifth Circuit, 1996).

30. USA Today/CNN/Gallup Poll, reported in Michael G. Franc, "Federal Race and Sex-based Preferences," in *Issues '96: The Candidate's Briefing Book* (Heritage Foundation), chap. 13, p. 13. Available at *www.heritage.org/heritage/issues96/ chpt13.html*.

31. Cohen, *Naked Racial Preference*, p. 231.

32. Cohen, *Naked Racial Preference*.

33. Cohen, "Race, Lies," p. 39.

34. Franc, "Federal Race and Sex-based Preferences," chap. 13, p. 13. Available at *www.heritage.org/heritage/issues96/chpt13.html*.

35. See William G. Bowen and Derek Bok, "Get In, Get Ahead: Here's Why," *Washington Post*, September 20, 1998, p. C1; Barbara Bergman, *In Defense of Affirmative Action* (New York: Basic, 1996).

36. Richard Cohen, "Affirmative Action for Whom?" *Washington Post*, September 9, 1997, p. A19.

37. Hull, "A Dream Denied."

38. Carol Morello, "The New Battleground for Affirmative Action," *USA Today*, November 28, 1997, p. 10A.

39. Hull, "A Dream Denied." See also Greg Gordon and Mary Jane Smetanka, "Issues of Race and Access," *Star Tribune* (Minneapolis, Minn.), June 24, 2003, p. 1A.

40. Rusty Hoover, "U-M Admission Fight Costly," *Detroit News*, October 30, 1997, p. A1.

41. Ibid.

42. Charles Lane, "High Court to Review Race-Based Admissions: Michigan Claims Set Stage for Fight Over College Access," *Washington Post*, December 3, 2002, p. A1.

43. As characterized by Robert Samuelson, "Affirmative Ambiguity," *Washington Post*, June 18, 2003, p. 25.

44. Charles Lane, "Affirmative Action for Diversity Is Upheld," *Washington Post*, June 24, 2003, p. A1.

45. David Von Drehle, "Court Mirrors Public Opinion," *Washington Post*, June 24, 2003, p. A1.

46. Quotations from Justice Sandra Day O'Connor's opinion reported in Charles Lane, "In Court's Ruling, a Nod to a Notion of a Broader Elite," *Washington Post*, June 24, 2003, p. A1.

47. Quoted in Jacques Steinberg, "University Admissions; An Admission Guide," *New York Times*, June 24, 2003, p. A1.

48. Quoted in David Goodman, "Split Court Ruling Relief to Affirmative Action Backers," the Associated Press State and Local Wire, June 24, 2003.

49. Steve Miller and Stephen Dinan, "More Lawsuits Likely on Affirmative Action," *Washington Times*, June 24, 2003, p. A12.

CHAPTER 17

1. Wesley J. Smith, *Forced Exit* (New York: Random House, 1997), p. 12.

2. Elena Muller, "Dr. Jack Kevorkian: From 'Dr. Death' to 'Mr. Kill,'" *Human Life Review*, Fall 1994, p. 40.

3. Jack Kevorkian, *Prescription Medicine: The Goodness of Planned Death* (Buffalo, N.Y.: Prometheus, 1991), p. 188.

4. Quoted in Michael Betzold, "The Selling of Doctor Death," *New Republic*, May 26, 1997, p. 22.

5. Smith, *Forced Exit*, p. 12. See also Kevorkian, *Prescription Medicine*, p. 211.

6. Nancy Gibbs, "Mercy's Friend or Foe," *Time*, December 28, 1992, p. 36.

7. Michael Betzold, *Appointment with Doctor Death* (Troy, Mich.: Momentum, 1993), p. 29.

8. Kevorkian, *Prescription Medicine*, p. 192.

9. Ibid., p. 194.

10. Ned Zeman, "Pushing the Button," *Newsweek*, November 13, 1989, p. 8.

11. Betzold, *Appointment*, p. 102.

12. Jack Lessenberry, "Kevorkian Is Arrested and Charged in a Suicide," *New York Times*, November 8, 1996, p. A19.

13. Nina Clark, *The Politics of Physician Assisted Suicide* (New York: Garland, 1997), pp. 57–58.

14. Brian Harmon, "Debate over Assisted Suicide Likely Will Reach the Supreme Court," Gannett News Service, May 24, 1996, p. S11.

15. "US: Kevorkian Turned Back as he Tries to Drop Off Body," AP Newsfeed (LEXIS-NEXIS database), April 10, 1998.

16. Smith, *Forced Exit*, p. 183.

17. Gibbs, "Mercy's Friend or Foe," p. 37. See also Betzold, *Appointment*, p. 95.

18. Greta Guest, "Michigan Sets New Ban on Aiding Suicides," *Washington Post*, July 4, 1998, p. A2.

19. Paul Greenberg, "Arranged Your Death Yet?" *New York Post*, April 13, 1998,

p. 25. Under Oregon's law, terminal patients with less than six months to live can request a lethal amount of medication for self-administration. A fifteen-day waiting period is required, as well as a second medical opinion. The act specifically prohibits "lethal injections, mercy killing or active euthanasia." Brad Knickerbocker, "Oregon Escalates Its Heated Right-to-Die Debate," *Christian Science Monitor*, April 8, 1988, p. 4.

20. Karen Cheney, "In Oregon, Medicaid Adds a Final Option," *Money*, May 1988, p. 32.

21. William Claiborne, "In Oregon, Suicide Option Brings a Kinder Care," *Washington Post*, April 29, 1998, p. A1.

22. Smith, *Forced Exit*, p. 213.

23. Quoted in Jack Lessenberry, "Kevorkian Goes from Making Waves to Making Barely a Ripple," *New York Times*, August 17, 1996, p. 6.

24. Phil Linsalata, "Prosecutor Races," *Detroit News*, August 7, 1996, p. A1.

25. Jack Kevorkian, "Fail-Safe Model for Justifiable Medically Assisted Suicides ('Medicide')," *American Journal of Forensic Psychiatry* 13, no. 1 (1992), pp. 11–12.

26. Stephen Schaefer, "HBO Shows Human Side of Dr. Kevorkian," *Boston Herald*, November 4, 1997, p. 39.

27. "Kevorkian Wins Again in Court," *Chicago Tribune*, May 14, 1996, p. 1; and Bruce Nelan, "Fasting for the Right to Die," *Time*, November 15, 1993, p. 89.

28. Jack Lessenberry, "Death and the Matron," *Esquire*, April 1997, p. 80.

29. Betzold, *Appointment*, p. 335.

30. Daniel Haney, "Six Percent of Physicians in Survey Say They Have Assisted Patient Suicides," *Washington Post*, April 23, 1998, p. A9.

31. Muller, "Dr. Jack Kevorkian," p. 40.

32. John Roberts and Carl Kjellstrand, "Jack Kevorkian: A Medical Hero," *British Medical Journal*, June 8, 1996, p. 1434.

33. Smith, *Forced Exit*, p. 184.

34. Ibid.

35. Kevorkian, *Prescription Medicine*, p. 201.

36. "A Peaceful Passing," *Hemlock Quarterly* 30 (January 1988).

37. Smith, *Forced Exit*, p. 6.

38. Knickerbocker, "Oregon Escalates," p. 4.

39. Christine K. Kassel, "Physician Assistance at the End of Life," in *Must We Suffer Our Way to Death?* ed. Ronald P. Hamel and Edwin R. Dubose (Dallas: Southern Methodist University Press, 1996), p. 128.

40. Kevorkian, *Prescription Medicine*, p. 192.

41. Quoted in Betzold, "Selling of Doctor Death," p. 22.

42. Clark, *Politics*, pp. 108–109.

43. Kathy Barks Hoffman, "Appeals Court Affirms Kevorkian's Conviction," Associated Press State and Local Wire, November 21, 2001.

44. "Kevorkian Seeks Prison Release for Poor Health," Associated Press State and Local Wire, December 9, 2002.

45. Mary S. Fischer, "To Live or to Die," *Reader's Digest*, May 2003, p. 111.

46. Julie Ray, "The Legality vs. Morality of Life and Death," *Gallup Poll Tuesday Briefing*, July 8, 2003.

CHAPTER 18

1. For a discussion of the AIDS awareness stamp and other disease stamps, see *Linn's U.S. Stamp Yearbook* (Sidney, Ohio: Linn's Stamp News), 1993.
2. Ibid., p. 232.
3. Ibid., p. 234.
4. See Kim Schneider, "AIDS Stamp Reportedly Confirmed," *Wisconsin State Journal* (Madison), December 24, 1992, for an earlier statement of this sentiment.

CHAPTER 19

1. A large number of local stories can be found on the Web sites discussed in the last section of this chapter.
2. *clinton6.nara.gov/1997/02/1997-02-28-remarks-by-president-on-teen-smoking.html*
3. See *angelfire.com/wy/saveourschools/pressrel.htm*
4. *clinton6.nara.gov/1997/02/1997-02-28-remarks-by-president-on-teen-smoking.html*. See also *www.fda.gov/features/896_tob.html*
5. Parents often play an important supporting role encouraging activism and making it possible. The Youth Activism Web site provides specific guidelines for parents wishing to support their child's activism. See *www.youthactivism.com/aparents.htm*
6. *www.glue.umd.edu/~molesko/resume.html*
7. *tobaccofreekids.org/campaign/yayas/1996yayas.shtml*. See also "Kids Undercover Crackdown on Illegal Cig Sales," *Chicago Tribune*, November 11, 1996, p. 3.
8. *www.glue.umd.edu/~molesko/resume.html*
9. *clinton6.nara.gov/1995/08/1995-08-12-radio-address-on-sales-of-cigarettes-to-children.html*
10. *www.fda.gov/fdac/features/896_tob.html*
11. *clinton6.nara.gov/1996/08/1996-08-23-president-on-fda-rule-on-children-and-tobacco.html*
12. *www.fda.gov/fdac/features/896_tob.html* and *www.cquest.com/LeskBrothers.html*
13. *www.timeforkids.com/TFK/magazines/printout/0,12479,93217,00.html*
14. Jo Becker, "Teens Simulated Cigarette Stealing Draws Welcome Attention," *Washington Post*, September 21, 2000, p. M2 (Montgomery Extra).
15. Hank Burchard, "Making Their Mark at the Memorial," *Washington Post*, November 18, 1994, p. N6.
16. Ibid. See also *www.susd.org/schools/high/Saguaro/leadership.html*
17. Burchard, "Making Their Mark."
18. *www.susd.org/schools/high/Saguaro/leadership.html*
19. See *new.crosswalk.com/news/1185050.html*
20. *www.conservativepetitions.com/petitions.php?id=136*. While 6,000 petition signers sounds impressive, interest in this issue was nowhere near as great as the over 90,000 petitioners who objected to the Senate's holding up of President George W. Bush's judicial nominations during the same time period.
21. *new.crosswalk.com/news/1185050.html*

22. Marc Morano, "Park Service Seeks to 'Modify' Controversial Lincoln Video," CNS News, March 4, 2003, available at *cnsnews.com*

23. *www.ceip.org/files/events/events.asp?EventID=163*

24. Manny Fernandez, "Carving Out a Place in History," *Washington Post*, July 27, 2003, A13.

25. Ibid.

26. *enh-os.org/johnson.htm*

27. Ibid.

28. *www.loe.org/archives/980424.htm*

29. Kory Johnson, "Children for a Safe Environment," *www.holisticpolitics.com/children.htm*

30. Ibid.

31. Ibid.

32. *enh-os.org/johnson.htm*

33. Claudia Feldman, "Environmentalist Inspires a Nation," *Houston Chronicle*, April 30, 1998, p. 7.

34. See *www.myhero.com/hero.asp?hero=KoryJohnson*.

CONCLUSION

1. From the first Lincoln-Douglas debate, August 21, 1858. See Suzy Platt, *Respectfully Quoted* (Washington, D.C., Library of Congress, 1988), p. 292.

2. In an era of preventive maintenance in which responsible vehicle owners have their wheels greased at regular intervals, the power of this phrase may well be lost. In earlier times, grease was such an expensive commodity that wagon owners waited until a particular wheel made noise before attending to it.

3. Attributed to eighteenth-century parliamentarian Edmund Burke but never found in such simplicity in his works. It may be a paraphrase of Burke's view that "when bad men combine, the good must associate; else they will fall one by one, an unpitied sacrifice in a contemptible struggle" (*Thoughts on the Cause of the Present Discontents*, April 23, 1770). See Suzy Platt, *Respectfully Quoted*, p. 109.

Photo Credits

Index

239

About the Author

Stephen E. Frantzich is professor and former chair of the department of political science at the U.S. Naval Academy, where he was selected as outstanding professor in 1991. He has written over a dozen books, largely focusing on technology and politics. He regularly serves as a consultant to the U.S. Congress, C-SPAN, the Dirksen Center, the Center for Civic Education, and a variety of foreign governments. Long a proponent of the judicious use of new technology in teaching, he recently published an interactive online textbook on the U.S. Congress and has a similar text on American government in the works. Twice selected as a senior Fulbright Scholar (Denmark 2001 and the Czech Republic 2002), he is widely sought as a speaker for both academic and nonacademic settings. Dr. Frantzich initially developed these stories to help break the cycle of unwarranted cynicism among his students. When not teaching and writing, he runs Books for International Goodwill (B.I.G.), a project that has sent over 1.5 million used texts to developing countries. He can be contacted at *frantzic@usna.edu* and he invites suggestions for future editions of *Citizen Democracy*.